The Which? Guide
to Money

About the author

Virginia Wallis spent the early years of her career working for the international division of NatWest before joining the Which? Money Group as a financial writer. As well as writing on a wide range of financial topics, she was responsible for Consumers' Association's response to the Jack Review Committee on Banking Services Law (whose findings led to the introduction of the Banking Code). Subsequently the editor of the annual *Which? Tax-Saving Guide* and an editor on *Which?* magazine, she is now a freelance writer and editor, author of *The Which? Guide to Insurance* and a regular contributor to the annual publication *Which? Way to Save Tax*.

The Which? Guide to Money

Virginia Wallis

CONSUMERS' ASSOCIATION

Which? Books are commissioned and researched by
Consumers' Association and published by
Which? Ltd, 2 Marylebone Road, London NW1 4DF
Email address: books@which.net

Distributed by The Penguin Group:
Penguin Books Ltd, 27 Wrights Lane, London W8 5TZ

The author and publishers would like to thank the following for their help in the preparation
of this book: Simon C Barnes, John Dolan, Teresa Fritz, Melanie Green, Ajay Patel, Philip
Telford, Pete Tynan, Neil Walkling and Peter Wilde.

First edition June 1999

British Library Cataloguing-in-Publication Data
A catalogue record for this book is available from the British Library

ISBN 0 85202 785 0

For a full list of Which? books, please write to Which? Books, Castlemead,
Gascoyne Way, Hertford X, SG14 1LH, or access our web site at www.which.net

Cover and text design by Kysen Creative Consultants
Cover photograph by AITCH

Typeset by ensystems, Saffron Walden, Essex
Printed and bound in England by Clays Ltd, Bungay, Suffolk

Contents

*An asterisk next to the name of an organisation in the text indicates that the address can be found in this section

Introduction

Money touches on every aspect of our lives – a fact that we are constantly reminded of by the steady stream of mailshots we receive and barrage of financial advertising, all aimed at 'helping' us with our finances. But what the marketing bumf is unlikely to tell you is that what is right for you depends entirely on your personal situation. Staying in control of your finances is about deciding what you want out of life and finding the financial tools that will help you to put your plans into practice. However, there is very little point in having financial plans if you don't have the money to pay for them. Financial institutions are fond of publishing figures which show that if you gave up going for a quick drink after work or said no to your daily chocolate bar, you could have saved thousands by the end of your working life. No doubt they are right. Alternatively, you could forget the penny-pinching and concentrate instead on the pounds you could save by losing 'loyalty' from your vocabulary and making changes to your existing financial arrangements.

Take the most basic of financial tools – a current account. Banks may like you to think that because they were nice to you when you were a student or they helped you through a particularly tough patch by upping your overdraft, you should stay put. But switching your current account from the most expensive could save £150 a year. Ignore the advice of your bank that one of the newer 'packaged' accounts would be more suitable for you and it could save you an unnecessary £60. Take advantage of competition in the credit card market and you could halve what you pay in interest. Keep a beady eye on the interest you are paid on your savings account, and you can make sure that what starts out as the best home for your money is not bettered by an account from a different savings provider.

Change the way you pay your bills or take time to do a little forward-planning for your holidays, and although it may not make you rich, the savings you make could more than cover a chocolate habit.

Switching your mortgage could save you hundreds of pounds and could mean that you create enough surplus cash to finance other essential plans such as paying into a pension. And understanding your pension choices can not only save you a small fortune in unnecessary charges but could mean the difference between an impoverished retirement and a comfortable one.

Making sure that you do not spend more than you need to on the financial tools that you need to run your day-to-day finances is only one way of saving money: another is making sure that you do not buy those that are unsuitable for your personal situation. If you have young children, for example, life insurance is an essential; if you have only yourself to worry about, it is not. If you are working and do not have a substantial cushion of savings to fall back on, you might need insurance against loss of income but if you are already retired and drawing a pension, it is highly unlikely that you do (even if you managed to find a policy that would pay out).

Just as important as understanding which financial tools you need and which you don't is getting a grasp of how the tax system can be made to work in your favour. If you are married, for example, one quick phone call could save you nearly £200; giving up your company car could make you thousands of pounds better off.

But saving money on your finances should not be seen as an end in itself. Finding a good home for your savings is just as important, especially if you need to make plans for the future such as buying a home with a partner, having children, paying for a university education or taking early retirement. Equally important is reviewing your financial plans to keep pace with your changing circumstances.

As for *how* we save – or, for that matter, how we borrow, – no one can complain that the options today are few and far between. The number of 'products' available for such purposes has burgeoned, seemingly at the speed of light, in recent years. In spite of the Financial Services Act and numerous voluntary industry codes of practice supposed to improve the information and advice given at the point of sale, consumers are still being sold the wrong products for their circumstances. Investigations conducted by *Which?* magazine routinely show that advice on mortgages can be flawed and misleading; that on pension choices little better. Even when the financial consequences of getting bad advice are less harmful to long-term financial well-being, it is still unhealthy that consumers are persuaded to buy bank accounts, credit cards, loans, savings plans and insurance which are expensive and often unsuitable.

Research by Consumers' Association over the years has found that many financial products are simply appalling; a recent survey showed that jargon and complexity are key barriers to proper consumer choice. It would be much easier to compare products if consumers could sort the good from the bad, the flexible from the inflexible and the good-value from the unnecessarily overpriced. Benchmarking of individual savings accounts (ISAs) is a step in the right direction but it should be extended to other financial products – in particular to those that affect consumers' day-to-day lives and their long-term financial health.

Staying in control of your finances means not spending more than you have to, knowing what you are buying, asking the right questions and walking away from the tools that are wrong for your personal circumstances. *The Which? Guide to Money* will help you to do just that.

Chapter 1

A practical guide to financial planning

How you choose to organise your money depends entirely on your personal circumstances: how financially independent – or dependent – you are; your financial responsibilities; where you live; what you do; the current state of your finances; how worried you are about the future and how well-equipped you are for it; how much income you have and where it comes from; what you need – and want – to spend your money on. All these factors, as well as your age and gender, will come into play when you work out your own financial plan.

Financial planning is not about fancy investment schemes. It is about with identifying which financial products best match your personal circumstances; which ones you can do without; and what adjustments you need to make to those you already have. That is not to say that investment will not feature in your financial plans, but it should not be top of your list of priorities if you have not yet taken steps to build firm financial foundations. This book will help you to build those foundations.

This chapter gives you an overview of what changes (if any) you need to make to your current financial arrangements and which financial products you should think about buying to suit your own personal situation. Once you have worked out your financial 'shopping list', use the detailed advice in the chapters that follow to find the most suitable version of each product in terms of both cost and convenience. The book also suggests ways of saving money on your existing finances, with practical advice on when switching product providers is worthwhile, together with tips on making better use of products you already have by changing the way you use them.

> **Tip**
>
> You can safely ignore advice that tries to tailor your financial plans according to your age: there are no hard and fast rules, and your other personal circumstances matter more. For example, someone in their twenties with no ties and a good salary will have different priorities for his or her money than someone of the same age who has not yet completed higher education. Similarly, thirty-somethings who have started a family will have less cash to spare than contemporaries who have not.

Getting the basics right

If you are serious about financial planning, the first thing you need to look at is the state of your current account, which is a key tool in controlling the flow of your money (see Chapter 2). A quick look at past bank statements will tell you whether you are in control of your finances but you should also consider whether you can improve the way you use your current account and check that you are not spending more than you have to on this most basic of financial services.

> **Tip**
>
> If you have a firm grip on your finances and you are happy with the service you are getting from your current account provider, it is unlikely that you need to make any changes. However, if your current account is out of control – either because you have too little money in it or too much – you should seriously consider changing your habits and/or your current account provider (see Chapter 2).

Increasing your financial flexibility

Using a credit card is a flexible way of paying for goods and services and, depending on how you use it, can either save or cost you money (see Chapter 3). If you use your credit card in tandem with your current account you can iron out dips in your finances and avoid what can sometimes be an expensive current account overdraft. In addition, provided you choose the right card, it can also be a good way of borrowing to pay for major purchases (see Chapter 13) and/ or financing your holidays (see Chapter 12). However, if you use a credit card to run up debts, it is a sure sign that you are not in control of your finances, and getting your spending back in line with your income should be a high priority.

Tip

Paying for goods and services by credit card gives you added protection if something later goes wrong with your purchase. If you cannot get redress from your supplier, you can ask the credit card issuer to pay. For more details, see Chapter 3.

Becoming financially solvent

If you have short-term borrowing – such as an overdraft on your current account or a debt on your credit card – on which you are paying interest, your priority should be to pay off these debts. If you have both an overdraft and a credit-card debt, you should pay off the most expensive one first. If your debts are more extensive (larger or more long-term) but still manageable, you may be able to save

---

Tip

Paying off a debt is a form of saving and makes sound financial sense if the interest you are paying on your borrowing is greater than the interest you could earn on any money you have available for clearing it – which is very likely to be the case. However, this is less likely if you are still a student (see Chapter 24) and/ or you have a free or cheap loan (see Chapter 13) or you are paying off a student loan. If you have savings and are running an expensive debt elsewhere, consider using them to clear as much of the debt as possible.

---

money by 'consolidating' them, either by transferring them on to one credit card, if you want to keep repayments flexible, or by taking out a personal loan (see Chapter 13), if you are happy to pay a fixed amount each month. How quickly you can clear your debts will depend on how much surplus cash you can put towards doing this and how much needs to be committed to your contingency plans (see opposite). If your debts are serious, and you are determined to do something about them, see Chapter 16.

Building up an emergency fund

Your first priority should be to clear any expensive short-term debts as quickly as possible, but if you do not have any borrowing to clear, your next priority is to create a cushion against the unexpected by building up an emergency fund in a suitable savings account (see Chapter 4). How big this fund needs to be depends on what you define as being an emergency: you might want to have enough money put away to be able to pay for household repairs; or you might want to save as much as a year's after-tax salary in case you cannot work for any reason. The size of your fund also depends on what other contingency plans you decide to put into place − see 'Making contingency plans', opposite.

Tip

The bigger your emergency fund, the more choice you have as to whether or not you buy certain types of insurance. For example, if you do not have to worry about where the money will come from to pay to repair or replace domestic appliances, you can reject expensive extended warranties (also known as appliance insurance), while having a more sizeable fund of spare cash also means that you can worry less about losing your income and so avoid expensive insurance designed to pay out − often for a limited time − if you become ill or are made redundant.

Making contingency plans

While an emergency fund will help you to deal with short-term emergencies, it is unlikely to be enough to enable you to cope with a major financial crisis, unless the amount is sizeable. So the main way of making contingency plans is to buy insurance. Although you can buy insurance for almost anything, your personal circumstances will dictate which types you really need. To ensure that the most important things are covered, you should consider the following types of insurance:

- **contents insurance** if you have belongings that you could not afford to replace
- **buildings insurance** if you are buying or own your own home (see Chapter 10)
- **income-protection insurance** if you would need to replace income if you were unable to work because of illness (see Chapter 5)
- **insurance against redundancy** if losing your job would mean that you could not meet certain regular monthly bills (see Chapter 6)
- **life insurance** if you are part of a couple, have children or you support a financially-dependent adult (see Chapter 7).

Tip

If you are an employee, you may find that you already have contingency plans in place through your job: many employers provide free life insurance as part of their salary package; some also provide a way of protecting your income in case of sickness. Paying into a personal pension can mean that you can buy life insurance reasonably cheaply. Depending on where you are in your working life, a pension can also provide a useful cushion if you are unable ever to work again. Once you are retired, you cannot be made redundant and your income will not be affected by sickness.

Planning further ahead

You cannot predict if you are going to become ill, lose your job or die young but you can be pretty sure that you will need a decent income once you retire. The main way to buy an income for retirement is by paying into a pension and this is well worth doing if you want to live on more than the state pension alone (see Chapter 8). Paying into a pension can also mean that you can save money on other contingency plans since a pension can also provide a cushion against other financial crises (because you may be able to start drawing on it early).

Tip

You should not put off paying into a pension. The earlier you start, the less you should have to pay in to achieve your desired retirement income and the more flexible you can be about your potential retirement date. Starting early (i.e. as soon as you start earning) also means that you can be more relaxed about periods when you cannot – for whatever reason – pay into your pension, (provided you choose a suitably flexible type of pension – see Chapter 8).

Paying for your financial plans

There is very little point making financial plans if you do not have the money you need to pay for them. Clearing your debts, paying into an emergency fund and buying insurance, for example, all require surplus cash. If you do not have enough money and you cannot increase your income, you will need to consider spending less. A good place to start is by seeing if you can cut down the amount you spend on your finances. This means:

- getting your current account into order and keeping an accurate running balance on it (see Chapter 2)
- using a credit card to help you to manage your spending (see Chapter 3)
- arranging a better home for any surplus cash in your current account by opening a savings account (see Chapter 4)

- checking that you are not paying too much for insurance against loss of income (if you need it) by choosing the most appropriate plan for your personal situation (see Chapters 5 and 6)
- making sure that you are not buying more life insurance than you really need (see Chapter 7)
- saving tax – and possibly money on insurance – by paying into a pension (see Chapter 8)
- checking that you are not paying too much on your housing costs (see Chapters 9 and 10)
- changing the way you pay your regular bills (see Chapter 11)
- keeping your holiday costs to a minimum (see Chapter 12)
- making sure that you have the right finance deal or loan for major purchases (see Chapter 13)
- reviewing the cost of running your car (see Chapter 14).

Tax point

One important way of saving money is by checking that you are paying the right amount of tax (see Chapter 17) and by making sure that you get all the tax subsidies that are on offer; these are outlined as appropriate in the following chapters.

If a thorough review of the cost of your financial arrangements does not produce the surplus you were hoping for, it would be well worth your while drawing up a detailed budget (see Chapter 18) to help you spend less on other things. Drawing up a budget would also be worthwhile if you want to put controls on your spending by setting certain limits or if you want to rearrange your spending to accommodate new plans or a change in your personal circumstances.

Tip

As well as saving money on the financial products your personal situation dictates you should have, you can also save money by getting rid of any that are not strictly necessary or which are unsuitable for your personal circumstances.

Financing other plans

If you have surplus cash after you have taken steps to build firm financial foundations, for example, by becoming solvent, building up an emergency fund, covering other contingencies and making provision for the future, you can start to think about other plans for your money. If you have no immediate plans to spend the surplus, you may decide that you want to start saving on a regular basis (see Chapter 20), perhaps for a holiday or the deposit on a home, or to build up a lump sum that you can then invest for a longer period of time (see Chapter 21).

If you have only yourself to consider, what you do with your money is entirely up to you. However, as soon as other people, such as a spouse or children, enter into the financial picture, your circumstances will change as will your financial priorities, which in turn may mean changing your financial arrangements, particularly if:

- you become one half of a couple (see Chapter 22)
- you decide to embark on parenthood (see Chapter 23)
- your children (or you) want to enter higher education (see Chapter 24)
- you are nearing your retirement or if you are already retired (see Chapter 25).

Part 1

The basic financial tools

Chapter 2

Current accounts

You will not get very far in the modern world of personal finance if you do not have a bank account – or more accurately, a current account with a financial institution that offers banking services. Once you have a regular income and financial commitments, you will need access to secure and convenient ways of paying and receiving money. A current account will provide this as well as acting as a passport to other financial products, such as credit cards, mortgages and other loans. In addition, having a current account can help you to convince a prospective landlord or lender, for example, that you are financially trustworthy.

This chapter explains how current accounts work, what to look for, how to compare charges and how to open and run your account (note that the extra features of current accounts specifically aimed at students are dealt with in Chapter 24). If you already have an account but you do not think that you are getting the best deal, you may wish to go straight to page 53, where you will find advice on how to switch accounts easily, with tips on cutting the cost of your account if moving it is not an option. Note that throughout this chapter 'bank' is used to mean any financial institution that offers a current account.

What a current account gives you

A fully fledged current account, which gives you access to the full range of banking services, should provide you with the following:

- **cheque book** Although banks would like to discourage their use because they cost so much to process and store, cheques are useful when you cannot use a plastic card, and for paying bills if you do not want to do so over the telephone (see pages 24–25). Cheques also provide you with a safe way of sending money through the post

- **paying-in slips** Also called Bank Giro credits, these are essential for paying cash and cheques into your account, either in person or by post. Banks prefer you to use personalised, pre-printed slips and may include some of these at the back of your cheque book to encourage you to do so. Otherwise, you can ask for a book of them. If you run out of these personalised slips, you can still pay money in by filling in what is called a 'counter credit' at any branch of your bank

- **cheque guarantee card** You are unlikely to be able to pay for goods and services – or withdraw cash – by cheque unless you can produce a cheque guarantee card, so called because it guarantees that the cheque will be paid up to a certain limit (typically £50 or £100 and sometimes as high as £250). If you pay by cheque for mail-order items, a cheque guarantee card is not necessary because your supplier can ensure that your cheque does not bounce before sending the item(s) you have ordered. Because banks are obliged to pay cheques backed by a cheque guarantee card (and there is very little they can do to stop you from writing cheques), some may not issue you with a cheque guarantee card until they are happy with the way you are running your account

- **cash card** A cash card can be used both in your own bank's cash machines (often referred to as ATMs – automated teller machines) and in those of certain other banks, although you may be charged to do this (see page 27). You access your cash by entering your personal identification number (PIN) into the machine. A cash card can also be used for getting currency in cash machines abroad (for more on holiday money, see Chapter 12)

- **payment or debit card** This is the plastic version of a cheque and cheque guarantee card rolled into one. Using a payment card rather than a cheque has several advantages: details of whom you paid should appear on your statement (with a cheque, you have to keep your own record); you are not restricted by a cheque guarantee card limit so you can buy goods up to any value provided you have enough money in your account; if you use your card in certain supermarkets, you can save yourself a journey to the cash machine by getting 'cash back' when you pay for your shopping because you can ask for cash (up to £50 usually) to be added to the bill – the person at the supermarket checkout then hands you cash from the till. From the bank's point of view, issuing someone with a payment card is less risky than issuing a cheque guarantee card, since the bank can control its use via computer

- **multi-function card** Most banks provide an all-in-one cheque guarantee, cash and payment card, which cuts down on the number of cards you have to carry around with you. The disadvantage is that if you lose it, you will be able to get cash only during normal banking hours
- **the ability to pay by standing order** This is a convenient way of paying regular bills of a fixed amount or of transferring money to another account on a regular basis. If the amount of the regular payment varies, standing orders are less convenient because you have to alter your instruction (or 'order') every time a change occurs. You can set up a standing order to anyone who has a bank account
- **the ability to accept payment instructions by direct debit** Heavy television advertising may have gone some way to improve the popularity of the direct debit, which is a convenient way to pay bills of both fixed and varying amounts, such as credit-card and utility bills. You can only pay organisations by direct debit if they have been approved by the banks that run the direct debiting scheme
- **regular statements** These are vital if you are to keep an eye on your balance and a check on your bank. Monthly statements are easier to deal with than quarterly ones and also mean that any mistakes come to light more quickly
- **an overdraft facility** This means that you can spend more money than you have in your account, but because this sort of borrowing is repayable on demand it is suitable only for short-term dips in your finances. Overdrafts are divided into two sorts: authorised, whereby a limit on what you can borrow is agreed in advance by you and the bank; and unauthorised, where you have not made an arrangement, thereby risking heavy penalties. Both types usually cost money in the form of interest on the amount borrowed and possibly bank charges – although some banks turn a blind eye if you overdraw only slightly or for not very long

- **interest when your account is in credit** The risible rates paid by most banks (less than 1 per cent before tax in a lot of cases) make the interest paid when your account is in credit hardly worth having. A current account is not a good home for your savings.

Tax point

Even though you are unlikely to get very much interest on your current account, you still have to pay tax on it at a rate of 20 per cent. Your bank will automatically deduct the tax from the interest payment before you receive it. If you are a higher-rate taxpayer extra tax will be due. If you get a tax return, make sure you keep all your bank statements for the relevant tax year and the annual interest summary that your bank may send you so that you can back up the details you give on your tax return. If you do not pay tax, you can register to have the interest paid in full: ask your bank for details.

Telephone banking

In addition to the traditional current account features, most banks offer a free telephone banking service, which lets you do a lot of the things you can do when visiting a branch, but outside normal banking hours. Whether you get to talk to a person or a computer or a combination of the two depends on the bank. To ensure that no one else can access your account, you use some form of security code when you make your call. Telephone banking is very convenient – particularly the 24-hour services – because you can sort out your finances at a time that suits you. It is also good for people who dislike writing letters, although some verbal instructions – putting a stop on a cheque, for example – may still have to be followed up in writing. The most useful telephone banking services offer you a facility for:

- checking your balance
- checking the most recent transactions on your account
- setting up and/or amending or cancelling standing orders
- cancelling direct debits

- paying regular bills
- transferring money to and from any other accounts you may have
- transferring money to another person's account
- ordering a statement
- ordering a new cheque and/or paying-in book.

Home banking on screen

An increasing number (but by no means the majority) of banks now offer screen-based home banking, although you may have to pay extra for this and you may also find that you are currently offered fewer facilities than you would get from the same bank's telephone service. However, because you can control and monitor your account on screen and are not reliant on someone at the end of a telephone to carry out your instructions, the best home banking services have more potential than telephone services. If you want to access your account on screen, you will need a computer, a modem and – depending which sort of system the bank offers – either special software from your bank or Internet access (which may come as part of the bank's package). If you do not have a computer, the alternative is to wait for television-based systems to become more sophisticated; those available in early 1999 were fairly limited in comparison with computer-based systems. However, improved television-based systems are on their way and the advent of interactive digital television is certain to bring other new developments.

The future of cash

Cash is an expensive commodity: it needs people to count it, security guards to look after it and secure places to store it in. As a way of cutting down on their costs, both banks and retailers have been experimenting with a replacement for notes and coins in the form of electronic cash – or 'e-cash'. Designed for small purchases where you would not or cannot use your payment card, e-cash is a smart card (a plastic card with a microchip rather than a magnetic strip), which you load with 'cash' from your bank account, either at cash machines or over the telephone. When you want to buy something the retailer puts your card into a terminal, which displays the value of your purchase so that you can check that you have been charged the right amount. However, you do not have to sign anything, and the transaction does not have to be authorised because the money is deducted from the amount of e-cash stored on the card rather than being taken directly from your bank account. When the e-cash runs out, you top it up by loading on more cash from your account. If you lose the card, you are in the same position that you would be in if you lost real cash. Mondex and Visa – the two main systems – are also developing ways to allow customers who use Internet home-banking to download e-cash from a computer into an electronic purse to pay for Internet shopping. Until e-cash becomes available nationally, it is hard to say whether it will catch on, given that the main benefits are for banks and retailers rather than for consumers. However, it could well be useful for people who do not like carrying a lot of change.

Let's hear it for cash

Alan found that it is generally no quicker to use Mondex than to use cash. He feels that for small purchases, where it is possible to offer the correct money, cash is quicker and the transaction is over in seconds. With Mondex, you have to watch the till and/or check the card with the balance reader, which according to Alan is not as easy as it sounds. You have to remember what was previously on the card and what your purchase cost, do the mental arithmetic and then check that your card holds the correct result. If you want a receipt, the machinery is embarrassingly slow. Alan once used Mondex on a bus: 'Never again,' he says.

Counting the cost of a current account

When building societies threatened bank territory by offering charge-free, interest-paying current accounts in the late 1980s, the banks predicted that it would not last – they were wrong. Nowadays a current account should cost you nothing, provided you never spend more than you have in your account. However, you are likely to see charges on your current account statements if:

- your bank charges for cash withdrawals from cash machines outside its free network (see below)
- your 'cleared' balance dips below zero (see 'The clearing delay' on page 28)
- you arrange an overdraft facility (see 'Always ask first' on pages 28–30)
- you do not arrange an overdraft facility but go overdrawn anyway, (see 'Unauthorised overdrafts' on page 31)
- you choose a 'packaged' account, which involves paying a monthly fee in return for a package of perks, see pages 31–32
- you make use of services (not necessarily related to your current account) for which there is a charge (see page 32).

Charges for cash

In general, you will not be charged for making cash withdrawals if you use your cash card at a machine in your bank's free network. However, as more links are being forged between the various cash machine systems, you may find that you are charged between 60p and £1.50 for using some linked machines. Ideally, the cash machines should notify you of the charge before you actually make the withdrawal, but this rarely happens. So you should refer back to the details that your bank should have sent you when it issued your card to find out which machines are free and which are not. If your card was not issued recently, ask your bank for an up-to-date list. Note that you will always be charged if you use your cash card abroad.

Convenience costs

Jonathan was pleased to discover he could use his cash card at the building society that he passed on his way to and from the office rather than having to take a ten-minute detour to his own bank's machine. However, he was a lot less pleased when his statement arrived showing a £1.50 charge for each withdrawal he had made from the convenient machine.

The clearing delay

With the exception of Abbey National and Barclays (other banks may follow suit), when you pay a cheque into your account, you do not actually get the benefit of that money until the cheque has 'cleared' (when your bank has received payment from the bank that issued the cheque). Until your bank receives payment, the cheque is referred to as 'uncleared'. If you withdraw money from your account before a cheque has cleared and your balance (excluding 'uncleared' cheques) falls below zero, technically you have an overdraft – i.e. you are borrowing – and you may have to pay interest and possibly other charges as well. The problem is that this technical overdraft will not show on your statement because most banks tend to show cheques credited to your account on the day you paid them in rather than the day the money really reached your account.

How long a cheque takes to clear depends on which bank issued it. If the person who wrote you the cheque has an account at the same bank as you (and you pay the cheque in at a branch of that bank), you usually have to wait only one working day before the money is available. If the person who wrote you the cheque uses another bank, the cheque will have to go through the clearing process, which takes three working days (weekend and bank holidays do not count). So, for example, if you pay in a cheque on Friday you will not be able to draw against it until the following Wednesday. With some banks you may have to wait a day or so longer so that the bank can be absolutely sure that the cheque you have paid in does not bounce. You will also have to wait three days if you pay in cash or cheques at a bank other than your own (this is not recommended because the other bank may charge you for doing this).

Warning

Do not rely on inspecting your balance to find out whether a cheque has cleared. Unless your bank gives information about your cleared balance (some do), the best way to find out if you can withdraw money against a cheque you have paid in is to phone your bank and ask where the cheque has got to in the clearing process.

An invisible overdraft

Ann paid a £2,000 cheque from her savings account into her current account to cover a cheque for £1,875 for a pension contribution, which she had put in the post the same day in the hope that it would not be paid until the building society cheque had cleared. She realised something was wrong when her payment card was refused in the supermarket so she phoned her bank to ask why. She was told that she was technically overdrawn and that her payment card had been refused because she was over her £1,000 overdraft limit. With her next statement she received notification that she would be charged £1 in overdraft interest made up of 45p for one day's interest up to her limit and 55p for the unauthorised part of the technical overdraft. Her statement showed that she was in credit for the entire charging period.

	what was on Ann's statement			what was really going on	
	payments out £	payments in £	balance £		real balance £
6 April			302.00		
7 April	110.35		191.65		191.65
Building society cheque is paid in		2,000	2,195.65	£2,000 building society cheque not yet cleared	191.65
8 April	1,875		316.65	Posted cheque for £1,875 is taken off account	1,683.35 overdrawn
9 April			316.65	£2,000 building society cheque is cleared	316.65

Always ask first

Your current account can start to cost you money if you overdraw. Even if you do not intend to borrow, there may be times when you do, for example:

- cheques you pay in and out may fall foul of the clearing system
- your employer may be a bit slow in paying your expenses
- you could forget to write down a cash withdrawal
- you could simply spend more than you meant to.

If you go overdrawn without your bank's agreement, it will cost you more than an 'authorised' overdraft – i.e. one that you have arranged before you make use of it. Cost is only one factor to consider; the other is convenience. If you do not arrange an overdraft, the bank is within its rights to refuse to pay (bounce) your cheques, standing orders and direct debits and may even put a stop on your cash withdrawals.

Up-front overdraft costs

The banks themselves are keen for you to arrange an overdraft to cover slight dips in your spending, and this is demonstrated by the fact that only a handful still charge an arrangement fee for making an overdraft facility available to you. However, you may face this charge if you want an overdraft limit of more than £250.

Tip

Even if you have to pay a fee for arranging your overdraft, it is likely to cost you less than the fees charged for borrowing without permission – see opposite.

Overdraft running costs

Whether or not you have to pay an arrangement fee for your overdraft, you will almost certainly have to pay interest on the amount you borrow. However, some accounts have a 'buffer zone', which means that interest is waived if you are only slightly overdrawn (up to £50 or £100, for example) or if you are overdrawn for only a few days. But even if you have to pay interest on the whole of your overdraft, it is not likely to cost very much: going overdrawn by £100 for a week every month, for example, could cost you less than £5 a year. The same overdraft will cost upwards of £55 if you choose a bank which, in addition to interest, charges a monthly fee – from £3 to £9 – for any month in which you are overdrawn. The most expensive overdrafts are those on which you are charged interest and a monthly (or quarterly) fee and are charged for every transaction you make during the charging period. For the example given above, this could push up the cost of your overdraft to nearly £150 a year. If you do not use the overdraft facility, it costs you nothing.

Unauthorised overdrafts

If you do not arrange an overdraft facility and you go overdrawn without your bank's permission (or you go over your agreed limit), you not only face the possible inconvenience (and embarrassment) of having your payments bounced, you may also have to pay a higher rate of interest on the amount you borrow (or the amount by which you exceed an agreed overdraft limit), a monthly fee for being overdrawn without agreement (or going over your overdraft limit) as well as charges for:

- **warning letters** telling you that you are borrowing without permission
- **returned items** if the bank bounces your cheques, standing orders or direct debits
- **card misuse** if you use your cheque card or debit card to cause – or increase – your borrowing.

Some banks also charge an additional daily fee for being overdrawn without permission. In most cases, this is charged only if the overdraft goes up or if, having cleared the debt, you go overdrawn again.

When you are charged

Whichever type of overdraft you have, any charges you incur will be calculated for a particular charging period, which can be either a month or a quarter. Since the introduction of the banking code (see pages 38–40), banks can no longer take the charges from your account without giving you at least 14 days' notice. In practice, banks send details of the interest and charges they intend to deduct – and the date the deduction will be made – with your regular statement.

Packaged accounts

Several banks now offer packaged accounts, which go by names such as 'gold service', 'advantage', 'option' or 'premium' and which offer special deals on other products and services in return for a monthly fee (even when you are in credit). The biggest draw is preferential overdraft rates on large overdrafts. Other 'benefits' may include commission-free travellers' cheques, free insurance of various kinds, legal helplines, free will-writing services and improved deals (although still not necessarily better than those you could get else-where) on personal loans and mortgages. If you have a large overdraft, a packaged account could be cheaper than a no-frills current account. Otherwise, unless you genuinely would have bought all the free extras they offer and they are suitable for your personal circumstances, a packaged account will be an expensive option. You would be better off buying the products they offer as and when you need them.

Current account lookalikes

Some accounts offer the same services as a fully-fledged current account (see pages 21–24), but fewer of them. Among these lookalike accounts are high-interest cheque accounts (HICAs) and savings accounts, typically those with a cash card aimed at young people aged 16 to 19. Although current account lookalikes can be useful for some people in certain circumstances – as a convenient way of accessing your savings (using a cash card or cheque book) or as a first step to financial independence, for example – they are unlikely to provide the flexibility and con-venience of a proper current account. It is also highly unlikely that you will find one that offers an overdraft facility.

Services that cost extra

Whatever the state of your bank balance, you will nearly always have to pay extra for one-off services. Your bank should tell you which services will cost extra before you make use of them, but, in general, you are likely to be charged for:

- **copy or replacement statements**, which you order in addition to the regular monthly or quarterly statements (which are provided free)
- **special cheque presentation**, which is when you want to speed up access to the proceeds of the cheque or you want to make sure that a cheque you pay in will not bounce
- **stopping a cheque**, although this service may be free if you are stopping a lost or stolen cheque
- **banker's drafts**, which you may need when you are buying

something – a car, for example – from a person/organisation who refuses to accept a personal cheque (see below)

- **automated same-day transfer**, which you use if you want to pay money into another person's bank account without waiting for the clearing system (also known as a CHAPS transfer, this is usually used for house purchase)
- **home banking**, although not all banks charge for their screen-based home banking service
- **sweeping**, which means that you ask your bank to transfer surplus cash regularly – usually over a set limit – from your current account into an account paying a better rate of interest. This facility is most common with accounts that charge a monthly fee, but keeping a close eye on your account balance and making the transfer yourself will cost nothing and is more flexible
- **safe custody** of valuables and documents – such as share certificates – which you want your bank to look after in a safe deposit box
- **foreign transactions** such as currency for your holidays or foreign money sent or received from abroad
- **foreign cash** you obtain using your cash card while you are abroad
- **travellers' cheques** in any currency
- **eurocheques and eurocheque card** if you want to be able to write your own cheques abroad (some eurocheque cards can also be used in foreign cash machines)
- **share dealing** if you want your bank to buy and sell shares on your behalf
- **status enquiries** if you want to obtain information about another person's financial standing.

Banker's drafts

A banker's draft is basically a cheque that a bank writes on your behalf. Because the cheque comes from a bank, the recipient knows that the money will be paid (this is less certain if he or she was to accept a personal cheque signed by you). So a banker's draft can be useful if you are paying for something large – a car, for example – and you do not want to pay cash. A cheaper alternative is a building society cheque, but you will need to have an account with a building society and enough money in it to cover the amount of the cheque.

Choosing a current account

The first thing to consider when choosing a bank account is convenience. For most people this will mean finding a bank that gives them easy (and free) access to cash machines in the places where they tend to need them. If you want to be able to visit your bank on a regular basis, you will need to find a bank that has a convenient branch. However, this is less important if the bank has a decent telephone banking service (see pages 24–25) and you are happy to run your account over the telephone. Even if you do not like the idea of doing business over the telephone, a convenient branch is not strictly necessary if you can do all your banking by post. If you are particularly keen to use your computer for your banking, choose a bank that offers you a home banking service (see page 25).

The second most important factor is cost. Once you have whittled down the number of banks that offer the services you require, you need to look in detail at what they will charge for running your account. Before you can do this you need to know whether you are always in credit or, if you are not, how big your overdrafts are and how long they usually last. If you are looking at several accounts, you may find it helpful to fill in the 'Step-by-step guide to comparing costs' (see opposite). You can also use this guide if you are thinking of switching accounts (see pages 53–56) and you want to compare the pros and cons of a new account with those of your existing one.

Tip

If you have not had a bank account before but suspect that you are likely to have dips in your finances in the future, make sure you open an account with a bank that lets you arrange an overdraft facility. This will avoid the expense of going overdrawn without permission.

A step-by-step guide to comparing costs			
Step 1: What will the account pay you?	Account A	Account B	Account C
Is the account free if you are in credit?			
Are withdrawals from the cash machines you are most likely to use free?			
Does the account pay interest on balances of £1 or more?			
What is the lowest rate of interest on credit balances?			
You can stop here if the answer to the first two questions is YES and you are genuinely always in credit. Choose the account that does not charge when you are in credit and that pays the best rate of interest. If you are ever overdrawn, go to Step 2.			
Step 2: Will the overdraft be free?	Account A	Account B	Account C
Can you arrange the size of overdraft you want without paying a fee?			
Is there an interest-free overdraft facility with sufficiently large limits to cover your overdrafts?			
Can you go overdrawn without paying a monthly (or quarterly) fee?			
You can stop here if the answer to all the questions in this step is YES because an overdraft will cost you nothing in interest or charges. If more than one account gives you a free overdraft, choose the one which pays the best rate of interest on credit balances. If your overdrafts are likely to go up or if none of the accounts offers a free overdraft, go to Step 3.			
Step 3: How much will your overdraft cost?	Account A	Account B	Account C
Does the account charge you for every transaction?			
What is the fee for arranging the size of overdraft you want? Enter zero if there is no arrangement fee.			
How much is the monthly fee? Enter zero if there is no monthly fee or if it will be waived for the size of overdraft you usually have. Enter a third of the fee if it is charged quarterly.			
What is the annual rate of interest for authorised overdrafts?			
Avoid accounts that charge per transaction. Choose, instead, the account with the lowest fees after adding the arrangement fee (if charged) to the monthly fee. If the fees for all the accounts are identical, choose the account with the lowest interest rate.			

Opening a current account

Once you have chosen the account that suits you best in terms of convenience and cost, you will need to fill in the bank's application form. In addition to this form, banks are required (under the banking code – see pages 38–40) to provide you with a written outline of the key features of the account, its terms and conditions and a list of charges. Banks are also legally required to ask you to produce some form of identity, such as:

- a current (and valid) passport
- a national identity card
- a full UK driving licence
- an armed forces identity card
- a National Insurance card (if you are under 20)
- an employer's identity card with a signature and photograph (although not all banks will accept this form of identification).

As well being able to prove who you are, you will also need to prove that you live at the address you have given on your application form. Most banks will ask you to produce two separate examples of proof of address, which could be a recent:

- utility bill (gas, electricity, water or telephone)
- council tax bill
- income tax statement
- statement from another bank or building society.

If you cannot produce any of the above, ask your prospective bank what it will accept as proof that you live where you say you do – a letter from your employer or parent, for example, or a copy of your entry on the electoral register.

Warning

Banks may use the fact that you are opening a current account with them as an opportunity to sell you other services such as a credit card. Do not take what they offer until you have found out what is available elsewhere.

Joint accounts

If you want to open an account with another person, the second account-holder will need to fill in his or her own details separately, and you will both (or all, if there are more than two of you) be asked to sign an extra declaration. This will state that you agree that you will be joint owners of the money in the account and jointly responsible for any debts (called 'joint and several liability'). This means that your current account provider can recover money to pay off debts from either account-holder regardless of who actually spent the money. It will also mean that if either of you dies, the money will automatically belong to the other person.

Warning

If you are setting up a joint account with friends – for paying the bills on your shared house, for example – check the bank's terms and conditions very carefully. Most standard terms and conditions say that the bank can act on instructions signed by any one of the account-holders. If you do not want just one person to be able to withdraw money from the account without the others' consent, you will have to 'change the authority to operate the account' – i.e. write to the bank to tell it that it should act only on instructions (which includes writing cheques) that have been signed by all the account-holders. If you do this, you will all have to sign the letter.

If a bank turns you down

A bank is perfectly entitled to refuse to take you on as a customer and does not have to give you its reasons for turning you down. The exception to this rule is if it uses a credit reference agency to check out your financial trustworthiness (whether you have been taken to court for non-payment of a debt, for example). For more on credit reference agencies and what to do if you are turned down for credit, see Chapter 15.

> **Tip**
>
> Some banks require you to agree to pay a regular amount of money – either a fixed amount such as £400 a month, for example, or your monthly salary – into your account before they will agree to open it. If you cannot show that you will be able to do this, you are most likely to have your application turned down. Always check whether a minimum monthly payment is required before you apply.

The banking code

If your chosen bank accepts your application and opens your account, you enter into a formal relationship with your bank, the terms of which are covered by the banking code. This is a voluntary code, which sets minimum standards of good banking practice and defines both a bank's obligations to you and your obligations as a customer. The detailed requirements of the code are taken account of as appropriate within the relevant sections of this chapter. In general terms, the banking code commits banks and building societies to:

- act fairly in their dealings with you
- ensure that all services and products comply with the banking code
- give you information on their services and products in plain language and offer help if you do not understand any aspect
- help you choose a service or product to fit your needs
- help you understand the financial implications of a mortgage, other borrowing, savings and investment products and cards
- help you to understand how your accounts work
- have safe, secure and reliable banking and payment systems
- ensure that the procedures followed by banking staff reflect the commitments set out in the code
- correct errors and handle complaints speedily
- consider cases of financial difficulty and mortgage arrears sympathetically and positively
- ensure that all services and products comply with relevant laws and regulations.

Disabled customers and the banking code

Under the Disability Discrimination Act 1995 it is unlawful for a bank to discriminate against disabled people by:

- refusing to serve them or deliberately not providing a service that is available to other customers
- offering a sub-standard service or less favourable terms
- offering a service that it is impossible or unreasonably difficult for a disabled person to use or charging more to meet the costs of making it easier to use a service.

In addition, banks will be required to take reasonable steps to make services accessible to disabled people by having specially-trained staff who can help or advise as well as providing:

for visually-impaired customers
- Braille, large-print and talking statements
- cheque and address templates to help customers with the layout and orientation of cheques and forms
- keyboards on cash machines to assist visually impaired customers
- information available in Braille, large print and audio tape
- contrasting décor in branches

for customers with hearing disabilities
- induction loops at counter positions
- special telephone facilities such as typetalk or text phones
- sign interpreters
- visual fire alarms

for mobility-impaired customers
- level or ramped access for wheelchair users
- lower counter positions, writing services and cash machines
- evacuation chairs in multi-storey buildings
- door openings of adequate width
- automatic doors.

Your bank should make a copy of the code available to you if you ask for one. If it refuses, or you have a complaint about the way your bank is putting the code into practice (or failing to), you can take your complaint to the Independent Review Body for the Banking and Mortgage Codes,★ which is responsible for monitoring the code.

Running your current account

Once you have received your cheque book, cards, passwords and have agreed the 'selected' personal information you will use to identify yourself when using your bank's telephone service (if applicable), you can start using the banking services on offer, which means:

- looking after your current account
- writing and paying in cheques
- setting up standing orders and direct debits
- keeping track of transactions
- checking up on your bank.

Looking after your current account

The banking code sets out the things that you, as a customer, should do to protect your money and to help prevent fraud:

- do not keep your cheque book and cards together
- do not allow anyone else to use your card PIN
- do not allow anyone else to use the password or other security code that you are given to access your account over the telephone or via computer
- always take reasonable steps to keep your card safe and your PIN, password and selected personal information secret at all times
- never write down or record your PIN on the card or on anything kept with or near it
- never write down or record your PIN, password or selected personal information without disguising it and never write down or record your PIN using the numbers in the correct order
- destroy notification of your PIN and/or password immediately

- always tell your bank as soon as possible if you discover or suspect that your cheque book and/or cards have been lost or stolen or that someone else knows your PIN, password or your selected personal information.

Under the banking code, if your card is misused before you have informed the bank of its loss or theft, or that someone else knows your PIN, you will not have to pay more than £50 of any loss unless you have acted fraudulently or with gross negligence – for example, failing to follow the security advice given above.

Tip

If your bank gives you the opportunity to choose your own PIN, take it: you will be able to choose a number that you can remember more easily than the one it sends you. All banks will have systems in place to let you do this by 1 July 2000.

Writing cheques

Most cheques are pre-printed with the crossing 'Account payee' or 'A/C payee', which means that they can only be paid into an account that carries the name of the person written on the cheque (the payee). In practical terms, this means that anyone stealing a cheque that you have written would have to open a bank account in order to pay it in – this will not be easy if the cheque is made out to your electricity company, for example. Although the 'account payee' crossing safeguards your cheques in certain situations, it will not protect them unless you make sure that you take the following precautionary measures to stop your cheques from being tampered with:

- always write cheques in ink
- keep your cheque book and cheque guarantee (or multi-function) card separate from each other
- write the name of the payee as close to the word 'pay' as possible
- never sign a cheque until you have filled in the name of the payee and the amount

- put 'only' after the amount in words or draw a line in the empty space
- if you make a mistake when writing a cheque, tear it up and start again or put your full signature next to any alterations.

How to stop a cheque

You cannot stop a cheque you have written – i.e. ask your bank not to pay it – if it is backed by a cheque guarantee card. You can stop other cheques, but note that you will still be liable for the debt that the cheque was due to pay. There is no guarantee that a cheque can be stopped because it depends on where it has got to in the clearing system: to be able to stop the cheque, your bank needs to receive your instruction before the cheque is presented for payment (see page 28). When you instruct your bank to put a stop on a cheque, you will need to give:

- your account number
- the cheque number
- the date you wrote the cheque
- the amount
- the name of the payee (i.e. the person the cheque is made out to).

Paying cheques in

If someone wants to pay you by cheque, do not accept it if you think it will bounce. You should also check that:

- the date on the cheque is not more than six months ago because it will be 'stale' or 'out of date', and the bank that issued it can refuse to pay (this is particularly important around New Year)
- it is not post-dated unless you are prepared to wait until the date on the cheque to pay it in (cheques cannot be paid before the date written on them)
- the amount in words and the amount in figures agree
- it is signed in your presence
- your name is spelled correctly. Some banks may turn a blind eye if it is clear that the cheque was intended for you – for example, your name is Clark but the writer of the cheque has added an 'e' or the cheque is written out to your nickname rather than your

full name – but strictly speaking the cheque should be returned to you.

To pay the cheque into your account, fill in a credit slip. You can then take this and the cheque(s) to a branch of your bank and pay it in over the counter. If there is a long queue, you can put it in the internal letter box that some banks provide for paying cheques in. Alternatively, you can post it.

Bounced cheques

Paying in a cheque does not guarantee that the money will reach your account. The bank that issued the cheque will return it unpaid if the person who wrote it – the 'drawer' – puts a stop on it. This will also happen if there is not enough money in the drawer's account or if something is wrong with the cheque – for example, the words and figures do not agree, the cheque is stale or you paid in a post-dated cheque too soon. The cheque will usually be stamped with the reason for refusal and the words 'refer to drawer', which means that you have to go back to the person who wrote you the cheque to sort out the problem.

How to set up a standing order

If you want to make regular payments of a fixed amount to another account – either yours or one belonging to someone else – you can either write a cheque every time you want to pay or you can set up a standing order. Whether you choose to write a letter (see the example below) or give your instruction over the phone, you will need to provide your bank with the account details of the person or organisation that is to receive the money. If you are intending to make regular payments to an organisation, it may provide a pre-printed form for you to fill in. If not, or if you are setting up a standing order to another person, you will need to provide your bank with the following details:

• the amount you want to pay
• how often you want to make payment – e.g. monthly, quarterly or annually
• the date each month (quarter, year) you want payment to be made

- whether you want payment to be made on the nearest working day before or after the date you specify (in case this falls at a weekend or on a bank holiday, for example)
- when you want the first payment to be made
- the name of the bank where the recipient's account is held
- the bank sort code (or the branch address if you do not know the sort code)
- the name of the account you want the money to be paid to
- the account number of the recipient.

Example of letter setting up a standing order

[Your Address]

The Manager
[Bank's address]
[Date]

Dear Sir

Account number: 0144905
Account name: J Smith

Please set up a standing order for [amount] to be paid monthly on the nearest working day after the [date] of each month starting in [month, year] to:
Savings Bank
Sort code: 13-70-06
Account name: Jason Smith
Account number: 06684758

Yours faithfully
Jason Smith

Changing a standing order

Once you have set up a standing order, it should carry on being paid in line with your original instructions until you tell your bank that you want it changed. For example, you may want to increase the amount or change the date on which the payment is made. If you write, you need only give details of the changes and the date when you want the change to take effect.

Example of letter changing a standing order

[Your Address]

The Manager
[Bank's address]
[Date]

Dear Sir

Account number: 0144905
Account name: J Smith

Please increase my monthly standing order to Savings Bank from [amount] to [amount] starting with the [month, year] payment.

Yours faithfully
Jason Smith

Cancelling a standing order

If you want to cancel a standing order, give your bank at least three weeks' notice and make it clear when the last payment is to be made.

Example of letter cancelling a standing order

[Your Address]

The Manager
[Bank's address]
[Date]

Dear Sir
Account number: 0144905
Account name: J Smith

Please cancel my standing order to Savings Bank after the [month, year] payment has been made.

Yours faithfully
Jason Smith

How to set up a direct debit

Setting up a direct debit is different from setting up a standing order because instead of telling your bank to make payments on your behalf, you tell the organisation you want to pay that it can collect money from your account. You do this by filling in a 'direct debit mandate', which you then send back to the organisation. This includes your authorisation to your bank to make payment to the 'originator' of the direct debit – i.e. the organisation that you wish to pay.

The advantage of using direct debit rather than standing order is that you do not have to amend your instruction if the amount you need to pay changes – which is likely to happen if you use a direct debit to pay your electricity or credit-card bill, for example. Under the rules of the direct debiting scheme, any organisation that uses 'variable' direct debits (where the amount collected can change) has to tell you in advance how much it will collect from your account and when it will actually do so.

The Direct Debit Guarantee

- This Guarantee is offered by all Banks and Building Societies that take part in the Direct Debit Scheme. The efficiency and the security of the Scheme is [sic] monitored and protected by your own Bank or Building Society.
- If the amounts to be paid or the payment dates change THIS ORGANISATION will notify you 10 working days in advance of your account being debited or as otherwise agreed.
- If an error is made by THIS ORGANISATION or your Bank or Building Society you are guaranteed a full and immediate refund from your branch of the amount paid.
- You can cancel a Direct Debit at any time by writing to your Bank or Building Society. Please also send a copy of your letter to us.

Changing a direct debit

If you want to amend the terms of your direct debit instruction – for example, you want to change the account from which payment is taken, or the date on which payment is made – you need to contact the organisation you pay rather than your bank. It will probably send you another mandate to fill in with the change in details.

Cancelling a direct debit

In theory, all you need to do to cancel a direct debit is to tell your bank. However, in practice, it is better to write both to your bank and to the organisation that you no longer wish to pay by direct debit. A copy of the letter you send to your bank should be sufficient but make sure that your letter quotes the reference number of the item you have been paying for – your credit card, insurance policy or mortgage account number, for example.

Tip

Whenever you write to your bank, always quote your account number and the name of your account – i.e. the name printed just underneath the amount box on your cheques.

Keeping track

Once you start writing cheques, using your payment card, paying money in and setting up standing orders and direct debits, you will need to keep track of all the money going in and out of your account. Keeping an accurate running total of your bank balance and your own record of all transactions helps you to know how much money you have available for spending and hence avoid going overdrawn. In addition, when your bank statements arrive, you have something to check them against. If you do not keep your own records, you will not be able to keep tabs on your bank's efficiency in running your account.

Keeping an accurate running balance

All cheque books either come with cheque stubs (counterfoils) or sheets at the front of the book for recording all your transactions. However, a piece of paper in your wallet, purse, personal organiser or diary is just as effective and may be more practical if you prefer not to carry your cheque book around with you. If you want to know how much money you have available at any given time, you need to write down every transaction as it happens and either add or subtract the amount from your running total.

You also need to take account of direct debits and standing orders. Provided you can remember the date and amount of every one, you can deduct them from your running total as they are deducted from your account. However, if you are liable to forget to do this, an alternative is to add up all your fixed-amount standing orders and direct debits for a month and deduct them as one amount when you add your monthly salary (or other source of monthly income). If you have variable direct debits coming off your account, you can subtract them from the running total when you get advance notice of what the amount will be. You should also do this when you get advance notice of bank charges and interest.

Warning

Balances or mini-statements, available from cash machines, tell you what the bank thinks your balance is, but this is not the same as what you have available to spend (because cheques might still be clearing). Keeping your own running balance will give a much more accurate and up-to-date picture of your finances and will enable you to take action to pre-empt an overdraft – for example, by topping up your current account from savings or by using a credit card rather than your payment card for your shopping.

Checking up on your bank

Your bank will keep you informed by sending you regular monthly or quarterly statements. However, although your statement will tell you what the bank thinks has been happening on your account, this will not necessarily be the same as what ought to have happened. Surveys conducted by *Which?* magazine★ have consistently revealed that the most common mistakes found on statements are to do with standing orders, direct debits, accounts being debited wrongly and incorrect charges being made. If you identify a problem, ask your bank to explain or put things right. Under the banking code (see pages 38–40), banks and building societies must have internal procedures in place for handling complaints and they must inform customers what they are. If your bank does not do this, report it to the Independent Review Body for the Banking and Mortgage Codes.* For more on effective complaining and getting problems sorted out, see Chapter 19.

> **Warning**
>
> Mistakes the bank has made on your account can have serious repercussions: for example, if it has messed up your mortgage payment, you may face charges for being in arrears. If the bank fails to pay certain insurance premiums, you may find that your policy has lapsed, and this could become an expensive problem if you cannot claim as a result or if you later reinstate the policy but have to pay higher premiums because of the lapse.

Making your statement tally

If you have kept an accurate record of your own, checking your bank statement should be fairly straightforward:

- tick off all the transactions on your statement that match those in your records
- from the final balance on your statement, deduct payments – cheques, cash withdrawals and so on – that you know have gone through since the statement date
- add cheques and other money paid in since the statement date
- deduct any future standing orders and direct debits that are already included in your own running total
- check that any interest and charges match up to the 'pre-notification of charges advice', which you should have received before they appeared on your statement
- add any interest the bank has paid to your own running total.

The figure you are left with after making the necessary adjustments listed above should now be the same as the running total (including interest, if appropriate) from your own records. If it is not, you will need to find out whether the problem lies with your own records or with your bank's. If you think that the bank is at fault – it has paid a standing order twice, for example, or it has deducted the wrong amount for a cheque – contact your bank as soon as possible either by phone or in writing (attach a copy of your statement to your letter if this would help to clarify the problem). The bank should then look into the matter and correct the mistake if it turns out to be its fault. If its mistake caused your account to go overdrawn, the bank should also pay back any charges and/or other deductions taken from your account in error. If it fails to solve the problem to your satisfaction, see Chapter 19.

Bank charges reversed

Over the past couple of months, Mike has had to write to his two banks about his standing orders. Both banks had ignored his instructions and had continued to make payments. After repeated attempts to get things put right, it struck him that when a bank thinks that he has made a mistake, it loses no time in charging a fee. Mike decided to take the same course of action and successfully claimed back £30 from one and £25 from the other. As he says: 'When banks mess up, why shouldn't they pay up?'.

How to check charges

When you open an account, your bank should give you a list of the charges that will be made as well as an explanation of the circumstances in which you will have to pay them. Your bank should also keep you up to date with any changes to those charges. If you receive advance notice that you have to pay charges, check that it tallies with the list you were last given (ask for a recent list if you no longer have one). If the figure that appears on your statement is different from the one on the published list, ask for an explanation, and a refund if you think the charge is more than it should have been or if you should not have been charged at all.

How to check interest

To check the amount of interest you have been charged, you need to count the number of days you were overdrawn by the same amount and you need to know the interest rate that your bank is charging you – this should appear on the advance notification of charges. If it does not, ask your bank. Interest rates can be quoted in two ways: as a flat rate (sometimes expressed as a percentage over bank base rate) or as an 'effective annual rate' (EAR) so check which your being given. Bank base rate is the minimum rate at which the bank will lend money. It moves in line with interest rates generally and is advertised in branches. Changes to base rate are also advertised in the national press. The EAR is supposed to help you compare the cost of overdrafts. However, in reality it does not because it ignores charges – see above. The EAR also assumes that you are consistently overdrawn by the same amount for a whole year, which is very unlikely to be the case. Some banks quote an annual percentage rate (APR) instead of an EAR but again this assumes that you are consistently overdrawn for the same amount for a whole year.

Neither the EAR nor the APR will give you the figure you need to check your bank's interest calculation (for which you need the flat rate of interest). If both an EAR and a flat rate are quoted, the flat rate is the lower figure and the one you should use to check the interest – use the 'Overdraft interest calculator' below to do this. If you have only the EAR to work with, use the table overleaf, which shows a range of EARs converted back into a flat rate.

Overdraft interest calculator	
Enter the amount by which you were overdrawn at **A** See note, below	**A**
Enter the flat rate of interest your bank charges at **B** If your bank quotes only an EAR – see table overleaf	**B**
Multiply **A** by **B** and enter the result at **C**	**C**
Divide **C** by 365 and enter the result at **D**	**D**
Enter the number of days you were overdrawn at **E**	**E**
Multiply **D** by **E** and enter the result at **F** **F** is the amount of interest you should have been charged on the overdraft amount entered at **A**	**F**
Note that if you were overdrawn by different amounts, you will need to go through the calculator separately for each amount and then add up all the answers at the end.	

Flattening out interest rates

Daily interest cost on an overdraft of:

EAR	flat rate	£50	£100	£200	£300	£400	£500	£1,000
10.4%	10%	£0.01	£0.03	£0.05	£0.08	£0.11	£0.14	£0.27
11%	10.5%	£0.01	£0.03	£0.06	£0.09	£0.12	£0.14	£0.29
11.5%	11%	£0.02	£0.03	£0.06	£0.09	£0.12	£0.15	£0.30
12.1%	11.5%	£0.02	£0.03	£0.06	£0.09	£0.13	£0.16	£0.32
12.6%	12%	£0.02	£0.03	£0.07	£0.10	£0.13	£0.16	£0.33
13.2%	12.5%	£0.02	£0.03	£0.07	£0.10	£0.14	£0.17	£0.34
13.8%	13%	£0.02	£0.04	£0.07	£0.11	£0.14	£0.18	£0.36
14.3%	13.5%	£0.02	£0.04	£0.07	£0.11	£0.15	£0.18	£0.37
14.9%	14%	£0.02	£0.04	£0.08	£0.12	£0.15	£0.19	£0.38
15.5%	14.5%	£0.02	£0.04	£0.08	£0.12	£0.16	£0.20	£0.40
16%	15%	£0.02	£0.04	£0.08	£0.12	£0.16	£0.21	£0.41
16.6%	15.5%	£0.02	£0.04	£0.08	£0.13	£0.17	£0.21	£0.42
17.2%	16%	£0.02	£0.04	£0.09	£0.13	£0.18	£0.22	£0.44
17.8%	16.5%	£0.02	£0.05	£0.09	£0.14	£0.18	£0.23	£0.45
18.3%	17%	£0.02	£0.05	£0.09	£0.14	£0.19	£0.23	£0.47
18.9%	17.5%	£0.02	£0.05	£0.10	£0.14	£0.19	£0.24	£0.48
19.5%	18%	£0.02	£0.05	£0.10	£0.15	£0.20	£0.25	£0.49
20.1%	18.5%	£0.03	£0.05	£0.10	£0.15	£0.20	£0.25	£0.51
20.7%	19%	£0.03	£0.05	£0.10	£0.16	£0.21	£0.26	£0.52
21.3%	19.5%	£0.03	£0.05	£0.11	£0.16	£0.21	£0.27	£0.53
21.9%	20%	£0.03	£0.05	£0.11	£0.16	£0.22	£0.27	£0.55
22.5%	20.5%	£0.03	£0.06	£0.11	£0.17	£0.22	£0.28	£0.56
23.1%	21%	£0.03	£0.06	£0.12	£0.17	£0.23	£0.29	£0.58
23.7%	21.5%	£0.03	£0.06	£0.12	£0.18	£0.24	£0.29	£0.59
24.3%	22%	£0.03	£0.06	£0.12	£0.18	£0.24	£0.30	£0.60
24.9%	22.5%	£0.03	£0.06	£0.12	£0.18	£0.25	£0.31	£0.62
25.5%	23%	£0.03	£0.06	£0.13	£0.19	£0.25	£0.32	£0.63
26.2%	23.5%	£0.03	£0.06	£0.13	£0.19	£0.26	£0.32	£0.64
26.8%	24%	£0.03	£0.07	£0.13	£0.20	£0.26	£0.33	£0.66
27.4%	24.5%	£0.03	£0.07	£0.13	£0.20	£0.27	£0.34	£0.67
28%	25%	£0.03	£0.07	£0.14	£0.21	£0.27	£0.34	£0.68
28.7%	25.5%	£0.03	£0.07	£0.14	£0.21	£0.28	£0.35	£0.70
29.3%	26%	£0.04	£0.07	£0.14	£0.21	£0.28	£0.36	£0.71
29.9%	26.5%	£0.04	£0.07	£0.15	£0.22	£0.29	£0.36	£0.73
30.6%	27%	£0.04	£0.07	£0.15	£0.22	£0.30	£0.37	£0.74
31.2%	27.5%	£0.04	£0.08	£0.15	£0.23	£0.30	£0.38	£0.75
31.8%	28%	£0.04	£0.08	£0.15	£0.23	£0.31	£0.38	£0.77
32.5%	28.5%	£0.04	£0.08	£0.16	£0.23	£0.31	£0.39	£0.78
33.1%	29%	£0.04	£0.08	£0.16	£0.24	£0.32	£0.40	£0.79
33.8%	29.5%	£0.04	£0.08	£0.16	£0.24	£0.32	£0.40	£0.81
34.4%	30%	£0.04	£0.08	£0.16	£0.25	£0.33	£0.41	£0.82

The flat rate is the figure you need to check your overdraft interest.

The table also gives you the daily interest cost for various levels of overdraft. If you just want a rough check of the interest your bank is proposing to charge, multiply the number of days you were overdrawn by the daily interest cost for the size of your overdraft nearest to yours.

If the figure you get from the calculator is the same as what your bank is proposing to charge you, your statement is correct. If it is slightly different, try adding a day or two to the number of days you were overdrawn to take account of the fact that cheques appear on your statement earlier than the money reached your account (see page 28). If the figure you get is still different, check that the amount by which you were overdrawn was within your overdraft limit. If it was not, the amount over the limit will be charged at the higher, unauthorised overdraft rate of interest (see page 31). If, after making these adjustments, you are still left with a figure that does not tally, ask your bank to give you an explanation of how it has calculated the interest.

Switching your current account

If you are unhappy with your bank, you may well be thinking of moving your current account elsewhere. Even if you are perfectly happy with the way your bank runs your account you may be less pleased with what it charges. Perhaps you want to change your account because you have moved house or job, for example, and your current bank does not have convenient cash machines or branches near to where you live or work. All these are good reasons for switching, and although the process may take a couple of months, it ought to be reasonably straightforward, provided you plan ahead and do it gradually.

Should you switch?

You should definitely consider switching your current account if your bank charges a monthly fee and/or a fee for arranging an overdraft. If you do not know how much your current account is costing you, you should go through your statements from the past 12 months and add up your bank charges and interest. If you are

. surprised by the figure you arrive at, you will almost certainly save money by switching.

How to switch: a step-by-step guide

Although some banks offer to transfer your old account for you, research by *Which?* magazine* found that people who looked after the switching process themselves were less likely to encounter problems.

Step 1: size up the task ahead

Ask your current bank for a list of all your standing orders, direct debits and, if you have set up a bill payment facility on your account (either by phone or using a home banking service) all the bills you pay in this way. There are two reasons for asking for this before you do anything else: you will get an idea about how complex switching is going to be; your bank is less likely to charge for providing the list than it would be if it knows you are about to take your account elsewhere. Having this list also gives you an opportunity to review the way you pay your bills – see Chapter 11.

Step 2: open your new current account

You do not have to close your old account before opening the new one and it makes sense to minimise disruption by waiting until you have your new cheque book and card(s) and any other services you have asked for. For more details, see page 36.

Step 3: deal with your direct debits

While you are waiting for your new bank to process your application, contact all the organisations that you pay by direct debit and ask each of them to send you a new mandate.

Step 4: wait for payday

Once your new account has been opened, and as soon after your next monthly salary (pension or benefit) has been paid, give your employer (pension provider or benefit office) your new bank details and ask that payments be made to your new bank account from now on. If you are paid by cheque (because you are self-employed, for example) or in cash (if you pick up your pension or benefit from a post office, for example) start paying your cheques or cash into your new account as soon as you have transferred all the regular payments from your old account to your new one – see Step 5.

Step 5: switch your regular payments

By now you should have received all the mandates you need to change your direct debits. Fill these in with your new bank details. Give your new bank all the necessary details for setting up your standing orders and cancel them at your old bank. In both cases, make sure the date you give for the first payment is after the date when your new account will have received your salary for the first time – see Step 4. For more on setting up, amending and cancelling standing orders and direct debits, see pages 43 to 47.

Step 6: pay bills at your convenience

If you have used your current bank's telephone or home banking service to arrange to pay regular bills, this facility will be cancelled when you close the account. If you are prepared to pay those bills by cheque for a while, you do not need to set up a bill payment facility with your new bank straight away. It could be worth waiting until you are sure that your new bank has dealt with all the other changes first.

Step 7: close your old account

As soon as you are happy with your new account, you can close the old one. Write to your old bank and send back your cards (cut in half), cheque books, paying-in books and so on.

Cutting costs without switching

If changing your bank is not a practical option, other ways of saving money are to:

- **arrange an overdraft** Borrowing without permission is expensive (see page 31)
- **check what else your current bank has to offer** It may be that your bank offers a different current account with better terms but it has just not told you about it
- **consider a half-way house** You can run two accounts at two

different banks in tandem – for example, using the one with the best overdraft terms for your bills, where you expect dips in your finances, and the other for cash withdrawals (you will benefit only if you keep the one with the most expensive overdraft in credit). For more on setting up a separate bill-paying account see Chapter 11

- **change your habits** If you find that you are regularly overdrawn at the end of the month, consider using your credit card more (see Chapter 3). If you find that you have high credit balances at the end of each month, consider setting up a standing order to your savings account, where you will get a better rate of credit interest (see Chapter 4)

- **look to the future** If you know that you will need to borrow more than your bank's limit and you will be buying items for which you cannot use a credit card, explain the situation to your bank and ask for a temporary increase in your overdraft limit to tide you over. This will always be cheaper than borrowing without permission – and probably less embarrassing as well

- **pay off your debts** If you are overdrawn by the same amount at the end of every month, consider using savings to bring your account back in line. The interest you lose on your savings is likely to be less than the interest you are paying on the overdraft

- **rearrange your borrowing** Overdrafts are good for occasional dips in finances. They are less good for borrowing to buy large items, for which a different type of loan might be more suitable (see Chapter 13)

- **look before you buy** Do not buy other financial services from your bank without checking what is on offer elsewhere. What your bank offers will rarely be the best deal

- **face up to facts** If you are never in credit, it is a sure sign that you are spending too much and you should do something about it before your debts get out of hand (see Chapter 16).

Chapter 3

Credit cards

A credit card is the modern way of paying on tick and a useful tool to have running alongside your current account (see Chapter 2). Using a credit card is little different from using the payment card which comes with your current account, with several important exceptions: you get a breathing space between making your purchases and having to pay for them; borrowing between statements can be free (unlike most overdrafts); and you get added protection in the form of the Consumer Credit Act (see page 59).

This chapter will tell you what is on offer, the kind of cards to avoid, how to choose the card that is right for your spending habits and how to apply for a card. If you think you may not be getting as good a deal as you could from your card, you may find it helpful to turn to 'Should you switch?' on page 82.

Which way will you use the card?

There are two ways of looking at a credit card: as a tool which will help you save money – as a potentially no-cost substitute for your current account payment card, for example – or as a flexible way of borrowing money when you need to smooth over dips in your finances. A credit card can also be a cost-effective and convenient way of spending when you are abroad (see Chapter 12).

A way to save

If you view a credit card as a substitute for your current account payment card when buying things it should cost you nothing (provided you choose the right card and always pay the bill in full each month – see pages 73–74). In addition, using it in this way may also *save* you money: if it stops your current account from going overdrawn, for example, and/or the delay between buying and having to pay for your purchases means that there is more money in your current account earning interest for longer. This is also true of savings you may have earmarked for large purchases – a washing machine, for example. Using a credit card means that you can leave your savings untouched until you get your statement; it is also a more convenient way to pay because the spending limit you get with a credit card is likely to be larger than the one you get with your bank payment card. A credit card can also help you to avoid overdrafts if you travel on business a lot and experience a delay between paying business expenses and getting them reimbursed by your employer. A credit card is not, however, a good substitute for a cash card on your current account (see page 22).

Tax point

If your employer gives you a company credit card and pays the bill for you, it may mean a tax bill. However, it will not cost anything in tax if you use the card purely for business expenses. What counts as a business expense depends on what line of work you are in, so check with your employer.

A way to borrow

Viewed as a flexible way to borrow (which is how card issuers prefer you to look at it since this is what feeds their profits), a credit card can often be cheaper than using a current account overdraft – especially if you have the kind of current account which charges monthly overdraft fees as well as interest. Using a credit card to meet short-term and occasional dips in your finances of the kind caused by heavy-spending months (Christmas, for example) can be a good way of managing your money. If you view a credit card as your licence to spend, spend, spend, it will start to get expensive – especially if you only ever pay the minimum you owe each month and/or regularly go over the spending limit you are given (see pages 59–60).

The Consumer Credit Act 1974

One of the main advantages of using a credit card instead of the payment methods offered by your current account when buying goods and services is the added protection you get from the Consumer Credit Act for items costing between £100 and £30,000. This means that if something goes wrong with the goods or services you buy – or if the company you buy from goes out of business or fails to supply what you ordered – you have the right to claim compensation from your supplier or from the card issuer (see 'Exercising your rights' on pages 81–82). Because of this valuable protection, it is always a good idea to keep your credit-card slips for goods and services for as long as you think that a problem may arise – until you have come back from a holiday, for example, or indefinitely for major purchases or work done on your house where problems may not come to light until after a few years. Most card issuers will extend this protection to items bought abroad. You will lose the protection of the Consumer Credit Act if you use a credit-card cheque (see overleaf) and this may also happen – depending on your card issuer – if an additional cardholder (rather than the principal cardholder who applied for the card) makes the purchase (see page 61).

What a credit card gives you

When credit cards first came on the scene, the choice was pretty much limited to Access or Barclaycard. These days there are any number of card issuers, although there are still only two main card networks – Visa and MasterCard. Credit cards are offered by banks, building societies, charities, petrol companies, supermarkets, other retail outlets, car manufacturers and so on. Yet despite this wealth of choice, the types of card on offer have not changed that much. All cards will give you:

• **a credit limit** This is your spending limit. If you go over it, your card may be refused and you may face charges (see page 72). Gold and platinum cards tend to have a high credit limit but may be available only if you earn over £20,000, say. Irrespective of their colour, most cards have a different limit for cash withdrawals – for example, no more than half your credit limit can be cash withdrawals

- **an interest-free period** This is the number of days you have after the date of your statement in which to pay the bill in full without having to pay interest. Many issuers give you 25 days, but some give you less time. Some cards have no interest-free period at all: you incur interest as soon as you make a purchase. These cards are not a good option if you want to use your credit card as a no-cost payment card, but they could be worth a look if you are running a debt from month to month as they tend to charge a lower rate of interest

- **the ability to borrow** The credit limit is not only your spending limit, it is also the most you can borrow on the card, which you do by not paying your monthly bill in full. The ability to carry debt over from one month to the next, rather than paying the bill in full by the due date each month, is what distinguishes a credit card from a charge card (see page 63)

- **the ability to withdraw cash** You can get cash on your card either over the counter at a bank or by using a cash machine, but it will cost you (see page 67)

- **a PIN number** This is the personal identification number which you need in order to use your card in cash machines displaying the sign of the network your card issuer belongs to. Tear it up and forget it if you do not want to use your credit card for cash

- **the ability to use your card abroad** It is usually worthwhile using your credit card abroad – either for purchases or to get foreign currency from cash machines or over the counter – because although there can be extra costs to pay, exchange rates used by card issuers are usually more favourable than normal tourist rates

- **credit-card cheques** A lot of credit cards come with a cheque book. These cheques work just like normal current account cheques except that the money is taken off your card account. However, there is no interest-free period so you incur interest on your purchase straight away. Using a credit-card cheque also means that you lose the protection of the Consumer Credit Act (see page 59), which may explain why card issuers are so keen to promote them

- **debt transfer** This can be useful if you are running a debt and want to take advantage of a lower interest rate on offer with a different card. Some card issuers will accept the transfer only if you close your account with your old card issuer. Others will let you keep the old card but may charge a slightly higher rate of interest than if you had got rid of the old card altogether
- **a choice of statement date** Not all issuers allow you to choose, but it can be useful if you are planning on using your card as a substitute payment card. This is because you can time your card statement to coincide with pay-day
- **the ability to pay the minimum by direct debit** If you sometimes miss making your monthly payment, the option of paying the minimum amount by direct debit can come in handy. It does not mean that you cannot pay more than the minimum by other means, but it does avoid unpleasant (and sometimes expensive) reminders and the possibility of getting a bad payment record
- **the ability to pay in full by direct debit** Some cards also give you the option of paying your entire bill by direct debit, which means that you will avoid paying interest and won't have to write a cheque each month. However, this is probably not suitable if there are going to be times when you want to pay less than the full amount because it could mean going overdrawn on your current account. Whichever direct debit method you choose, the card issuer should always send you the statement at least seven days before the money comes off your account in order to give you time to update your current account records (see Chapter 2), and transfer money from savings to meet the bill if you need to
- **the ability to name an additional cardholder** Arranging for someone else to have a card on your account is of questionable value unless that person is unable to get a credit card in his or her own right. You will be held responsible for the other person's actions and for getting the card back from him or her if you decide to end the arrangement. You may also lose the protection of the Consumer Credit Act for purchases made by the additional cardholder.

Additional angst

When Kate split up with her boyfriend Ben, she was naturally keen that he shouldn't continue buying things on the additional card she had arranged for him on her credit card. She didn't want to encourage him to go off on a spending spree by asking him for the card back directly, so she asked her card issuer to retrieve it instead. The card issuer refused to help and to add insult to injury said that Kate would be responsible for anything Ben spent on the card until it expired. The card issuer was within its rights to do this since buried in the small print of the terms and conditions for her card were instructions that if Kate wanted the additional card cancelled, as principal card-holder she would have to put it in writing and send the card back. Only after Kate threatened to cancel her own card did the card issuer agree to cancel the additional card.

Added protection

Several card issuers include purchase-protection insurance as part of their credit-card deal. If you lose or damage things you have just bought with your card – or if they are stolen – the insurance will pay out if the mishap happens within 90 to 100 days from the date of purchase. However, there is usually a maximum limit on what purchase protection will pay, and it will not cover:

- second-hand purchases
- animals
- cars or other vehicles
- currency
- perishable goods
- plants
- tickets
- watches or jewellery in luggage (unless carried by hand).

Purchase-protection insurance is of limited value if you already have 'all-risks' cover for your belongings under your house insurance policy.

Some issuers also offer a card-protection service – either free or as an optional extra which you pay for when you take out the card. You register the details of all your plastic cards (bank cards, other credit cards, shop cards and so on) with an insurance company. If your wallet or purse goes astray, you can report all your cards missing by phoning just one number. Other benefits often include an emergency loan of up to £1,000 if you are stranded abroad without access to money and up to £1,000 insurance cover against fraudulent use of the cards. However, the law already protects you against fraudulent use of the card: your liability is limited to £50 per card unless your card issuer can prove that you have been grossly negligent. If this is the case, the insurance will not cover you anyway.

Credit-card lookalikes

When is a credit card not a credit card? When it is a charge card. The difference between the two is that a credit card allows you to borrow within a pre-set limit, while a charge-card issuer will offer unlimited free credit on condition that you pay your bill in full every month – with heavy penalties if you don't. If what you are really after is a flexible way of borrowing, charge cards are best avoided. The two most well-known charge cards are American Express (Amex) and Diners Club, but some banks offer their own platinum and gold charge cards (some of these are genuine credit cards, so check the terms and conditions carefully if you are offered one). What all charge cards have in common is a fairly high annual fee, access to a large overdraft facility (upwards of £10,000) and free travel insurance, plus various other up-market perks aimed at the well-heeled. Note that charge cards do not carry the protection offered by the Consumer Credit Act (see page 59).

Credit-card perks

As well as the standard features you get with most credit cards, some issuers also offer perks as an added inducement to sign up for a card. If you intend to use your credit card as a substitute payment card, there is no harm in looking at what is on offer if you are attracted by the added extras. However, borrowers – or forgetful payers – should be wary of perks and should concentrate on finding a card which gives a good deal on the basics. The one major exception to this rule are the types of card that offer a cash rebate on your spending, a cash equivalent in the form of gift vouchers from certain shops (useful only if you are a fan of the shop in question), or money off your regular bills.

Points mean prizes

Most of the cards which offer perks work on a points system: the more you spend, the more points you get. However, the number of points you get for every £1 spent varies between card issuers, as does the number of points you need to exchange for the perks available, which include:

- **free flights** Check how many air miles you get for every £1 spent and choose the most generous card
- **new-car discounts** (usually with a particular car manufacturer). The points buy you a discount on top of any discount you negotiate with a car dealer but there may be a maximum limit. Check that there is no time limit for redeeming points if you have no firm plans to buy a new car
- **free gifts** The late twentieth-century equivalent of Green Shield stamps. The points you get are redeemed against specific items in the scheme's gift catalogue. This perk is only worth having if you like the 'gifts'
- **holiday discounts** These are only good for package holidays and you have to spend more to get a bigger discount. Some issuers also offer cash discounts if you use their card to book holidays from certain tour operators
- **free tickets** Your points earn free entry to certain popular leisure attractions, theatres and cinemas
- **special deals on financial products** For a really good deal on products such as mortgages, insurance and investments, you are usually better off looking elsewhere.

Giving to charity

Cards which let you give as you spend work by donating a fixed sum (usually in the region of £5) to the charity, or range of charities, of your choice when you first use it, and then a small percentage of the value of your purchases after that – typically 25p for every £100 spent. One of the first of these 'affinity' cards, the Oxfam card, raised nearly £100,000 by the end of its first year in the late 1980s. If you take the view that every little helps, choosing a charity-linked card will certainly benefit the charity concerned. However, if you are serious about giving you would be better off drawing up a deed of covenant which gives a far better 'perk' by enabling the charity to claim back the tax you have paid on your donation.

Shop until you drop

Most shop cards, which you can use to pay for things (as opposed to shop loyalty cards which earn you points – see Chapter 11) work exactly like credit cards, but can generally be used only in the shop, or group of shops, from which you get the card – with the exception of cards offered by the banking arms of large retailers such as supermarkets. Shops like people to apply for shop cards because it helps them to get to know customers' purchasing patterns. They also hope that it will enable them to retain customers, especially if they can supply the kind of goods shoppers want. The perceived kudos of being able to shop 'on account' harks back to grander days when this privilege was reserved only for very special customers. Since most shops also accept other credit cards, whether a shop card is worth getting depends on whether you like the look of other perks such as free catalogues, 'special' shopping evenings and discounts on certain products. The main reason for avoiding shop cards is that interest rates tend to be higher than those for ordinary, accepted-anywhere cards. However, if you want to shop on credit at Marks and Spencer or John Lewis, the in-house card is your only option.

Counting the cost

A credit card can cost you nothing if you always pay your bill in full every month. However, a credit card will cost you money if you:

- choose a card with an annual fee (see below)
- do not get an interest-free period (see below)
- use your card to get cash (see opposite)
- pay by credit-card cheque (see opposite)
- use your card abroad (see page 68)
- don't pay your bill in full every month (see pages 68–70)
- break the terms of your agreement with the card issuer (see page 72)
- are made to pay extra for using your credit card (see pages 72–73).

Avoiding annual fees

It used to be the case that only charge cards carried an annual fee. Then in the late 1980s, many credit cards followed suit. However, the trend is now away from annual fees largely due to increased competition in the market – particularly from cheaper no-fee, low-interest cards coming in from the United States.

If you intend always to pay your bill in full, you should avoid annual fees. If you use your card for borrowing, an annual fee could conceivably make sense, but only if the fee plus interest on your debt is lower than the interest you would pay on a no-fee card, or you spend enough on your card to get the fee waived. However, since this is very hard to judge before you have used the card for a year, as a general rule you are better off choosing a no-fee card.

No interest-free credit

Some newer cards do not give an interest-free credit period, which means that interest is charged on transactions and cash withdrawals from the day they reach your credit-card account. These cards are aimed at people who are running a debt on their credit card – the draw is a lower rate of interest.

Cards that do not offer an interest-free period are best avoided if you always pay the balance in full or pay less than the full amount only occasionally. The small print of the terms and conditions of this type of card should say something like:

There is no interest-free period. Interest is charged from the date any transaction or transfer reaches the account.

Charges for cash

Irrespective of whether you pay your bill in full every month, it will always cost you money if you use your credit card to get cash. This is because a handling fee (usually 1.5 per cent of the amount withdrawn, or £1.50 if you withdraw less than £100) is added; this may be subject to a maximum. The rate of interest charged for cash withdrawals will always be higher than the rate of interest charged for purchases. With some cards, you pay interest on cash withdrawals only if you do not pay your bill in full. Look for phrases such as:

> If you pay the statement balance on or before the payment date we will not charge interest on any of the items shown in that statement. If you do not pay the statement balance on or before the payment date we will charge interest and add it to your account on the next statement date.

A card which charges just a handling fee will always make getting cash cheaper than one that also charges interest from the date you make the withdrawal. So avoid cards where the terms and conditions say something along the lines of:

> We will charge interest on any cash transaction and handling charge, starting on the transaction date and ending on the date of full payment.

Charges for cheques

If you use a credit-card cheque to pay for goods and services, interest is usually charged on the amount of your purchase from the day the cheque hits your account, irrespective of whether or not you pay your

---

Tip

If you have a choice between using a credit-card cheque and using the card itself, always use the card. You will not lose the protection of the Consumer Credit Act (see page 59), and it will usually cost less.

bill in full. Some cards also charge a handling fee similar to that for cash withdrawals (see opposite). Note that you will not usually be charged if you can use your credit card as a cheque guarantee card.

Foreign credit

A credit card can provide a very convenient and cost-effective way of both making purchases abroad and getting foreign currency (charges will be the same as for any cash transactions – see opposite). However, some cards can be twice as expensive as others because of the loading that card issuers add to the exchange rate used to convert foreign currency transactions into sterling. The exchange rate is the wholesale rate – typically better than the tourist rate – used by the card networks (Visa and MasterCard), plus loading or a 'conversion fee' decided by individual card issuers: some make the loading clear (see example, below); others do not. If you plan to use your card abroad a lot you should look for a card with the cheapest charging method.

> The amount of any transaction in foreign currency will be converted into sterling at a rate of exchange determined by the bank at the time the item is debited to the account. In determining the rate of exchange, the bank will use the market rate obtained by Visa International. The rate of exchange will also incorporate the bank's conversion fee of 1.75% of the transaction amount. We make a charge of 2.5% of the transaction value for each foreign currency transaction and the calculation of the sterling amount shown on your statement takes this into account.

The cost of borrowing

A card should cost you nothing to use if you avoid cards with an annual fee (and those without interest-free credit), never use your card to get cash or make foreign purchases, don't use credit-card cheques and always pay your bill in full each month. However, as soon as you become a part-payer (i.e. use your card to borrow) you will have to pay interest. How much depends both on the interest rate – usually expressed both as a percentage per month and as an annual percentage rate (APR) – and on the method that the card issuer uses for calculating the interest charge. The different methods used can mean that two cards apparently charging the same rate of interest can apply quite different rates when it comes to the actual cost of borrowing. See table on page 71.

Statement-date charging

This charging method is rare these days. Interest on purchases is calculated from the date of the statement on which they first appear. Interest on cash advances is usually charged from the date of the withdrawal (see 'Charges for cash' on page 67), while if you make a part-payment, interest is charged from the statement date on the amount remaining after your payment has been deducted from the outstanding balance. You therefore do not have to pay interest on the days between making a purchase and your statement date. This should be clear in a card's terms and conditions. For example:

> Interest at the rate shown will be charged on any part of the balance outstanding at the beginning of the monthly accounting period [i.e. statement date] which remains unpaid 25 days later. Interest is not charged from the date of purchase.

Transaction-date charging

This method is much more common and more expensive than statement-date charging because interest starts to clock up from the day your purchase (or cash advance, if applicable) reaches your account. Interest is charged from the statement date on the daily balance of your account. Any part-payment will reduce the balance but further purchases (and cash advances) will increase it. This effectively means that you lose any interest-free period until you pay your bill in full. There are two ways of defining full payment:

- **method one** With most cards, full payment means the balance (including interest charges) given on the last statement. So (assuming that you do not use your card for cash) if you make part-payment one month followed by full payment the next month, no interest charges will appear on the third monthly statement. Following is an example of the wording you may find for a card which uses this method:

Interest will be calculated on a daily basis on the outstanding balance of all transactions from the date the transaction is processed to your account until the date of payment in full. Accrued interest will be debited to your account on each statement date. However, you will not have to pay interest on any purchases posted to your account after the date of your previous statement if you repay the full amount of the new balance by the due date for payment (shown on your monthly statement). You cannot avoid interest charges on cash advances but the earlier you make your payment, the less interest charges you will incur

- **method two** An increasing number of cards use a different definition of full payment. They will stop charging interest only after you have made full payment in two consecutive months after making a part-payment. So if you make a part-payment in month one, you need to make full payment in months two and three. Interest charges will then not appear on the fourth month's statement (assuming you did not use the card to get cash). Avoid cards with statements like this in their terms and conditions:

    a) Interest will be charged on a daily basis at the rate of 1.6% per month on the daily outstanding balance from the date the card transaction is debited to the card account until any repayments are credited to the card account and there-after on the reduced balance up to and including the next statement date when interest will be debited to the card account.

    b) If the total balance outstanding on the monthly statement date is repaid by close of business on the 20th day following that date, no interest will be charged on that balance after the date on that statement.

    c) If the total balance outstanding on the monthly statement date is repaid by the close of business on the 20th day following that date *and* the whole of the balance which was outstanding on the immediately preceding monthly state-ment date was repaid in full on or before the close of business on the 20th day that followed that date, no interest at all will be charged on those transactions.

How the charging method affects the interest you pay

	statement-date charging	transaction-date charging method 1	method 2
15 February make purchase			
1 March date of statement 1	interest calculation starts	interest calculation starts	interest calculation starts
20 March part-payment reaches account			
1 April date of statement 2	interest calculation stops because statement 2 is paid in full	interest calculation stops because statement 2 is paid in full	interest calculation stops
20 April full payment reaches account			
1 May date of statement 3			interest for the period between statement 2 and the date of full payment appears on statement 3
20 May full payment reaches account			
1 June date of statement 4			no interest charge because statements 2 and 3 paid in full
Number of days interest is charged for:	31	44	64

Extra charges

Some card issuers will apply charges if you break the terms of your agreement or ask them to do something out of the ordinary. These may include:

- **late payment charge** (up to £20) if you do not make payment by the due date or do not pay the minimum required
- **returned payment charge** (about £10) if the cheque you use to pay your bill bounces or your direct debit is returned unpaid
- **letter charge** (about £10) if the card issuer has to write to you because you have broken the terms of your agreement – you have gone over your credit limit, say
- **charge for duplicate statements** (about £5) – some card issuers double this if you ask for over six, for example
- **charge for duplicate vouchers** (about £5 per copy) – although if you have asked for a copy voucher because an amount on your statement is in dispute, there should be no charge.

Why it pays to stay within the limit

John was shocked to find a £10 charge for being £160 over his credit-card limit, and phoned his card issuer to say that he was going to pay the bill at once. But he discovered that since his statement, his card issuer had refused a continuous authority transaction (see page 76) and had twice bounced his credit-card cheques. On top of his embarrassment at having these payments refused, the bank had charged him £60 for its trouble. Later the same day another payment was refused, resulting in a further charge of £20. When his next statement turned up, he found he had been hit with a second fee for being over his credit limit. In total he was charged £100.

Credit-card surcharges

Until 1990, retailers and service providers were not allowed to charge you extra if you chose to pay by credit card. Now that they are, how much extra is up to them. By law, you must be told about any surcharge before you choose your method of payment. It may be worth paying the surcharge if you want to keep the protection of the Consumer Credit Act.

You can minimise the surcharge but keep the protection by paying at least £100 of the cost – the minimum required to be covered by the Act – with your credit card (the deposit on a holiday, say) and the remainder by some other means.

Choosing a credit card

The first thing to look for when choosing a credit card is no annual fee. Such cards are in plentiful supply and often have the best rates of interest on borrowing.

What you look for next will depend on how you propose to pay the bill and what you intend to use the card for:

- If you always pay your bill in full every month (i.e. you are a 'full payer') and never use your card to get cash, you should look for a card with a generous interest-free period (avoid no-free-credit cards – see page 66) and choose the perks that attract you (see pages 63–65).
- If you are a full payer but like to use your card to get cash, look for all of the above plus a card that does not charge interest on cash withdrawals (see page 67).
- If you intend to pay your bill in full most of the time but may occasionally make use of the credit, look for a card with low interest and check the method used for calculating interest (see pages 68–70).
- If you keep a running debt on your card, you should choose a card with a low rate of interest. You are the kind of customer card issuers are particularly interested in, so look out for special deals and incentives to transfer your debt (see pages 82–83).
- If you want to use your card to get foreign currency and/or make purchases abroad, make sure that the card you choose has all the features appropriate to your bill-paying method plus low exchange-rate loading (see page 68).

Tip

If you plan to use a credit card for your holiday spending but the one you possess has high charges for foreign transactions, consider taking out another card with better terms. For more on using your card abroad, see Chapter 12

How to apply for a credit card

You must be at least 18 before you can have a credit card. Applying for a card is very straightforward: you simply get hold of an application form (from a bank, via newspaper adverts or mailshots) and fill it in.

Warning

Do not apply for a card without first reading the terms and conditions. The type may be painfully small but you could face a nasty shock if you choose a card without knowing what you are letting yourself in for. Check carefully to make sure the card is appropriate for your bill-paying method and intended use.

Payment-protection insurance

While preparing your credit-card application, watch out for gimmicks encouraging you to take out 'payment-protection' or 'credit-care' insurance. This is designed to pay out if you are too ill or injured to work or if you are made redundant. If it does pay out, the insurance will pay only a small proportion – typically 10 per cent – of your outstanding balance and then usually for only a year. This sort of insurance will not pay off the full amount you owe even if you are able to make a claim, and will not cover you if you are retired, not in paid employment or work for fewer than 16 hours a week. If you are self-employed or you work on short-term contracts (of less than six months), the policy is unlikely to cover you for periods of unemployment but may pay out if you are too sick to work.

However, you would do better to consider taking out income-protection insurance (see Chapter 5).

Some credit-card application forms ask you to sign a declaration confirming your eligibility for the insurance. Even if you are eligible, this sort of insurance is of questionable value and the policy terms are often very restrictive. Also, the cost of the insurance will go up and down each month in line with the outstanding balance on your account – and you will have to pay the premium even if you pay your bill in full. For each £100 outstanding just before your statement date, expect to pay around 70 pence.

Warning

Watch out for application forms which ask you to state that you are eligible for payment protection insurance: by doing so, you may be saying that you want the insurance.

What happens to your application?

Once the card issuer has received your completed application form, it will usually be put through two checks to see whether you are an acceptable risk. The first is a check on your general creditworthiness, for which the card issuer will use a credit reference agency. The second is to see if you meet the card issuer's own lending criteria, for which a process called 'credit scoring' is commonly used.

As well as looking at your credit record, card issuers will also want to know whether you are the kind of customer that they want. For example, some card issuers do not want full payers because they are a

---

Tip

If you know you are a good credit risk – you have always kept up repayments and have never defaulted on a loan, for example – it would be well worth your while challenging a refusal because it may be that something is wrong with your credit file. For more details on appealing against rejection and getting your credit file corrected, see Chapter 15.

---

less attractive proposition than customers who make only part-payment and so pay interest; others may be interested only in home-owners; others in people who have a debt to transfer. If your application is unsuccessful and you are turned down for credit, see Chapter 15.

Using your credit card

If your application is successful, sign your card as soon as you receive it. After memorising your personal identification number (PIN) – which should arrive separately from the card – destroy the paper it was printed on. If you do not intend to use the card for cash, do not bother memorising the PIN. Depending on the card issuer, you may also be asked to sign and return a form confirming that you have received the card. After that, all you have to do is produce your card, sign your name and keep the receipts. Note: when paying your bill always allow at least four to five working days for your payment to be processed if you are paying by cheque.

Making regular payments

If you want to make regular payments using your credit card, you can do this by setting up a continuous authority transaction (CAT), or continuous payment authority as it is sometimes known. To do this you authorise the company or person you wish to pay to charge your credit card whenever payment is due. Generally, you fill in a pre-printed form from the organisation you want to pay – a magazine subscription, for example. Note that your agreement is not with the card issuer but with the person or organisation you are paying.

If you want to cancel a CAT, you will have to tell the recipient of the payment. Unlike direct debits on a bank account (see Chapter 2), telling the card issuer to cancel the agreement will not work. Even if you get rid of a credit card, the issuer is still obliged to make regular payments of this kind.

Keeping track of your account

Keeping track of your account should be quite straightforward provided you have kept all your credit-card chits (and those of any additional cardholder), noted details of phone transactions such as theatre bookings or mail-order purchases, and have a record of all CATs set up on your account. When your monthly statement arrives, check that all the transactions listed match up to your records.

Warning

If you do not keep all your credit-card receipts, you will not be able to check that your card company has got your statement right. If you query a transaction and it turns out that it was indeed your mistake, the card issuer may charge you for supplying a copy voucher (see page 72).

Making your statement tally

Some card issuers make checking a statement easier than others. A clear statement will show the date of the transaction – i.e. the day you made the purchase or withdrew cash – while a less helpful statement will give only the date that a transaction was 'posted to' (i.e. reached) your account. You may also find that while the date of purchase and its amount match up to your receipt, the name of the retailer does not. However, this does not necessarily mean that there is a mistake. It may simply mean that the retailer has linked up with a larger company in order to lower costs, and the name on your statement belongs to the organisation handling the retailer's card transactions.

If you have cancelled a subscription or resigned from a club or society which you used to pay by CAT (see opposite), check that no charges have been billed to your account since the date you cancelled. If a person or organisation you used to pay by CAT is still charging you, you must contact them direct and ask for your money back – your card issuer cannot help you.

How to check interest

If you did not pay your bill in full after your last statement, you are bound to be charged interest on the amount outstanding. Some cards will also charge interest if you did not pay the previous two bills in full (see page 70). If the interest you have been charged seems rather high or you do not think it should have been charged at all, first check your card's terms and conditions. It may well be that the reason for the charge is buried in the small print. If you do not have the terms and conditions any more, ask your card issuer for an explanation of how the interest was calculated. If you are not satisfied with the explanation and think that you have been overcharged, you should complain. For more information, see Chapter 19.

Tip

If you did not pay your last credit-card bill (or last two bills) in full, you will save on interest charges if you make the current month's payment as soon as possible after receiving your statement.

Dealing with discrepancies

If you find an entry on a statement that you genuinely cannot account for and did not authorise, you should query it with the card company straight away. You can do this by letter (see opposite) or by phone but whichever method you choose, make it clear that you will not be paying the disputed amount. If you pay your bill in full by direct debit, ask for an assurance that the disputed amount will not be included in the direct debit payment. Alternatively, ask your bank not to pay the direct debit, which means that you will have to make payment by cheque until the problem has been sorted out. You should also contact your card company if:

• there seems to be a duplicate entry on the account
• you have not received goods that you ordered but your account has been charged
• you have been issued with a refund voucher but the refund does not appear on your statement.

If you phone the card company, you will usually be sent a form to fill in confirming your reason for disputing your statement (see example, page 80). This may also happen if you write a letter. As soon as the card issuer receives your form, it should exclude the disputed amount from its interest calculations while the transaction is under investigation. If the issuer's investigations reveal that you are in the right, your account will be credited with the amount. If the card issuer failed to exclude the amount from its interest calculations, you should also receive a credit for the interest that has built up on it.

If you are not happy with the way your card issuer has dealt with your query or if it has taken too long to sort a problem out, follow the guidance given in Chapter 19.

Warning

If it turns out that you were in the wrong, you face paying interest on the disputed amount – usually from the date when the transaction first appeared on your statement.

Example of letter disputing a transaction

[Your Address]

Disputes Manager
[Credit Card Company]
[Address]
[Date]

Dear Sir

Credit card account number: 5566 1234 7891
My recent statement includes a transaction which I did not authorise. The details are as follows:

Date of transaction: [date]
Date transaction posted to the account: [date]
Transaction reference number: 1234
Supplier: [name]
Amount: £1,234

Please investigate the matter without delay. Please will you also confirm that you have suspended this transaction from my account and that I will not incur interest on it. I enclose a cheque for payment to my account excluding the above disputed amount.

I look forward to hearing from you within the next 14 days.

Yours sincerely
Jason Smith

Example of card issuer's standard form for disputed transactions

[Your address]

[Credit Card Company]
[Address]
[Date]

Credit card account number: 5566 1234 7891

Dear Mr Smith

Further to your recent contact regarding a disputed item, please complete the transaction description and amount details and enclose any relevant documentation you may have to support your claim.

Transaction description

_____ I did not authorise the transactions, nor did any other party to the account

_____ I only authorised one of the transactions and there would appear to be a duplicate entry

_____ Although I did engage in this transaction I have not received the goods/part of the order to the value of £ _____

_____ I was issued with a refund voucher which does not appear on my statement, copy of the refund voucher enclosed (if no voucher is available, please contact the merchant direct)

_____ Other (please explain).

Cardholder Signature   Date

Yours sincerely
A Jones
Manager
Card Disputes

Exercising your rights under the Consumer Credit Act

If you have paid your credit-card bill but have not received the goods or services for which you have paid, you can claim on your credit-card company under the Consumer Credit Act. If your supplier is still in business, the card issuer is likely to put pressure on the supplier to deliver whatever you ordered. However, if your supplier has gone out of business the card company is your only hope (see below). Note that if the card company refuses to meet its responsibilities by settling your claim, you can take it to court using the small claims procedure.

Example of letter claiming a refund from a card issuer when the supplier has gone out of business

[Your address]

[Credit Card Company]
[Address]
[Date]

Dear Sir

Credit card account number: 5566 1234 7891

On [date] I ordered [item] from [supplier] at a cost of [amount], for which I paid using the above credit card. I have paid the relevant bill covering this purchase.

The [item] has not been delivered, despite letters to the supplier on [dates], and I have discovered that the supplier has gone into liquidation.

I understand that under Section 75 of the Consumer Credit Act 1974 the credit-card company is liable to the customer for any breach or misrepresentation along with the supplier of goods and services.

The failure of [supplier] to deliver [item] is a breach of our contract and as I paid by credit card I hold you liable for this breach. I therefore expect you to credit my account with the full purchase price of [amount] within the next 14 days. If you fail to reimburse me I shall have no alternative but to issue a summons against you in the county court for recovery of the money without further reference to you.

Yours sincerely
Jason Smith

Should you switch?

You should definitely switch your credit card if you are paying an annual fee – especially if you always pay your bill in full every month. You can also save money by switching if you use your card to get cash or for your holiday spending, and your current card does not offer a good deal for these sorts of transaction.

If you use your card to borrow – either occasionally or all the time – you will certainly save money if you can find a card charging a lower rate of interest.

Switch to save and switch again

If you run up a debt on your existing credit card, look into the special introductory offers – which typically last for six months to a year – that an increasing number of cards are offering these days. Card issuers like customers who pay interest and so are usually very keen to get you to transfer your debt to them. Some offer better rates to people who close down their old credit-card accounts as soon as the switch is made. Always check:

- what the interest rate will be
- when the special offer period comes to an end
- how much of your balance the special low-interest rates will apply to: it may be only to the balance that you transfer and not to any new purchase you make with the card, although you can find cards which apply the low rate to all transactions
- whether the transferred balance is treated as a purchase or as a cash advance; if the latter, the interest rate will be higher
- how your repayments will be used – most card issuers use your repayments to pay off your transferred balance first.

There is nothing to stop you switching cards again – and to carry on switching – when the special-offer rate on each card comes to an end. But be wary of cutting up an old card or transferring your balance to a new card until you know what your credit limit is going to be.

Caught out by the small print

When Alastair transferred his credit-card debt of £2,800 to a lower-charging card, he used his card to make a few purchases. He was surprised to be charged more interest than the APR of 7.9 per cent he had been led to expect, and stopped using the card when he found that his repayments were being used to clear the debt he had transferred, rather than to pay for the new purchases.

How to switch cards

Switching credit cards is much more straightforward than switching current accounts (see Chapter 2): you simply fill in an application form for the new card. This will probably have space for you to transfer your old credit-card balance at the same time as you apply – but note that if your new credit limit is smaller than the balance you want to transfer you will have to leave some debt on your old card. Do not cut up your old card until you have found out what your credit limit is going to be.

If you have CATs (see page 76) on your old card, you have a choice: you can either contact all the organisations involved as soon as you get your new card; or you can wait until you get a statement showing that they have been charged to your old card (which is what will happen if you do not rearrange them immediately). You can then change them as they happen. Alternatively, keep your old card on specifically for your regular payments – especially if you plan to switch cards on a regular basis.

Tip

If you have decided that the time has come to clear your credit-card debt, consider becoming a full payer on your old card while transferring your existing balance to a lower-charging card – even one that does not give free credit. You will be able to pay off the debt gradually but at a much lower rate of interest – while not incurring interest on your old card.

Chapter 4

Savings accounts

If you run your current account in credit and pay your credit card bill in full every month, you should seriously consider paying any spare money into a savings account. Not only will your money earn more interest than it does in a current account – not least because some of the interest on your savings can be tax-free if you save cash in an individual savings account (ISA) (see pages 92–94) – but it will build up a cushion against the unexpected. Creating an emergency – or rainy day – fund in this way is an essential part of sensible financial planning, and you should not consider other forms of saving and investing until you have a sufficiently large fund to cover what you view as an emergency (see Chapter 1).

However, setting aside a fund of spare cash for unexpected expenditure is only one use for a savings account: you can also use it to earmark money for predictable short-term future spending such as next year's holiday, a large piece of furniture or the deposit on a flat, for example.

This chapter covers the types of savings accounts that are most suitable for building up an emergency fund and for funds you plan to spend in the short term. It tells you what to look for, how to choose the most convenient account, and examines ways in which you can avoid paying tax on the interest you earn. Whether you are thinking of changing your savings account or you are opening one for the first time, you will find advice on avoiding penalties and getting the best deal on interest rates. If you already have an emergency fund and your other short-term spending plans are sorted out you may want to look into other ways of saving and investing (see Chapters 20 and 21).

How much should you save?

There is very little point in saving if you have expensive debts (see Chapters 2 and 3), but once you have cleared these, the amount you should save will depend on how much surplus cash you have available after meeting all your other commitments. To get an accurate picture of how much this might be on a monthly basis, it would be worthwhile filling in the 'Personal budget calculator' in Chapter 18. For a more ad-hoc approach, consider transferring however much is left in your current account just before pay-day (assuming that this amount is genuinely surplus to requirements). If you want to be more disciplined, another approach is to fix the amount you want to save each month and to work this amount into your budget (which may mean cutting your spending on other things).

> **Tip**
>
> When working out how much you can afford to put towards your emergency fund, don't forget to allow for the cost of covering other contingencies. Depending on your personal circumstances, you may need to spread your surplus cash between savings and spending on insurance (see Chapter 1).

What is on offer

Traditionally the preserve of high-street banks, building societies and the government (in the form of National Savings), nowadays savings accounts are on offer from the banking arms of insurance companies and other financial institutions, and those of large supermarkets. Regardless of who offers them, in terms of the basics all savings accounts work the same way: you pay your money into the savings account of your choice and it earns interest until you withdraw it.

If you decide to close the account altogether, you get back what you paid in plus whatever interest has been earned. There is no risk to your capital (the money you pay in) provided the account earns interest at a rate equal to or above inflation (at the time of writing about 2.5 per cent). If the interest rate on your savings is lower than inflation (as is the case with the interest paid on most current accounts, for example), the spending power of your capital will gradually diminish over time.

Although all savings accounts operate in basically the same way, they differ in terms of:

- how quickly you can get at your savings (see below)
- how much money you can withdraw, and how often (see opposite)
- how you pay money in and get it back again (see pages 87–88)
- the interest rate and how frequently interest is paid (see pages 88–90)
- how the interest is taxed (see pages 90–94).

Access to your cash

The most suitable types of savings accounts for emergency funds and short-term investments are those which give you reasonably quick access to your cash:

- **instant-access accounts** let you withdraw your money immediately and can be named as such only if you get immediate access to your money in cash, whether over the counter, from a cash machine or by instantaneous transfer to another account (your current account, for example) from which you can then withdraw cash. However, if you want to withdraw money using a method that does not involve cash, you may have to wait a few days, so the account effectively stops being instant-access and becomes a no-notice account
- **no-notice accounts** are savings accounts which do not require you to give advance warning of wanting to withdraw money, but which make you wait a few days either for a cheque for your withdrawal to be posted to you or for the money to be transferred to your current account. The wait may be worth it if you do not like the idea of withdrawing large amounts in cash. Some accounts come with a cheque book (and sometimes other features of a current account), and withdrawals are made by writing a cheque – these are typically called 'high-interest cheque accounts'
- **notice accounts** require you to give anything from 7 to 90 days' advance warning or 'notice' of wanting to withdraw your savings (or sometimes longer). It used to be the case that you got a much

better rate of interest in exchange for this notice period but nowadays you may find that an instant-access or no-notice account offers a similar or better deal with greater flexibility.

Tip

Using a credit card to buy goods and services you have saved up for means that you can leave the money in your savings account earning interest for longer. If you time your purchase to happen just after the date when your monthly statement is due, you will earn more than a month's worth of extra interest.

Paying the penalty

As well as looking at how quickly you can get at your cash, you also need to make sure that you will not fall foul of the terms and conditions of the account. New rules for the advertising of savings accounts which came into force at the beginning of 1999 mean that the conditions and penalties attached to an account can no longer be buried in the small print, so it should be easier to spot whether an account:

- requires a minimum investment to open the account
- restricts the number of withdrawals you can make each year
- imposes a charge if you make more than a set number of withdrawals
- allows free withdrawals only if the balance on your account remains above a certain amount
- imposes a limit on the size of each withdrawal or deposit
- pays 'bonus' or extra interest only if you make no withdrawals in a year
- makes you give up interest if you do not give sufficient notice of wanting to withdraw your money.

A question of convenience

If you are going to get the best from a savings account it needs to be convenient, which means that you should be able to pay money in and get money out in a way that suits you. All accounts let you pay money in by standing order (and more rarely by direct debit), which is fine if you want to save a regular amount every month. However, if you will be saving on an as-and-when basis, you need to decide if you will be happy to queue at a branch (or cash machine) to pay your money in and get it out, or whether you would prefer to use one of the increasing number of postal or telephone-based accounts.

With these, paying-in arrangements usually involve you being issued with a paying-in book. You post a cheque for the amount you want to save – many companies offer pre-paid envelopes to keep your postage costs down. To get money out, you either ask to receive a cheque through the post or ring up to arrange to have the money transferred directly to your current account (or some other account which you specify when you open the account). Some postal and telephone accounts also offer a cash card to give you instant access to your cash, although if you are unhappy about getting out substantial amounts of cash, this may not appeal.

Warning

Do not automatically assume that a savings account from the same institution which provides your current account will be the most convenient. Postal and telephone-based accounts from other providers make transferring money in and out of your savings account just as easy as transferring money between accounts at the same bank. You are also likely to get a much better rate of interest than that on offer from your current account provider.

Assessing the interest

Most savings accounts pay interest at a variable rate, which means that the interest rate will go up and down more or less in line with interest rates generally. You may also find accounts which pay interest at a fixed rate for a specified period of time, although these are unlikely to be suitable for an emergency fund or other short-term savings – both because of restrictions on withdrawals and because you may have to lock your savings away for a fixed amount of time.

A lot of accounts – sometimes called 'tiered' accounts – pay a higher rate of interest once the money you have in the account goes over a certain level (or levels).

Accounts typically pay interest monthly, quarterly, half-yearly or yearly. Interest can be paid out to you – direct to your current account, for example – or it can be 'compounded' which means that you can leave it in your account earning more interest as part of your savings. This is probably the best course of action for short-term savings. The more frequently interest is added to your account, the more interest you will end up earning.

Warning

When the Bank of England announces a cut in interest rates, check that the interest on your savings account is not cut by more than the general cut in rates. If it is, consider switching (see page 98).

How to compare interest rates

Since the beginning of 1999 (when a new code of conduct for the advertising of interest-bearing accounts came into force), it has been a lot easier to compare the interest rates on savings accounts because advertisements have to give an 'annual effective rate' (AER) which enables you to make direct comparisons between accounts that pay interest at different intervals. In effect, the AER is the financial equivalent of the 'price per kilo' labelling that you find on supermarket shelves which enables you to compare the price of different-sized packets of the same product. If the account offers bonus interest (see page 87), an AER including the bonus can also be quoted but it must state clearly that the bonus is included in the figure and cannot be given greater prominence than the AER without the bonus.

As well as the AER, advertisements must also quote the 'contractual' rate, which is the flat rate of interest before taking into account how often interest is paid. The flat rate must be quoted as a gross figure (i.e. before tax) but it can also be quoted as a net figure (after-tax) or as a tax-free figure. The following table shows how differences in the frequency with which interest is paid can affect what you actually get, and demonstrates why the AER is a better tool for comparison than the flat rate.

Using the AER as a comparative tool

AER if interest is paid:				
Flat rate	Monthly	Quarterly	Half-yearly	Yearly
3%	3.04%	3.03%	3.02%	3%
4%	4.07%	4.06%	4.04%	4%
5%	5.12%	5.09%	5.06%	5%
6%	6.17%	6.14%	6.09%	6%
7%	7.23%	7.19%	7.12%	7%
8%	8.3%	8.24%	8.16%	8%
9%	9.38%	9.31%	9.2%	9%
10%	10.47%	10.38%	10.25%	10%

The table assumes that you make no withdrawals and that you leave the interest in the account.

Savings accounts and tax

Although the AER is a useful tool for comparing the interest rates of accounts which are taxed in the same way, it will not tell you how two accounts compare after tax has been taken into account. To be able to compare like with like, you need to know whether the interest is tax-free or taxable and what your highest rate of tax is (to work this out, see Chapter 17). If you choose tax-free savings (see pages 92–94), you do not have to pay tax on the interest your savings earn and so the AER is the interest that will be paid, irrespective of your top rate of tax. If you choose taxable savings, the interest that you will get depends on what sort of taxpayer you are:

- non-taxpayers will get the AER rate because all interest from a savings account will be tax-free
- lower-rate taxpayers need to multiply the AER of taxable interest by 0.8
- basic-rate taxpayers need to multiply the AER of taxable interest by 0.8

- higher-rate taxpayers need to multiply the AER of taxable interest by 0.6.

Note that these figures relate to the 1999–2000 tax year and assume that interest is taxed at 20 per cent for lower- and basic-rate taxpayers and at 40 per cent for higher-rate taxpayers. If interest is tax-free, all types of taxpayer get the same rate of interest.

Calculating the after-tax rate of interest

AER before tax	Tax-free	non-taxpayers	lower- and basic-rate taxpayers	higher-rate taxpayers
1%	1%	1%	0.8%	0.6%
2%	2%	2%	1.6%	1.2%
3%	3%	3%	2.4%	1.8%
4%	4%	4%	3.2%	2.4%
5%	5%	5%	4%	3%
6%	6%	6%	4.8%	3.6%
7%	7%	7%	5.6%	4.2%
8%	8%	8%	6.4%	4.8%
9%	9%	9%	7.2%	5.4%
10%	10%	10%	8%	6%

Rates of tax are for the 1999–2000 tax year.

Tax point

With the exception of National Savings accounts (see page 94), lower-rate tax on interest is deducted before interest is paid to you. If you do not pay tax on any of your other income, it may be that you do not need to pay tax on your income from savings either. You can register for interest from your savings to be paid without tax being deducted by filling in form R85, available from the institution where you hold your account. If you are a higher-rate taxpayer, you should give details of your interest from savings on your tax return and you will pay the extra tax due directly to the Inland Revenue.

Tax-free savings

There are two types of tax-free savings accounts which are suitable for an emergency fund and other short-term savings:

- an individual savings account (ISA)
- a National Savings Ordinary Account.

Warning

Do not choose a savings account just because it is tax-free. If you can get a better rate of interest after taking tax into account, paying the tax will be worthwhile.

Individual savings accounts (ISAs)

ISAs have been available since 6 April 1999 and unlike their predecessor TESSA, they do not make you lock your savings away for five years. This means that they can be a good home for surplus cash if you do not already have an emergency fund or other savings.

You can have an ISA if you are a UK resident who is aged 18 or over. Husbands and wives can each have their own ISA. As well as being able to save cash in an ISA, you will also be able to invest in stocks and shares, including unit trusts, open-ended investment companies (OEICs) and investment trusts and investment-type life insurance (for more on these types of investments, see Chapter 21). All income and gains on ISA savings and investments will be completely free of tax. Because of this, there are limits on how much you can invest in each component as well as other rules:

- in the 1999–2000 tax year (the first year of the scheme), you can invest up to £7,000 in total. Within this overall limit, the most cash you can save is £3,000 and the most you can spend on investment-type life insurance is £1,000. You have the option to invest the full £7,000 in stocks and shares but if you want to do this, you lose the ability to save cash or buy insurance
- from 6 April 2000, the limits will be a maximum of £1,000 in

cash, £1,000 in investment-type life insurance and £3,000 in stocks and shares with an overall limit of £5,000
- the tax rules do not stipulate a minimum investment, but companies offering an ISA may do.

Maxi or mini ISAs?

ISAs are run by 'ISA managers' – i.e. the financial institutions which offer them. Although you cannot choose to invest more than the limits given above, you can make a choice between having a 'maxi ISA' or up to three 'mini ISAs':

- If you opt for a **maxi ISA**, you use one manager which must offer stocks and shares but does not have to offer the cash or insurance components – avoid these if you are interested in saving cash.
- With a **mini ISA**, you choose a separate manager for each component of your ISA. So you could have a mini cash ISA with a bank or building society, a mini insurance ISA with an insurer and a mini stocks and shares ISA with an investment company, for example.

Warning

You cannot have a maxi ISA *and* a mini ISA. If you try to open both you will face Inland Revenue fines. Your choice of ISA also affects the amounts you can invest (see Chapter 21).

CAT marks

CAT marks are the Government's attempt to ensure that ISAs meet certain minimum standards so a CAT mark is not a guarantee that you are getting the best deal possible. CAT stands for: fair Charges, easy Access and decent Terms. In general, to meet the CAT standards, an ISA cannot be bundled with other products or limited to existing customers, and the managers of CAT-marked ISAs cannot suddenly decide to withdraw them. The particular standards applied to CAT-marked cash ISAs are that:

- there must be no charges (with the exception of charges for things like duplicate statements or lost cash cards)
- the minimum you can invest cannot be set at more than £10

- you should not have to wait more than seven working days to get at your money
- there must not be any conditions attached to running the account (for example, a limit on the number of withdrawals you can make)
- the interest paid must be no less than 2 per cent below bank base rate
- if bank base rate goes up, the interest you are paid should go up within a month of the increase.

National Savings Ordinary Account

The attraction of a National Savings Ordinary Account is that the first £70 of interest (£140 for joint accounts) is tax-free – but to earn that amount you would have to have £5,800 in savings. The off-putting part is that the rates (in April 1999) are quite low – 1 per cent on savings up to £500 and 1.2 per cent for total savings exceeding £500. If you look at the table on page 91, you can see that an account which pays taxable interest is likely to give you a much better deal. However, rates may improve so it is always worth comparing this account with what you can get elsewhere.

Unlike the ISA, anyone can open an account. You can do this at any post office with a minimum opening investment of £10, which is also the minimum amount you can pay in. The most you can withdraw in cash is £100, unless you have a regular customer account (to qualify for this you need to use the same post office for six months, at which point you can fill in a form enabling you to withdraw £250). If you want more than the maximum cash withdrawal, you will have to apply in writing and wait about a week before getting your money. With cheque withdrawals, you can withdraw the total amount you have in your account.

Choosing a savings account

The best home for an emergency fund is either an instant-access or no-notice account. If you do not already have any savings, but want to start putting money aside, consider an ISA which gives you reasonable access to your cash. However, bear in mind that once you have taken money out of an ISA, you cannot replenish it until the following tax year – this will be a problem only if you have paid in the maximum amount allowed for the year at the time you take the money out. If you already have some savings, it may be worthwhile transferring them to an ISA. If your savings exceed the limits of what you can save in an ISA (see pages 92–93), it may be better to use an ISA for money you do not want to touch and a taxable savings account for your emergency fund. If you are saving up for something specific and you know when you will need to pay for it, you could consider a notice account.

Once you have decided which sort of account you want, the next priority is to make sure that it is convenient both in terms of paying cash in and retrieving it, and regarding the conditions placed on the account. If you plan to withdraw some savings in the future, an account that limits the number of withdrawals you can make may not pose a problem – but if you are not sure how often you will need to withdraw money (as is the case with an emergency fund), it would be better to choose an account which gives you unlimited and penalty-free access to your cash.

The final consideration is the interest rate. You should choose the account which offers the best rate (use the AER to compare them – see page 90) after taking tax into account. To get information about interest rates, check the regular surveys of saving rates in *Which?* magazine, other personal finance magazines and the personal finance pages of newspapers.

Tip

Most surveys of savings rates concentrate on accounts which are nationally available. It is also worth checking the rates being paid by smaller building societies in your area.

Are your savings safe?

Financial institutions which offer savings accounts must be authorised and regulated by the Financial Services Authority.* In the unlikely event that a bank or building society should fail, you are guaranteed to get back 90 per cent of the first £20,000 of your savings – although the rest will be lost. With a joint account, each account holder is separately protected up to £20,000.

Opening a savings account

Once you have chosen the savings account that will suit you best and which pays the best rate of interest, obtain an application form and complete it, then either post it off with a cheque (if you are opening a postal or telephone-based account), or open the account in person at a branch. Note that you may need to provide some form of identification when you open the account (see 'Opening a current account' on page 36).

If you have decided that you want to make regular payments into your account, ask for a standing order form for your savings account. Alternatively, use the sample letter for setting up a standing order on page 44.

Keeping track

If you have a branch-based account, or a National Savings account where you need to visit the branch (or a post office) to pay in and withdraw money, you will usually be issued with a passbook where all transactions will be recorded as they happen, so there is no need to keep any records other than your passbook (unless you have a cash card, in which case you should keep the chits you get when you use the cash machine). You should keep your own records if you have a postal or telephone-based account so that you can check them against the regular statements you receive (you must be sent a statement at least once a year). You can also check that your account is in order by checking your balance on a regular basis. If you find a mistake on your statement, contact the institution where you hold your account as soon as possible. If you are having problems getting a mistake sorted out, see Chapter 19.

Changes to interest rates

As well as making sure that your account is being run properly, you should also keep a regular check on the rate of interest that your savings are earning. If interest rates change during the year, you must be told about the change. How this is done depends on the type of account you have. If you have a:

- **telephone or postal account** you will receive personal notification (i.e. a letter, email or mailshot) of changes to interest rates within 30 days of the change
- **branch-based account** you may receive personal notification within 30 days; otherwise you have to look out for advertisements in the branch or national press.

Whichever kind of account you have, the notification must show both the new and the old rate of interest. In addition, every year you must be sent a summary of all the savings accounts on offer from your savings institution (unless you have a passbook account with less than £100 in it) with details of current interest rates and the different rates which have applied to the account throughout the year.

Changes to terms and conditions

As well as changes to interest rates, you must be given at least 30 days' notice of any changes to the terms and conditions of your account. If the change is clearly not in your favour, you must be given:

- personal notification of the change – with a copy of the new terms and conditions if they are significantly different from the old ones
- 60 days in which to change or close your account – without penalty if you make the change during the 60 days given.

If your account is obsolete
Thanks to intensive lobbying by Consumers' Association, if savings institutions stop actively promoting an old savings account (or close it to new customers entirely) and launch a new and better replacement, they must:

- keep interest paid on the old account at the same level as the interest paid on a similar new account
- switch your old account (with your agreement) to the new account if it is similar to but a better deal than the old account
- tell you about other accounts which may be better for you if there is no direct replacement for your old account, and allow you to switch accounts without penalty if this is what you want to do.

> **Tip**
>
> Although it is harder for banks and building societies to leave you in the dark about changes to your account, it is still worth keeping your own regular check on your account – not least because you may find a better offer from a different institution.

Should you switch?

Unless you are saving with a building society in the hope that it will convert to a bank and you will get a handsome payout, you should lose 'loyalty' from your vocabulary when it comes to finding a good home for your savings. The institutions that offer savings accounts regularly change the interest rates they pay as well as the terms and conditions relating to the account, and new accounts frequently appear on the market, often with temptingly high interest rates to get new customers to sign up. Because switching savings accounts is very straightforward, you should certainly switch accounts if you can get a better rate of interest or better terms such as fewer restrictions on withdrawals, for example, or easier access to your money. Switching from a branch-based account to a telephone or postal account will also mean that you will be informed about changes to your account automatically.

How to switch

If you find an account that offers a better deal, switching is relatively straightforward:

- open the new account
- cancel any standing order to your old account (if applicable) and reinstate it at your new account
- give the required amount of notice to withdraw all your savings from your old account (unless it is an instant-access or no-notice account)
- withdraw your savings and pay them into your new account
- cut your cash card in two (if applicable) and send it back.

Part 2

Contingency plans

Chapter 5

Income-protection insurance

Having an emergency fund to fall back on will help you to cope with short-term blips in your finances, but unless you have a sizeable amount of cash put aside, it is unlikely to be sufficient to cope with the potentially long-term effects of being unable to earn due to sickness. This is not anything to worry about if you do not yet have regular earnings, or if you are retired and have a pension income since this will carry on being paid whatever your state of health. You should, however, give serious thought to what you would do if sickness or a disabling accident put a stop to your earning power. It is also worth considering how sickness would affect your family if you look after children full-time and your long-term sickness would mean that childcare would have to be paid for (see page 109).

This chapter looks at the different ways in which you can get financial help if sickness strikes. It also tells you how to assess whether you need to make additional contingency plans by buying insurance. You will find details of the types of insurance available, advice on choosing the right type for your personal circumstances and tips on keeping the cost to an absolute minimum. The financial help available if you lose earnings through redundancy is dealt with in Chapter 6.

Where to go for help

Before you can decide whether you need to buy your own insurance, you should find out what other possible methods of replacing income are available to you and how much you are likely to get from each source. The main sources of income if you are unable to work because of illness are:

- **a sick-pay scheme** through your job (see below)
- **state benefits** (see below)
- **early retirement** (see pages 103–104)
- **your own resources** (see pages 104–105).

Help from your employer

If you do not know whether your employer runs a sick-pay scheme, it would be worth finding out by checking your contract of employment, studying your staff handbook or asking your boss or human resources (personnel) department. The most generous sick-pay schemes carry on paying your full salary for the first six months of any long-term illness, with a reduced salary (typically half) for the next six months. If you still have not recovered after a year, you may have a case for early retirement on the grounds of ill-health (see pages 103–104). Less generous schemes limit payment of full salary to one month's sickness, followed by half-salary for a second month. Instead of running a sick-pay scheme, your employer could pay for you to belong to a 'group income-protection insurance scheme', also called 'group permanent-health insurance', which is income-protection insurance (see pages 105–110) bought in bulk for a group of (usually senior) employees.

If your employer does not run a sick-pay scheme and group insurance is not on offer, your employer should pay you statutory sick pay of £59.55 per week (in the 1999–2000 tax year) provided you earn enough to pay National Insurance and you are off work sick for at least four consecutive days. If you do not earn enough to pay National Insurance or you are still ill after 28 weeks of receiving statutory sick pay, you may be able to claim state benefits instead.

Help from the state

If you do not qualify for statutory sick pay (because you are self-employed or out of work, for example), you may be entitled to incapacity benefit through the Benefits Agency* if your doctor certifies that you are not well enough to do your job and provided you have paid sufficient National Insurance (currently at any time in your working life but due to be changed to at any time in the last two years). There are three rates of benefit:

- for **the first 28 weeks of illness** you get short-term incapacity benefit of £50.35 a week, which is tax free
- **from week 29** the short-term incapacity benefit goes up to £59.55 but becomes taxable and you will receive it only after you have been through the 'all work' medical test (although the government plans to replace this with the 'personal capability assessment', which will look at ability to work rather than focusing on inability) and this shows that you are incapable of doing *any* job
- **from week 53** you get the higher – but still taxable – long-term incapacity benefit of £66.75 a week. However, if you are terminally ill or very seriously disabled, the long-term rate is paid from week 29.

Extra benefits are available if you have children, a partner who looks after the children or who is over state pension age. Extra benefits for children are tax free while those for a partner are taxable. If you do not qualify for incapacity benefit, you may be able to claim other benefits, depending on your personal circumstances. As we went to press, the government planned to change the rules relating to entitlement to incapacity benefit. For up-to-date information on state benefits when you are ill, contact your local Benefits Agency.

Your pension

If you are unlikely to be able to return to work at all and you pay into a pension scheme (see Chapter 8), you may qualify for early retirement on grounds of ill health. If you belong to an employer's final-salary scheme, you may qualify for a 'disability pension', whereby you get a bigger pension than you would from normal early retirement. It is often calculated by assuming that you have built up the number of years' service that you would have at normal retirement age but based on your current salary. Whether this would be an option depends on the rules of the scheme and on whether you would meet Inland Revenue guidelines, which say that you must be unable to follow your normal occupation due to physical or mental deterioration.

If you have a personal pension, retiring early will not have the advantages of a disability pension from your employer, where a minimum amount is guaranteed. The Inland Revenue allows you to take a personal pension early on health grounds but the benefits you get will depend entirely on the amount of the fund you have built up – see Chapter 8 for how to work out how much pension your fund will buy you. Note that the government has put forward proposals that will mean that a claim for incapacity benefit will be reduced if you receive a weekly pension of more than £50.

Tip

If you are not yet paying into a pension or you have been paying into a personal pension for only a short time and you are worried about how you would cope if you were too ill to work, consider making other arrangements to replace your income.

Helping yourself

Once you have found out how much income you could expect to receive from your employer, the state and/or your pension, you need to compare this 'income if ill' figure with the figure for the bare minimum that you would be happy to live on (you may find it useful to use the 'Personal budget calculator' in Chapter 18). If there is a shortfall between your expected income and the amount you would want to live on, but you have savings that you would be prepared to use to make up for the shortfall, you need to work out how long you could manage before you had to take a sharp cut in your standard of living. To do this:

- work out the minimum you would be happy to live on each month
- subtract the monthly amount of income you would expect to receive from external sources (if the figure is zero or a minus figure, there is no shortfall)
- divide any savings that you would be prepared to use to top up your income by the figure for the monthly shortfall (if there is one).

If you would have to take a sharp cut in your standard of living and you are not prepared to do this, or your sums show that you would be able to maintain your current, or reduced, standard of living for only a limited time (less than six months or a year, say) before feeling the pinch, you need to arrange your own protection against loss of income through illness. The main way of making sure that you would have enough to live on is by taking out insurance, which will pay out if you become seriously ill or disabled. The three main types of insurance available are:

- income-protection insurance (see below)
- critical illness insurance (see pages 110–112)
- accident and sickness insurance (see pages 112–113).

Sums for the self-employed

David and Janice and their son Christopher live and work in a small Surrey village. David gave up the security of a job in the Civil Service to become self-employed. When he left his job, he also left behind a good sick-pay scheme. Fortunately, David has never had a long illness but if he did, he and his family would find life very hard indeed. David and Janice reckon that they need about £350 a week to cover basics such as rates, mortgage, food, heating and so on. But if David were to become ill and could claim incapacity benefit, the family would still have to find about £300 a week. To make ends meet, they would have to eat into their savings, and if David were ill for a year or more they would be really struggling. Since they couldn't manage on state benefits and Janice's income alone, they decide that they need to buy income-protection insurance.

Income-protection insurance

Income-protection insurance, which you buy yourself, pays out a regular tax-free income (referred to as the 'benefit') if you become ill or suffer an accident that leaves you unable to work. If you have this sort of insurance through your job (see page 102), the replacement income is taxable. How 'unable to work' is defined varies from policy to policy and can be any of the following:

- an inability to do your own job
- an inability to do your own job or a similar job for which you are qualified
- an inability to do any kind of paid work.

A policy that pays out if you cannot do your own job is clearly better than one where you have to be unfit to do any job. Normally, you carry on getting the income either until you get better or until you reach retirement, whichever comes first – although newer 'budget' schemes may limit payment to a maximum of five years. Provided you keep paying for it – i.e. you do not let the 'premiums' lapse – your policy will pay out as many times as you need it to.

As well as paying out if you are never able to work again, some policies also top up your earnings by paying a 'partial' or 'rehabilitation' benefit for a limited period if you are able to return to your original job but in a reduced capacity – part-time, for example. If you take a different and lower-paid full-time job, either with your existing employer or with a different employer, some policies will pay 'proportionate' benefit, which again is a way of topping up your earnings but it usually carries on being paid until retirement.

How much replacement income?

To make sure that no one is better off by staying away from work, all insurers put a limit on the income they will pay out if you claim. The most common rule is that the income paid out by the policy – plus income from any similar insurance – plus any statutory sick pay and state benefits must not come to more than 65 per cent of your average before-tax earnings over the previous 12 months; the limit may be 50 per cent of before-tax earnings if the insurer does not take social security benefits into account. If you are self-employed or you are an employee whose income fluctuates – for example you earn a proportion of your income as bonuses – your average earnings will usually be taken to be an average of three-years' worth of taxable earnings.

When the insurance will not pay out

Most income-protection policies will not pay out for illness that starts within three weeks of the policy being issued. Even after this 'waiting period', most policies will not pay out until you have been off work sick without pay for what is called a 'deferred period' of at least four weeks. However, because no policy pays out while you are still receiving your full salary, it can make sense to extend the deferred period to coincide with the length of time you can expect to receive full sick pay, for example, or for as long as you could survive on savings. If you become ill and recover during the deferred period, no payment will be made. As well as not paying out until after you have been ill and off work for a certain number of weeks, no payment will be made if you are unable to work as a result of:

• medical conditions, other health defects or participation in danger-ous sports that you did not tell the insurer about when you took out the policy
• intentional self-inflicted injury
• alcohol or drug abuse
• pregnancy or childbirth
• air travel – apart from ordinary passenger flights
• HIV- and AIDS-related illnesses
• war, riot or other civil disturbance.

Counting the cost

How much you pay for income-protection insurance depends on how much you want to be insured for, whether you choose optional extras such as increases in cover and payouts (see page 109) and how long you are prepared to wait before claiming – i.e. the length of the deferred period. The cost also depends on how likely it is that the insurer will have to pay out: the greater the risk of you claiming, the more the insurance will cost. To assess the risk, the insurer takes into account a broad range of factors including:

• **your job** This is a key factor in determining what you will pay since some jobs carry bigger health risks than others. Insurers generally split jobs into four occupational groups, ranging from low to high risk. Jobs in the lowest-risk group include office jobs, such as accountants and lawyers, and attract the lowest premiums. Each insurer uses its own claims experience to determine which occupations it puts in which group, and their lists are not identical.

107

If you find that you are in a particularly high-risk occupation, it will be worth approaching several different insurers to compare prices

- **your sex** Women typically have to pay about half as much again as men for the same cover. This is because women tend to make more claims and for longer periods
- **your age** The older you are the more expensive income-protection insurance becomes. This is because older people tend to have more health problems
- **your health** It will come as no surprise to learn that this sort of insurance will cost more if you have a history of medical problems. However, once you have taken out the policy, the insurer cannot refuse to renew the policy, and your premiums cannot be increased on the basis of your *own* claims record – but they can go up for other reasons, provided that all policyholders would face an increase
- **your leisure activities** If you indulge in what insurers term 'hazardous' sports, such as rock-climbing, flying light aircraft or pot-holing, for example, your insurance will cost more
- **your habits** Smokers are generally charged more for income-protection insurance, as are heavy drinkers. You will be expected to admit to how much you smoke and/or drink on the application form.

Choosing an income-protection policy

If you are considering buying income-protection insurance because you are worried about the financial consequences of being too ill to work, you need to make sure that the insurance will not add to your worries by not paying out when you need it to or by not paying out enough. As well as checking that the definition of 'unable to work' is as generous as possible (see pages 105–106), make sure that:

- you choose a deferred period that fits in with the length of time you could manage without needing extra income (see pages 106–107)
- you do not pay for more replacement income than the insurer will pay out once the rules about benefits and other income have been brought into play (see page 106)

- the policy will pay a replacement income until retirement
- you ask for 'waiver of premium' cover if you do not want to pay premiums while you are claiming.

Tip

Do not automatically insure for the maximum allowed by the insurer. You will save money if you insure only for the amount of replacement income you really need.

It may be a long time before you need to make a claim, and when you do, the payment may have to continue for a long time, so you need to allow for increases both in the amount you are insured for – to reflect the fact that your earnings are likely to rise in the future – and in the income that will be paid out in the event of a claim. Most insurers offer index-linking – which means that increases are linked either to price inflation or to earnings inflation – either as part of their standard policy or as an optional extra that you arrange at the time you take out the policy. Depending on the insurer, you may also be able to arrange for the cover and/or the replacement income paid when you claim to rise by a fixed percentage each year or in line with inflation. Note that if you do not arrange for increases when you take out the policy, you will not be able to have the replacement income increased once it is being paid out.

Cover for unpaid work

The amount you can claim on income-protection insurance is linked to your earnings from work, which means that there is no point taking out a policy if you are out of work. The exception to this rule is the unpaid role of housewife or househusband. If you are responsible for running the home, you can take out a policy that pays out when you are ill. Your earnings are assumed to be about £10,000, which is an estimate of the cost of replacing your unpaid services.

Waiting saves money

David has worked out that he needs to buy cover to replace £18,000 a year (£350 a week). He has also decided that although he is self-employed, he won't opt for the standard four-week deferred period but will save on premiums by choosing a 26-week (6-month) deferred period. As he says: 'it's a question of balancing the extra premiums against the probability of being ill for a long period and if I wait 26 weeks before the policy starts to pay out, the premiums are halved. Janice and I have come to the conclusion that if the worst happens, we would be prepared to manage on Janice's income and dig into our savings for a while rather than pay out extra in premiums'.

Keeping track

Once the insurer takes you on, you *must* be offered the chance to renew your policy each year except when:

- you have changed your job to one that is considered to be an 'unacceptable' risk. Most occupations are viewed as acceptable but changing jobs can mean having to pay a higher premium if it is in a different risk category
- you have moved to live outside Europe permanently (for more than one year).

If you let the policy lapse – by failing to renew it, for example – the insurer may ask for evidence that your health has not deteriorated before agreeing to carry on insuring you as before. The insurer cannot ask for this information if you carry on paying the premiums without a break.

Critical illness insurance

Critical illness insurance – previously called 'dread disease insurance' – is designed to pay out a tax-free lump sum if you are diagnosed as having one of a defined list of serious or life-threatening conditions or you suffer 'total and permanent disability'. However, you should not get side-tracked into worrying about the illness; you should focus instead on the financial consequences and you need to consider how you would manage if *any* illness or injury, a broken leg for example, prevented you from working.

So critical illness insurance should not be regarded as a substitute for income-protection insurance (see pages 105–110), and if you have already decided that the latter is the type of insurance you need, you are unlikely to need critical illness insurance as well. The

reason for this is that income-protection insurance covers more illnesses and can provide a monthly income for as long as you cannot work (up to retirement age if necessary), which is particularly important for self-employed people, who cannot rely on the cushion of sick pay from an employer. Although income-protection insurance will pay out only after you have convinced the insurer that you are unable to work, it will cover both critical and non-critical illnesses such as stress and back pain if they prevent you from earning.

On the face of it, critical illness insurance is cheaper than income-protection insurance. However, it is worth bearing in mind that you may pay less because you get less in terms of what is covered. You should also be aware that because the payment from a critical illness policy is a lump sum, once it is spent, you do not get any more. With an income-protection policy, the replacement income carries on being paid as long as it needs to be paid; there is also no limit on the number of claims you can make – provided you are still paying the premiums and provided that the claims are valid.

Warning

Critical illness insurance is often sold in conjunction with a mortgage, with the lump sum (if it gets paid) being used to pay off the outstanding loan if you suffer from the 'right' sort of illness. However, you should resist the lure of the lump sum if what you really need is replacement earnings. Having a large lump sum that will pay off the mortgage may sound like a good idea but only if you would still have enough money coming in to cover other expenses.

The table below shows how much non-smoking 30-year-olds would have to pay for an income-protection policy that provides a replacement monthly income of £1,500 and a critical illness policy which could pay out a lump sum of £90,000 (the size of lump sum you would need to pay an equivalent monthly income for five years). As you can see, the critical illness policy is substantially cheaper when compared with an income-protection policy with the standard four-week deferred period. However, if the same 30-year-olds were prepared to wait six months before the income-protection policy started to pay out (to coincide with sick pay from an employer coming to an end, for example), the income-protection insurance would be cheaper than critical illness insurance for the man and not that much more (but for better cover) for the woman.

Income-protection v critical illness insurance

	Income-protection policy paying a monthly income of £1,500 after:		Critical illness policy paying a lump sum of £90,000
	four weeks	six-months	
Man aged 30	£57.15	£26.85	£42.52
Woman aged 30	£95.05	£43.55	£36.57
Both man and woman are non-smokers			

Source: Norwich Union

Accident and sickness insurance

Personal accident insurance is often offered free as an inducement to buy other financial products, and this should alert you to the fact that you are unlikely to suffer the particular injuries covered by this sort of policy. Some policies will pay out a modest lump sum if you die from bodily injuries as a result of a violent accident; some will pay out a lump sum if you suffer an injury that is specified in the policy. This might include loss of hearing, loss of an eye or a limb or temporary or permanent disability as a result of an accident. The amounts paid out are usually fixed according to the nature of the injury.

Accident insurance is often linked to sickness insurance (it is not possible to buy sickness insurance on its own) and as well as paying out a lump sum for certain specific injuries they may also pay a set amount for a limited period – usually up to a maximum of two years if you cannot work because of illness or accident.

The possible attraction of accident and sickness insurance is that it is cheap but that is because the chances of the insurance ever paying out are very low because the conditions and exclusions can be stringent and restrictive. Income-protection insurance gives much better cover.

Chapter 6

Insurance against redundancy

If you would not be able to cope without the earnings from your job, you would be wise to make plans to minimise the financial trauma of being made redundant. The steps you have to take to protect your finances in the face of unemployment are very similar to those you have to take to protect your income in the face of long-term sickness (see Chapter 5), with one main exception: the kind of insurance designed to pay out on redundancy is often restrictive, expensive and, for many people, a very poor buy indeed. This means that it is especially important to look at the alternatives to insurance.

This chapter tells you the minimum you can expect in the way of redundancy pay, explains what other help is available from the state and looks at what you can do to prepare your finances for possible redundancy. For many people, losing their job would seriously affect their ability to repay their mortgage and or/other loans. You will find details of the kind of insurance that is available to protect loan repayments on pages 120–123. If you are already having difficulties with mortgage and other loan repayments see Chapter 16. For more details on the financial help available if you lose earnings as a result of sickness or injury, see Chapter 5.

Redundancy pay

If you are made redundant, your employer should give you any outstanding salary and/or holiday pay, any pay that you receive instead of working your notice period and – if you qualify for one – a redundancy payment. This can either be the legal minimum or whatever your employer chooses to offer, which may be substantially more than the legal minimum, especially if you are given the choice of volunteering for redundancy.

You are legally entitled to a statutory redundancy payment – i.e. the legal minimum – if you have worked for the same employer for at least two years and you are at least 20 years old (because years of work before the age of 18 do not count). The amount of redundancy payment you get depends on the number of years that you have worked for the same employer, your age at the beginning of each year worked and your age when made redundant. For each year worked (up to a maximum of 20 years), you get either one week's before-tax pay (at the date you receive your redundancy notice) or £220 – whichever is lower – multiplied by:

- one and a half for each year after your 41st birthday
- one for each year between the ages of 22 and 41
- a half for each year between your 18th and 22nd birthdays.

The most you can get is £6,600. The table on pages 116–117 tells you the most you can expect to get if you earn more than £11,440 (the annual equivalent of the maximum £220 per week) according to your age and the number of years in your current job.

Note that if you are made redundant because your employer has gone out of business, the government will pay any statutory redundancy due to you – ask the receiver or liquidator for a claim form.

Tax point

Any lump-sum redundancy pay you get is tax-free up to a limit of £30,000. If you get a bigger lump sum than this, the amount over £30,000 is taxed at your highest rate of tax (for how to work this out, see Chapter 17).

Not entitled to the legal minimum?

If you have worked for an employer for less than two years but you have been paying into your employer's pension scheme, you may be entitled to a refund of your pension contributions (less tax at 20 per cent). Taking the refund will mean that you lose valuable provision

Statutory redundancy payment

Number of years of service

Age	2	3	4	5	6	7	8	9	10	11	12	13	14	15	16	17	18	19	20
20	£220	£330	£440																
21	£220	£330	£440	£550															
22	£220	£330	£440	£550	£660														
23	£330	£440	£550	£660	£770	£880													
24	£440	£550	£660	£770	£880	£990	£1,100												
25	£440	£660	£770	£880	£990	£1,100	£1,210	£1,320											
26	£440	£660	£880	£990	£1,100	£1,210	£1,320	£1,430	£1,540										
27	£440	£660	£880	£1,100	£1,210	£1,320	£1,430	£1,540	£1,650	£1,760									
28	£440	£660	£880	£1,100	£1,320	£1,430	£1,540	£1,650	£1,760	£1,870	£1,980								
29	£440	£660	£880	£1,100	£1,320	£1,540	£1,650	£1,760	£1,870	£1,980	£2,090	£2,200							
30	£440	£660	£880	£1,100	£1,320	£1,540	£1,760	£1,870	£1,980	£2,090	£2,200	£2,310	£2,420						
31	£440	£660	£880	£1,100	£1,320	£1,540	£1,760	£1,980	£2,090	£2,200	£2,310	£2,420	£2,530	£2,640					
32	£440	£660	£880	£1,100	£1,320	£1,540	£1,760	£1,980	£2,200	£2,310	£2,420	£2,530	£2,640	£2,750	£2,860				
33	£440	£660	£880	£1,100	£1,320	£1,540	£1,760	£1,980	£2,200	£2,420	£2,530	£2,640	£2,750	£2,860	£2,970	£3,080			
34	£440	£660	£880	£1,100	£1,320	£1,540	£1,760	£1,980	£2,200	£2,420	£2,640	£2,750	£2,860	£2,970	£3,080	£3,190	£3,300		
35	£440	£660	£880	£1,100	£1,320	£1,540	£1,760	£1,980	£2,200	£2,420	£2,640	£2,860	£2,970	£3,080	£3,190	£3,300	£3,410	£3,520	
36	£440	£660	£880	£1,100	£1,320	£1,540	£1,760	£1,980	£2,200	£2,420	£2,640	£2,860	£3,080	£3,190	£3,300	£3,410	£3,520	£3,630	£3,740
37	£440	£660	£880	£1,100	£1,320	£1,540	£1,760	£1,980	£2,200	£2,420	£2,640	£2,860	£3,080	£3,300	£3,410	£3,520	£3,630	£3,740	£3,850
38	£440	£660	£880	£1,100	£1,320	£1,540	£1,760	£1,980	£2,200	£2,420	£2,640	£2,860	£3,080	£3,300	£3,520	£3,630	£3,740	£3,850	£3,960

Age																			
39	£440	£660	£880	£1,100	£1,320	£1,540	£1,760	£1,980	£2,200	£2,420	£2,640	£2,860	£3,080	£3,300	£3,520	£3,740	£3,850	£3,960	£4,070
40	£440	£660	£880	£1,100	£1,320	£1,540	£1,760	£1,980	£2,200	£2,420	£2,640	£2,860	£3,080	£3,300	£3,520	£3,740	£3,960	£4,070	£4,180
41	£440	£660	£880	£1,100	£1,320	£1,540	£1,760	£1,980	£2,200	£2,420	£2,640	£2,860	£3,080	£3,300	£3,520	£3,740	£3,960	£4,180	£4,290
42	£550	£770	£990	£1,210	£1,430	£1,650	£1,870	£2,090	£2,310	£2,530	£2,750	£2,970	£3,190	£3,410	£3,630	£3,850	£4,070	£4,290	£4,510
43	£660	£880	£1,100	£1,320	£1,540	£1,760	£1,980	£2,200	£2,420	£2,640	£2,860	£3,080	£3,300	£3,520	£3,740	£3,960	£4,180	£4,400	£4,620
44	£660	£990	£1,210	£1,430	£1,650	£1,870	£2,090	£2,310	£2,530	£2,750	£2,970	£3,190	£3,410	£3,630	£3,850	£4,070	£4,290	£4,510	£4,730
45	£660	£990	£1,320	£1,540	£1,760	£1,980	£2,200	£2,420	£2,640	£2,860	£3,080	£3,300	£3,520	£3,740	£3,960	£4,180	£4,400	£4,620	£4,840
46	£660	£990	£1,320	£1,650	£1,870	£2,090	£2,310	£2,530	£2,750	£2,970	£3,190	£3,410	£3,630	£3,850	£4,070	£4,290	£4,510	£4,730	£4,950
47	£660	£990	£1,320	£1,650	£1,980	£2,200	£2,420	£2,640	£2,860	£3,080	£3,300	£3,520	£3,740	£3,960	£4,180	£4,400	£4,620	£4,840	£5,060
48	£660	£990	£1,320	£1,650	£1,980	£2,310	£2,530	£2,750	£2,970	£3,190	£3,410	£3,630	£3,850	£4,070	£4,290	£4,510	£4,730	£4,950	£5,170
49	£660	£990	£1,320	£1,650	£1,980	£2,310	£2,640	£2,860	£3,080	£3,300	£3,520	£3,740	£3,960	£4,180	£4,400	£4,620	£4,840	£5,060	£5,280
50	£660	£990	£1,320	£1,650	£1,980	£2,310	£2,640	£2,970	£3,190	£3,410	£3,630	£3,850	£4,070	£4,290	£4,510	£4,730	£4,950	£5,170	£5,390
51	£660	£990	£1,320	£1,650	£1,980	£2,310	£2,640	£2,970	£3,300	£3,520	£3,740	£3,960	£4,180	£4,400	£4,620	£4,840	£5,060	£5,280	£5,500
52	£660	£990	£1,320	£1,650	£1,980	£2,310	£2,640	£2,970	£3,300	£3,630	£3,850	£4,070	£4,290	£4,510	£4,730	£4,950	£5,170	£5,390	£5,610
53	£660	£990	£1,320	£1,650	£1,980	£2,310	£2,640	£2,970	£3,300	£3,630	£3,960	£4,180	£4,400	£4,620	£4,840	£5,060	£5,280	£5,500	£5,720
54	£660	£990	£1,320	£1,650	£1,980	£2,310	£2,640	£2,970	£3,300	£3,630	£3,960	£4,290	£4,510	£4,730	£4,950	£5,170	£5,390	£5,610	£5,830
55	£660	£990	£1,320	£1,650	£1,980	£2,310	£2,640	£2,970	£3,300	£3,630	£3,960	£4,290	£4,620	£4,840	£5,060	£5,280	£5,500	£5,720	£5,940
56	£660	£990	£1,320	£1,650	£1,980	£2,310	£2,640	£2,970	£3,300	£3,630	£3,960	£4,290	£4,620	£4,950	£5,170	£5,390	£5,610	£5,830	£6,050
57	£660	£990	£1,320	£1,650	£1,980	£2,310	£2,640	£2,970	£3,300	£3,630	£3,960	£4,290	£4,620	£4,950	£5,280	£5,500	£5,720	£5,940	£6,160
58	£660	£990	£1,320	£1,650	£1,980	£2,310	£2,640	£2,970	£3,300	£3,630	£3,960	£4,290	£4,620	£4,950	£5,280	£5,610	£5,830	£6,050	£6,270
59	£660	£990	£1,320	£1,650	£1,980	£2,310	£2,640	£2,970	£3,300	£3,630	£3,960	£4,290	£4,620	£4,950	£5,280	£5,610	£5,940	£6,160	£6,380
60	£660	£990	£1,320	£1,650	£1,980	£2,310	£2,640	£2,970	£3,300	£3,630	£3,960	£4,290	£4,620	£4,950	£5,280	£5,610	£5,940	£6,270	£6,490
61 to 64	£660	£990	£1,320	£1,650	£1,980	£2,310	£2,640	£2,970	£3,300	£3,630	£3,960	£4,290	£4,620	£4,950	£5,280	£5,610	£5,940	£6,270	£6,600

for the future but you have to balance this against your needs in the short-term, where a lump sum could be useful for tiding you over while you find another job.

Help from the state

If you are an employee and you have paid enough National Insurance, you will be entitled to claim Jobseeker's Allowance for the first six months that you are unemployed irrespective of how much you have in savings and irrespective of what your partner (if you have one) earns. Jobseeker's Allowance is not available to the self-employed, although you may be able to claim Income Support (paid at the same rates) – check with your benefit office.

The rates for Jobseeker's Allowance for the 1999–2000 tax year are given in the table below.

Jobseeker's Allowance for the 1999–2000 tax year

Age	weekly amount
Under 18	£30.95
Between 18 and 24	£40.70
25 or over	£51.40

Tip

If you are paid monthly and you want to compare what you earn with what you might get in state benefits, multiply your monthly after-tax salary (from your pay slip) by 12 then divide by 52. Alternatively, multiply the weekly benefit by 52 and divide by 12.

If you are still unemployed after six months, your entitlement to Jobseeker's Allowance will become means-tested. You will qualify only if you have savings of less than £8,000, you work fewer than 16 hours each week and your partner (if you have one) works fewer than 24 hours each week. You get the full amount of the allowance if your savings are less than £3,000. However, for every £250 of savings you have over £3,000, you are assumed to have an extra £1 of weekly income, which will be taken into account along with any other earnings when calculating how much benefit you are entitled to. If you are eligible to claim the means-tested Jobseeker's Allowance, you may also be entitled to extra payments for children, and you should get help with your housing costs in the form of Housing Benefit and Council Tax Benefit. If you are a single parent or are caring for a dependent adult, you may be better off claiming Income Support – check with your local Benefits Agency.*

Tip

Even if you are not entitled to any state benefits, it is worth signing on at your local unemployment office or Job Centre as soon as you leave your job. This is so that you receive National Insurance credits for the period while you are not working. This means that your right to other benefits (including basic state retirement pension) is protected even though you are not earning.

Early retirement

If you are a member of your employer's pension scheme or you have a personal pension and are over the age of 50 when you are made redundant, you may have the choice of taking early retirement. This simply means that you start drawing your pension earlier than you would have if you had carried on working to normal retirement age – but it also means that you get a smaller pension. Once you start taking your pension you cannot change your mind so you need to think seriously before taking this option. However, if you are not confident that you will get another job or you think that you will be able to find only lower-paid or part-time work, it could be worth taking your pension early. Drawing a pension does not stop you from earning money by working.

Helping yourself

If you are made redundant, there will inevitably be a time lag between leaving your job and getting all the payments due to you, wherever they come from. So it makes sense to have enough cash saved up to tide you over for at least a couple of months. The next step is to see how long you could manage for before finding another job or taking a sharp cut in your standard of living. To do this:

- work out the minimum amount you need to live on each month
- subtract the monthly amount of state benefits or pension (if you would retire early) to arrive at your monthly shortfall (if the figure is zero or a minus, there is no shortfall)
- add all the lump-sum payments you would expect to receive to any savings you would be prepared to use
- divide the total lump-sum payments and savings by your monthly shortfall.

This will tell you how many months you could carry on as normal. If you think this gives you enough time to find a new job, you know that you could cope without making any changes to your current financial arrangements. However, if you think that you would not be able to find another job before your funds run out you should seriously consider building up your savings (see Chapter 4) and/or finding ways to reduce your monthly expenditure (see Chapter 18). Buying insurance could be an option (if you meet the criteria for it to pay out – see page 122), but you still need to think about how you would make ends meet after a year.

Redundancy insurance

Most redundancy insurance is linked to the repayment of loans – whether it is your mortgage (see Chapter 10), a personal loan (see Chapter 13) or a debt on your credit card (see Chapter 3). If you do not have any loans, it is extremely unlikely that you will be able to buy any kind of insurance against redundancy. The exception to this is if you have bought income-protection insurance to cover your income against long-term sickness (see Chapter 5) because you may be able to buy add-on insurance that will pay a replacement income in case of redundancy (although in early 1999, only Norwich Union was offering this option).

The kind of insurance that you can buy to cover your loan repayments has a variety of different names and often it is bundled with insurance against loss of income as a result of an accident or sickness:

- loan payment protection insurance
- creditor insurance
- loan protection
- credit care
- payment care (or similar)
- payment protection plan
- accident-sickness-unemployment cover
- mortgage payment protection insurance (MPPI).

Warning

Don't confuse mortgage payment protection insurance with mortgage protection insurance (see Chapter 10), which is life insurance designed to pay off the whole of your mortgage loan if you die before it comes to an end.

Should you buy?

The government would like you to buy this sort of insurance, and lenders are keen to sell it, but buying it can add considerably to the cost of each type of loan that you have. You cannot buy a single insurance policy to cover all your debts; instead you will have to buy insurance for each loan.

If you could manage for at least a year by using your other resources (see page 119–120), it is unlikely that you will need to buy redundancy insurance. This is because it is very rare to find insurance that will pay out for more than 12 months. You also need to be

---

Warning

If you already have income-protection insurance (see Chapter 5), you should not buy redundancy insurance that is bundled with accident and sickness insurance. Paying twice for the same insurance does not mean that you get twice the payout if you claim.

---

aware that you will have to wait between one and three months before you are able to claim so you need to make some sort of provision for this waiting period anyway.

Note that insurance sold to cover mortgage repayments must make you wait only two months if it was sold to you after 1 July 1999. Existing policies must be amended (if necessary) by July 2001.

You should not buy redundancy insurance if any of the following apply (because the insurance company will not pay out):

- you are already unemployed
- you are over normal state retirement age
- you work fewer than 16 hours a week
- you have been in employment for less than six months
- you work on short-term contracts of less than six months
- you know that you are going to be made redundant or there is a possibility that your job is under threat – there has been a recent round of redundancies at your place of work, for example
- you know that you will be able to take voluntary redundancy or early retirement
- you are frequently unemployed.

You should also be wary of redundancy insurance if you are employed on fixed-term contracts: most policies will pay but only if your contract comes to an end early and unexpectedly and then only if the contract was due to run for more than six months to a year. However, if you work on fixed-term contracts for one employer and your contracts have been consistently renewed for at least two years (a year for new mortgage payment protection policies), you may find that an insurer will treat you as though you are in permanent work, with the result that the policy should pay out if your contract comes to an abrupt end.

If you are self-employed or a company director and you are considering taking out this sort of insurance against the risk of periods of unemployment, tread very carefully. Some insurers will pay out only if you have permanently ceased trading – you have been declared bankrupt, for example – or if the company of which you are a director has failed. It is very unlikely that redundancy insurance will pay out if you have stopped trading temporarily or if you are simply faced with a shortage of work.

Unforeseen disaster

When Ian bought his new car, he paid for half of it up front and signed up for an 18-month finance agreement to pay the rest. At the same time he bought insurance to cover his repayments in case he lost his job. Four months later, the company he worked for went into receivership, and Ian was made redundant. He claimed on the insurance but the insurer refused to pay up. Ian had been a director and minority shareholder of the company he worked for and the insurer argued that he must have known about the impending receivership. Ian hadn't known and not only that, the company had been declared a viable proposition by its bank. The insurer still refused to pay up and said that it had proof that the company had been in trouble before Ian had taken out his insurance.

What will the insurance pay for?

If you are eligible, how much the insurance company will pay out depends on the loan you have bought the insurance for:

- **mortgage payment protection insurance** covers the whole of your monthly mortgage repayments but usually up to a maximum of about £750 to £2,000 per month. You can usually pay for an extra allowance to include your house insurance payments and other regular outgoings
- **insurance for personal loans** will cover your monthly loan repayments, including the insurance premium
- **insurance for credit cards** and store cards will pay a set amount – typically 10 per cent – of your outstanding balance each month for a set period of anything between 6 and 36 months, but most often 12 months.

State help with your mortgage

The state offers limited help with the interest payments on a mortgage of up to £100,000, provided you are eligible for means-tested Jobseeker's Allowance or Income Support (see pages 118–119). If you took out your mortgage before 1 October 1995, you will have to wait two months after claiming benefit before any payment is made and then you will receive half the mortgage interest for four months. After this period, you should receive the full amount of interest. If you took out your mortgage on or after 1 October 1995 and you qualify for income support, you will receive all the interest on a mortgage of up to £100,000 after nine months of unemployment (or sickness). Payment from the state is for the interest part of your mortgage repayments only: you will receive nothing towards any capital repayments (which you start to make after the first few years of a repayment mortgage) or towards any insurance linked to your mortgage.

What it costs

Insurance against unemployment only is cheaper than cover against unemployment, accident and sickness. The cost also depends on the type of loan you are insuring:

- **mortgage payment protection policies** cost from about £5 to over £7 for every £100 of your monthly repayments. So if your usual monthly mortgage repayment is £400, the insurance will cost between £20 and £30 per month. The cost of the insurance will rise if your monthly repayments go up but it will fall if your monthly repayments go down. Some lenders offer free – but limited – cover as an incentive to new borrowers.
- **personal loan insurance** can push up the cost of borrowing quite considerably, not least because the insurance nearly always includes cover for accident and sickness: for example, on a three-year loan of £5,000, insurance could cost upwards of £20 a month, which is on top of the loan repayment.
- **credit- and store–card insurance** costs about 70 pence for each £100 of your outstanding credit-card balance so the cost goes up and down according to how much you owe each month.

How to buy

It is likely that when you take out a loan or apply for a credit card, the lender will offer you insurance to go with it. However, where mortgage payment protection policies are concerned, you can buy this form of insurance from brokers and direct insurers as well as from your lender. In response to criticism that loan payment protection policies were being sold to people who would be unlikely to benefit from them, the Association of British Insurers (ABI)★ issued a Statement of Practice for the sale of and treatment of claims under all such policies issued after 1 July 1996. This says that insurers offering this sort of policy must make sure that prospective policyholders understand what they are buying and that they should be given:

- **an explanation of the suitability of the policy** for the self-employed, people on contract work or in part-time work and people with pre-existing medical conditions
- details of the **main features of cover as well as the main restrictions** – i.e. the circumstances in which the policy will not pay out
- **written material that is clear and not misleading**
- full **details of cover** after completion of the contract – i.e. after you have signed on the dotted line.

As well as making sure that the person selling you this sort of insurance gives you the information as detailed in the ABI guidelines, you should also check:

- that you satisfy any qualifying criteria – for example, how long you need to have been in work before you count as 'employed'
- how long you have to wait before you are allowed to make a claim under the policy
- how long you will have to wait before payments are made
- how long payments will carry on for if you have to claim
- whether doing temporary work will affect your claims
- for credit-card and store-card insurance, what percentage of your outstanding balance will be paid off each month
- for personal loans and home-improvement loans, whether you will be able to cancel the insurance if you pay off the loan early

- whether the cost of the insurance is added to the loan (which means you will pay interest on it) or whether you pay for the insurance separately
- whether you will have to carry on paying the premium while you are claiming.

Breaking the code

The standard of current compliance [with the ABI selling code] by those one might expect to have in-house training facilities, the banks, seems appalling. In mystery shopping exercises ... only half the time did banks explain the cover, or draw attention to exclusions and restrictions. This is a pretty dismal record.

1998 Annual Report of the Insurance Ombudsman Bureau*
published March 1999

Chapter 7

Life insurance

The main reason for buying life insurance is to provide financial protection in the event of your death for the people who are dependent on you. If you are single and have no financial dependants, you may not need to give life insurance a second thought. It may also be unnecessary if you and your partner have no children and each of you could fend for yourself if the other died. However, if you have a non- or lower-earning partner and/or children or you support a financially dependent adult, life insurance is definitely worth considering.

This chapter tells you how to work out the amount of life insurance you need, how to recognise any cover you may already have – such as life insurance through your job or linked to your mortgage – and gives advice on choosing the right sort of policy for your personal circumstances. If you already have life insurance, you can use the 'Life insurance calculator' (on page 132) to check that you have the right amount, and the advice on whether to switch to a different policy (see pages 141–142) to help you to save money. Note that this chapter deals with only those types of life insurance that are appropriate for protecting your dependants. For information on buying life insurance as a way of saving and investing, see Chapters 20 and 21.

How much life insurance do you need?

You cannot put a price on human life but you can quantify the amount of life insurance you need to ensure that your nearest and dearest do not suffer financially in the event of your death. Some people in the insurance industry feel that this figure should be at least ten, if not twelve, times your annual salary; others say that you should buy as much cover as you can afford. Neither method is particularly helpful and both could result in your spending far more on life insurance than is strictly necessary or, less probably, not buying enough. What you really need to do is to sit down and work out how your death will affect the financial position of your dependants or how you will be affected by losing your partner's income. The calculator on page 132 will help you to work out the amount of insurance you need but you cannot fill it in until you know:

- whether your dependants will need a lump sum to spend after you die (see below)
- how much your dependants can expect to receive as lump-sum payouts (see opposite)
- how much income your dependants will need to live on after your death (see pages 130–131)
- how much income will be available for your dependants after your death (see page 131)
- how long the income will be needed (see page 135).

Lump-sum spending

Your dependants' most immediate need for a lump sum after your death will be for your funeral (unless you have decided to donate your body to medical science). An average funeral in the UK costs about £1,100 for a cremation or £1,600 for a burial, but what it will cost depends on where you live and how simple or elaborate you want the funeral to be. In addition, your dependants may need to:

- pay off debts – including the mortgage
- replace costly items such as a computer or a company car, which would no longer be available after your death
- replenish savings if these have to be used to meet other immediate expenses for a month or so
- pay inheritance tax bills if any
- meet the cost of gifts of money for people (other than your dependants) that you have made in your will.

Tax point

If you leave everything to your spouse, no inheritance tax will need to be paid. If you and your partner are unmarried, or you leave everything to your children, there may be an inheritance tax bill if the total value of your money and possessions (excluding those that are jointly owned) comes to more than the inheritance tax threshold (£231,000 for deaths occurring in the 1999–2000 tax year).

Lump-sum payouts

It may well be that you already have life insurance or other financial products that are designed (or can be made) to produce a lump sum on your death, such as:

- a mortgage protection policy or endowment policy with your mortgage (see Chapter 10)
- insurance that you have taken out with a loan which will pay off the loan if you die before it has been repaid
- a pre-paid funeral plan
- a savings plan or investment bond from an insurance company or friendly society (see Chapters 20 and 21)
- life insurance – often called 'death-in-service benefits' – through your job
- a lump sum from your pension that would be paid to your partner (if a widow's or widower's pension is not available)
- a personal pension plan that will give a refund of your contributions or the value of the fund built up (see Chapter 8)
- cash savings or investments such as shares and unit trusts
- Premium Bonds, which have to be cashed in when you die
- life insurance you have already bought (if you are reviewing your life insurance needs).

If you leave a widow, she may be entitled to a widow's one-off payment of £1,000 from the state if you have paid sufficient National Insurance.

Mortgage protection policies

If you have an endowment mortgage, life insurance is automatically included as part of the package, but if you take out a repayment mortgage, most lenders will insist that you buy separate life insurance in the form of a mortgage protection policy. This is a kind of term insurance (see page 136) designed to pay off your mortgage if you and/or your partner (if applicable) die before the mortgage has come to an end. The amount you are insured for goes down in line with the reducing amount of the mortgage loan.

If you are buying a home on your own and you have no dependants, unless you particularly want to leave your home to someone in your will, you do not need to have this sort of life insurance. This is because your mortgage should be paid off after your death using the proceeds from the sale of your home.

Mortgage protection policies are not the same as mortgage *payment* protection policies – see Chapter 6 – which is insurance against not being able to pay your mortgage because you lose your earning power.

Income needed

Unless you are calculating how much life insurance you may need in order to provide for children only, the adult who will have to manage after your death is probably the best person to make an estimate of the income that he or she will need to live on. This involves taking your current monthly expenditure (or the figure from your payslip if you contribute the whole of your monthly earnings to joint spending) then adding extra expenditure that will be incurred, such as:

- paying for services currently provided for free, say, cleaning and childcare
- running a car, if, say, you would need to replace a company car
- replacing other perks from your job.

You then need to subtract spending on things that would no longer need to be paid for after your death which may include:

- all or part of your mortgage payments – if the mortgage will be paid off (which it will be if you have a mortgage protection policy or an endowment mortgage)
- the amount by which your living expenses will be reduced – food bills, travelling expenses and so on, but bear in mind that the cost of heating and lighting your home is unlikely to fall dramatically
- personal spending on clothes and leisure activities
- payments into a personal pension
- life insurance premiums.

Tip

If you have a firm grasp on your monthly spending and you have already drawn up a detailed budget (see Chapter 18), you can work out after-death expenditure quite quickly by deleting all the items that will no longer be needed. Using a detailed budget also means that you are less likely to overlook the essentials.

Income available

The income that will be available after your death includes the surviving partner's after-tax pay if he or she carries on – or starts – working after your death. If he or she goes part time, the amount of income available will be reduced – to zero if he or she gives up work altogether. If you are paying into an employer's pension (see Chapter 8), you need to find out whether it will pay a pension either to your partner (although a pension to an unmarried partner may be at the discretion of the scheme) or to your children (if applicable). If you are paying into a personal pension (rather than into an employer's scheme), it will not provide a pension for your partner and/or children. However, it may provide them with a lump sum (see page 129). If you are retired and your pension comes from an annuity, which you bought with the fund you built up in a personal pension, your partner will get a pension only if you have bought a 'joint life' annuity, which will carry on paying an income after you die. If you leave a widow, she may be entitled to state benefits, provided you have been paying National Insurance contributions for at least 12 years.

Life insurance calculator

Step 1: Do you need a lump sum?	
Enter total lump-sum spending at A	A
Enter the total of the lump-sum payouts that your dependants would receive after your death at B	B
Subtract B from A and enter the result at C	C

If C is a plus figure, you need at least this amount of lump-sum life insurance. If C is a minus figure, you do not need to buy insurance for lump sum spending.

Step 2: Do you need income?	
Multiply the monthly amount that your dependants will need to live on by 12 and enter the result at D	D
Enter the total yearly amount of income that your dependants would have available after your death at E	E
Subtract E from D and enter the result at F	F

If F is a plus figure, this is the amount of income that you need to insure for. If F is a minus figure, your dependants are already well provided for. If both C and F are minus figures, you have more life insurance than you need.

Step 3: Which type of insurance do you need?

If the figure at F is a plus figure, you have a choice:
- you can buy a family income benefit policy (see page 136) to provide this amount of income, or
- you can insure for a lump sum which can then be used to provide an income (which will probably be the better option if C is a minus figure). To work out the size of lump sum you need, go to Step 4.

Step 4: What size of lump sum?	
Multiply the figure at F by the number of years you want the income to be paid for (if you want the income to carry on being paid indefinitely, see 'How long will the income be needed? on page 135) and enter the result at G.	G
If C is a minus figure (and you want to use this lump sum to provide an income), subtract it from G. If C is a plus figure add it to G.	H

The figure at H is the total lump-sum insurance you need.

Lisa and Paul do their sums

If 40-year-old Paul died tomorrow, the insurance his wife Lisa will get from his employer, together with the insurance they already have in place to pay off the mortgage – plus a couple of other policies that they had forgotten about – will be more than enough to maintain the standard of living that Lisa and their two children Clare (aged nine) and Ben (aged six) currently enjoy. However, if Lisa died, Paul would be worse off so they need to consider insuring Lisa's life too.

Do they need a lump sum?

If Paul dies, Lisa would need to meet the cost of Paul's funeral, pay off their £70,000 mortgage and she would have to buy a car to replace Paul's company car. This would not be a problem because she will get a lump sum of £188,000 in the form of death-in-service benefits from Paul's employer and their various other insurance policies would pay out £99,000.

Do they need income?

Paul's death would mean that their monthly household budget of £1,700 would no longer have to cover the monthly mortgage repayments of about £380 or pay the £130 in premiums on their endowment policies, and Lisa would probably save about £100 a month on the household bills. However, Lisa would have to find extra cash to run a car, pay for private health insurance, which Paul gets as a perk, and to pay for the baby-sitting Paul now does when she goes out with friends and to her evening meetings as a governor of the children's school. She would still have her freelance earnings, but Paul's pension scheme would also pay her a widow's pension of £10,140 after tax. She might also be entitled to state benefits but the actual amount is uncertain (since they depend on Paul's National Insurance record at the time of death) so they disregard them. Taken together, the figures show that Lisa would need an extra £7,540 a year to maintain their current standard of living. The lump sum of £200,000 would be more than enough to provide this income until the children leave home.

The situation is less rosy if Lisa dies. Although Paul would still have his income and perks, he would lose Lisa's freelance consultancy income of about £10,000 a year (which they set aside for family holidays and work on the house) and he would have to make more substantial provision for childcare to enable him to carry on working. Although the mortgage would be paid off (as for Lisa), the only lump sum he would receive would be in the form of a return of Lisa's personal pension fund currently valued at just over £35,000. To be absolutely sure of being able to pay for childcare, they need to insure Lisa's life for about £53,000.

How the sums add up	if Paul dies	if Lisa dies
Funeral costs	£2,000	£2,000
Pay off mortgage	£70,000	£70,000
Replace company car	£15,000	
Total lump-sum spending (A)	**£87,000**	**£72,000**
Death-in-service benefits	£188,000	
Return of pension fund		£35,000
Mortgage endowment policy	£70,000	£70,000
Other insurance policies	£29,000	£29,000
Total lump-sum payouts (B)	**£287,000**	**£134,000**
Lump sum available (A − B = C)	**- £200,000**	**- £62,000**
Current monthly spending (total for year)	£20,400	£20,400
Spending on holidays and the house etc.	£10,000	£10,000
add extra costs childcare	£2,600	£10,000
car running costs	£1,000	
health insurance	£1,000	
Subtract savings mortgage repayments	£4,560	£4,560
life insurance premiums	£1,560	£1,560
reduction in bills	£1,200	£2,400
Income needed to live on (D)	**£27,680**	**£31,880**
Paul's contribution to family spending		£20,400
Lisa's freelance earnings	£10,000	
Widow's pension	£10,140	
Income available (E)	**£20,140**	**£20,400**
Replacement income required (D − E = F)	**£7,540**	**£11,480**

How long will the income be needed?

The 'Life insurance calculator' assumes that you will want the income from your life insurance to be paid for a fixed number of years – until the children have left home, for example, or until your mortgage is paid off. The calculator also assumes that:

- the lump sum will be invested to provide an income
- the lump sum will grow in line with inflation
- the income taken will rise in line with inflation
- the lump sum will gradually be reduced to zero.

However, if you do not want to use up the lump sum or you want it to provide an income that will carry on being paid indefinitely, you will have to leave the whole of the lump sum invested to produce the income needed (for the types of investment suitable for producing an income – see Chapter 21). You will have to insure for a larger amount and you will have to guess at future investment returns.

You also have to know how big a lump sum you need to produce the income required. To do this, divide the income figure by the rate of return that best reflects your assumptions. For example, if you want an income of £8,500 a year and you think that you will be able to achieve a rate of return on the lump sum of 4 per cent after tax, divide 8,500 by 0.04; this tells you that the lump sum you need is £212,500.

Tax point

Pensions and benefits (except for the state widow's payment) are taxable. If you want to work out the after-tax amount of income from these sources, see Chapter 17.

Choosing life insurance

Once you have worked out whether you need life insurance and how much cover you have to buy, you need to choose the right sort. The two types of insurance that are most suitable for protecting your dependants are:

- term insurance (see overleaf)
- flexible whole-life insurance (see pages 138–139).

Term insurance

The cheapest and simplest way of protecting your dependants is to buy 'term' insurance. This pays out only if you die within a specific period of time (the term), which is usually between 5 and 25 years – although it can be longer. If you survive to the end of the term, you get nothing back (in the same way as you get nothing back if you don't claim on your contents or car insurance). There are three types of term insurance policy:

- **lump-sum policies** pay out a one-off lump sum when you die, and this can be spent or invested. The policy pays out the same amount whether you die near the beginning or the end of the term
- **family income benefit policies** tend to be cheaper than lump-sum policies and pay out a series of regular lump sums on your death which can be used as income for as many years as the policy has to run. For example, if you die after six years of a 15-year policy, it pays out for nine years (fifteen minus six). Family income benefit policies are useful if your dependants do not want the worry of investing a large lump sum, and they are also a good way of providing cover for a specific period
- **pension-linked policies** are lump-sum term insurance policies that you may be able to buy if you are paying into a personal pension (see Chapter 8). The advantage is that you get tax relief on the premiums you pay (within limits). The disadvantage is that the amount you pay for the life insurance reduces the amount that you can pay into your pension.

Tip

Do not automatically assume that a lump-sum payout is best: family income benefit policies are usually cheaper and can provide a guaranteed income for a fixed period of time. Whichever type you choose, make sure that you take your dependants' wishes (or their guardians' wishes if you are insuring for children) into account. Not everyone will relish the prospect of investing a large lump sum.

Types of cover

Both lump-sum and family income benefit policies can pay out a 'level' (i.e. fixed) amount, which means that the amount you are insured for stays the same over the term of the policy. However, if you want the amount you are insured for to go up – note that your premiums will also increase – you can choose:

- **escalating cover**, where the amount you are insured for goes up each year either by a fixed percentage or in line with the Retail Prices Index (RPI). This is a good way of making sure that the value of your cover keeps up with inflation – a particularly important factor if you are insuring for more than ten years, for example
- **increasable cover**, where you pay for the option to increase the amount you are insured for either at set intervals – such as on each anniversary of taking out the insurance – or when a particular event occurs – marriage or the birth of a child, for example.

Tip

Because your state of health affects the cost of cover, the advantage of having increases built into your policy is that the price is worked out on the basis of your health at the time you first took out the original policy, even if your health is not as good as it was.

Other optional extras

As well as paying extra to increase the amount you are insured for, you can also pay extra for other options such as:

- **term extension**, which means that you have the option to increase the length of time the policy runs for – i.e. extend the term of the policy – before it has come to an end. This should be cheaper than taking out a new policy at the end of the term because premiums increase as you get older
- **renewable insurance** allows you to take out another policy regardless of your state of health at the time. Premiums will be based on your age at the time you renew but there will be no

increase as a result of possible deterioration in your health. This option could be worth considering if you are worried about future health problems which would make life insurance expensive (or even unobtainable)

- **waiver of premium** ensures that cover continues even if you cannot afford the premiums because you have stopped earning as a result of illness or disability. This can be a useful extra safeguard (unless you already have insurance against sickness – see Chapter 5) but normally it comes into effect only after three to six months' sickness
- **convertible insurance** is relatively rare but gives you the option to convert your term insurance into a flexible whole-life policy (see below) without a further assessment of your health.

Flexible whole-life policies

If you want life cover to carry on indefinitely rather than finishing at the end of a fixed amount of time, a useful alternative to lump-sum term insurance is a flexible unit-linked whole-life policy, which – as the name suggests – gives you cover for the whole of your life (provided you have paid the required premiums). Unit-linked refers to the fact that part of your premium pays for units in an investment fund while part pays for life cover. This sort of insurance is called 'flexible' because you can choose the balance between investment and insurance. If you choose the 'maximum protection' option nearly all of your premium goes towards life cover. The advantage of flexible whole-life insurance policies is that cover is guaranteed for the rest of your life whatever your state of health. With term insurance, unless you pay extra for a renewable policy (see above), you may not be able to renew your policy if your health has deteriorated.

However, with whole-life policies, as you get older, the units in the investment fund are used to pay for the higher cost of life cover. With the maximum protection option, the investment fund is relatively small and so, after a few years, it may not be sufficient to pay for the life cover. If this happens, your premiums are likely to rise unless you are prepared to accept a lower amount of cover. Another disadvantage of unit-linked whole-life insurance is that you cannot buy purely on price because to get the best deal, you need to make sure that the investment part will perform well. This may mean taking financial advice, which can also be expensive.

What life insurance costs

What you pay for life insurance is set when you take out the policy you buy: with term insurance, the price is set when you take out the policy; with flexible whole-life policies, the price you pay is set at the outset but may need to be increased in the future depending on how well the investment part of the policy performs (see above). The cost of life insurance of whichever type also depends on a number of other factors. Naturally, the larger the sum you want to be insured for and the longer the length of time you want the policy to cover you, the more expensive your premiums will be. The other main factors that influence how much your premium will be are your:

- **age** The older you are when you take out your policy, the more it will cost for a given level of benefit
- **sex** Policies are cheaper for women because they have a longer life expectancy than men
- **health** Premiums for life insurance are calculated on the assumption that you are in good health. If you smoke or have a medical condition, your term insurance will usually cost more
- **family history** If your family has a history of serious illness or there is a risk that you carry the gene for certain hereditary conditions, the price of life insurance can increase
- **occupation** If you have a high-risk occupation – such as deep-sea diving or working on an oil rig – you are likely to have to pay more than someone who does office-based work
- **leisure pursuits** If you indulge in dangerous sports such as hang-gliding and scuba diving, expect to pay more.

If you and your partner both need life insurance for roughly the same amount, it is generally cheaper to take out a joint policy. A 'first death' policy pays out when either of you dies so would be suitable for covering a large joint debt such as your mortgage. A 'last survivor' policy pays out only after both of you have died (it does not have to be at the same time). This type of policy can be useful if you and your partner are not financially dependent on each other but your children (or other dependants) would suffer from losing both your incomes.

Buying life insurance

One of the advantages of buying term insurance is that you can buy purely on price so it is worth checking the term insurance rates that are published in the personal finance pages of the national press if you want an idea of which insurers are likely to offer the cheapest deals. Buying flexible unit-linked whole-life insurance is less straightforward because you need to consider investment performance as well as price. You should also check that the person or company you are buying from is authorised by the Financial Services Authority.*

Whichever type you buy, make sure that the policy is 'written in trust' for the benefit of whoever you want the money to go to. This means that your dependants will get the money as quickly as possible and also that it does not form part of your estate for inheritance tax purposes. An alternative to writing a policy under trust is to arrange for the policy to be on a 'life-of-another' basis. This is also useful if you depend on someone financially but you are not sure that you can depend on them to have arranged life insurance – an estranged partner who is paying you maintenance, for example. You can take an insurance policy out on that person's life so that if he or she dies, you, as owner of the policy, receive the proceeds. Note that you cannot take out a life-of-another policy on anybody's life: you must stand to lose financially if the other person dies – i.e. you must have an 'insurable interest' in the other person. You are assumed to have an unlimited insurable interest in your own life and that of your spouse. When it comes to other people, your insurable interest is limited to the amount you would lose if they died.

Applying for life insurance

When you apply for life insurance, you will need to give details of your medical history on the application form. If you have had health problems in the past, your insurer is likely to ask you to provide a medical report from your GP and/or you may be asked to attend a medical examination by a doctor chosen by the insurer.

The insurer is also likely to ask for details of any genetic tests that you have had. The exception to this is where you are applying for life insurance (up to a maximum of £100,000) directly linked to a new mortgage for a home you plan to live in. For other life insurance, you cannot be asked to take a genetic test but if you have had genetic tests you must tell the insurer about them (and possibly what the results were).

Warning

Failing to tell the truth on your application form or failing to disclose the fact that you have had genetic tests could invalidate the policy, which means that your dependants would receive nothing on your death.

Keeping track

Once you have received your policy, make sure that the person who is going to benefit from it knows where it is kept. You should also check that your premiums are being paid correctly so that you do not run the risk of the policy lapsing and cover disappearing. You then have very little to do until your financial circumstances change, when you should review the amount you are insured for.

Should you switch?

You should not switch if you have serious health problems as it is likely to be cheaper to stick with your current policy. If you want to change a whole-life policy, you should get advice before switching. If you have calculated that you have too much life cover (and there is nothing in the foreseeable future that suggests that your insurance needs are going to rise), you should cancel rather than switch.

If you have the right amount of cover, it is very likely that you can save money by switching to a cheaper policy. It could also be worthwhile checking the rates offered by your current insurer because you may be paying more than they charge new customers. If you find a cheaper deal, switching is very simple: get the new policy in place and then cancel the old one.

Cover cancelled

When 26-year-old Jason bought his flat, his lender encouraged him to take out a life insurance policy to cover his mortgage of £65,000. However, Jason is single, has no dependants and already has free life insurance of four times his annual salary from his employer. When he checked how much cover he had, Jason realised that he could save himself nearly £200 a year by cancelling the policy his lender had encouraged him to take out.

Chapter 8

Pensions

If you pay National Insurance, you have already made a start on your pension planning by buying entitlement to a pension from the state. However, a state pension alone is unlikely to provide adequate income for your retirement. If you want to live on more than the state pension when you retire and/or you do not want to carry on working until you are 65, you should give serious thought to paying into a pension of your own. Saving now to buy an income in the future – which is basically what pension planning is all about – does not just hold the prospect of a more comfortable retirement: it can also mean that you will be better protected against losing your earning power as a result of long-term illness (see page 103) or redundancy (see page 119). A pension is also a good way of providing a financial cushion for your dependants after your death (see pages 129–131).

This chapter looks at the types of pension available, explains what your pension choices are and tells you how you can boost your pension power with help from the Inland Revenue. If you are already paying into a pension, you may wish to go straight to pages 157–172 where you will find advice on assessing how much income you will need in retirement, as well as practical guidelines on how to work out how much you should be paying into your pension and tips on keeping track of your pensions. If you want to know what to do when you change jobs and what steps you can take to improve your chance of a decent income in retirement by switching pensions, turn to page 172. For information on what to do about your pension if you are nearing retirement, see Chapter 25.

Although pensions come in many different guises – largely depending on who is providing the pension – there are basically only two types of pension: those which carry a guarantee and those which do not.

Tip

The biggest attraction of choosing to save for your retirement through a pension scheme rather than using other savings and investments is the fact that part of the cost is met by the Inland Revenue in the form of tax relief. This means that if you pay tax at the basic rate, a £100 contribution costs you only £77; if you are a higher-rate taxpayer, a contribution of £100 costs only £60. However, in return for paying part of your pension, the Inland Revenue will not let you touch your money until you are at least 50. If you do not want to lock your money away until you retire, or you want to keep your options open as to how you will eventually use your savings, consider investing in an individual savings account (ISA) instead (see Chapter 21).

Guaranteed pensions

With pensions that carry a guarantee, your pension contributions buy you the entitlement to a specific amount of income which is guaranteed to be paid at retirement. What you pay in is not directly linked to what you get out because the onus is on the pension provider to make sure that you are paid the pension you have been promised. This sort of pension includes:

- **the basic state retirement pension** Commonly called the old-age pension, this is a flat-rate pension, the amount of which varies according to your National Insurance record when you reach the state retirement age of 65 (60 for women born before 6 April 1950). The full amount for a single person in the 1999–2000 tax year is £66.75 a week (£3,471 a year).
- **the state earnings–related pension scheme (SERPS)** You build up entitlement to this extra state pension only if you are an employee. You cannot pay into SERPS if you are self-employed. The amount you get on retirement is linked to the National Insurance you have paid and your average earnings (hence the name) up to a cash maximum which is currently about £100 a week – in practice, most people get less. You can choose to opt out of SERPS by 'contracting out', which may happen automatically if

you join an employer's scheme. If your employer's scheme is not contracted-out, you can contract out by taking out a personal pension (see page 146) specially designed for contracting out: these personal pensions are referred to as 'rebate only' or 'appropriate'. The pension scheme through which you contract out aims to replace the SERPS pension you would otherwise have got. If you have a choice of whether or not you contract out, you should bear in mind that you will lose the certainty of a predictable income in retirement by contracting out. The Department of Social Security (DSS) produces a useful leaflet: PM7: 'Understanding contracted-out pensions', which is available from DSS Pensions.*

- **the state second pension** This is the scheme with which the government plans to replace SERPS, but it is not scheduled to be introduced until 2002 at the earliest. Unlike SERPS, you will not necessarily have to be earning to build up entitlement to the state second pension since it has been proposed that full-time mothers and other carers will be able to build up entitlement; it may also be open to the self-employed. You will be able to contract out of the state second pension, and the government plans to encourage you to do so.

- **employers' final-salary schemes** These are available only to employees of the employers which offer them. Your pension contributions buy you a pension which is guaranteed to be a definite proportion of your salary at retirement or when you leave the scheme, if earlier (which is why these schemes are referred to as 'defined benefit' schemes)

Tip

You can get a forecast of your basic state retirement pension and also any SERPS pension to which you may be entitled by filling in form BR19 from the Retirement Pension Forecasting and Advice Service* or DSS Pensions.* Note that if you are a married woman (or widow) who pays the married woman's reduced rate of National Insurance (which you could choose to do before 6 April 1977), your state pension is based on your husband's National Insurance record. Any forecast you get will take account of this.

- **employers' hybrid schemes** Also called mixed-benefit schemes, these are a combination of a final-salary scheme and a money purchase scheme (see below). The pension you get at retirement is guaranteed to be the greater of whichever method of calculating your pension gives the better result.

Pensions which are not guaranteed

With pensions that do not carry a guarantee, what you get out when you retire is (among other things) directly linked to what you pay in – which is why these schemes are sometimes referred to as 'defined contribution' schemes. Your contributions are invested to build up a fund which, at retirement, is converted into cash and used to buy an annuity which provides your pension income. These schemes are also referred to as 'money-purchase' schemes because the money from the fund is used to purchase the pension. There is no guarantee with money-purchase schemes because the pension you eventually get depends on the size of your fund and how much income it will buy, which in turn depends on annuity rates when you convert your fund into a pension. This sort of pension includes:

- **employers' money-purchase schemes** These are available only to employees of the employers which offer them
- **additional voluntary contribution schemes (AVCs)** These are schemes which employers have to offer alongside their main scheme to allow employees to make extra payments towards their pension. Most work on a money-purchase basis (even if the main scheme is a final-salary one), so the extra pension that the additional payments buy is not guaranteed. The exception is employers (mostly in the public sector) who allow the members of their final-salary schemes to buy 'added years' – i.e. extra guaranteed entitlement to the main pension
- **free-standing additional voluntary contribution schemes (FSAVCs)** work like the employer's version but are sold by insurance companies
- **personal pensions** These are currently the only non-state pension option for the self-employed and employees who cannot join an employer's scheme. Personal pensions replaced retirement annuity contracts on 1 July 1988 but if you took a retirement

annuity contract out before that date, you can carry on paying into it

- **group personal pensions** These are personal pensions arranged by an employer for a group of employees. By buying in bulk, the employer is usually able to negotiate lower charges or special terms
- **stakeholder pension schemes** The government is proposing these as a simpler, cheaper and more flexible alternative to a personal pension for people who cannot join an employer's scheme. As we went to press the government's proposals were still going through the consultation process, and the final details of how the schemes will work had not been decided. However, it is very unlikely that stakeholder pensions will be available before April 2001.

Warning

With pensions that are not guaranteed, you can only estimate how much income you will get at retirement – you will not know for definite until you actually retire. In recent years buying a pension has become more expensive because annuity rates have been falling (as have interest rates generally). For someone who has built up a fund of £100,000, a cut of one percentage point in annuity rates – from 9 per cent to 8 per cent, for example – would mean a reduction in retirement income of £1,000 a year.

Your pension choices

Pensions are inextricably linked to earnings, so if you do not have any earnings you cannot pay into a pension. The exception to this (at least until the state second pension replaces SERPS – see page 145) is the entitlement you can gain to the basic state pension, either by paying extra to make up for gaps in your National Insurance record or by making sure that your National Insurance record gets the appropriate credits or protection for periods when you are not working or stay at home to look after children or a dependent adult. For more details, contact DSS Pensions.* If you do have earnings, the pension options open to you depend on whether you are an employee (see overleaf), or self-employed (see page 152).

> **Tip**
>
> If you have recently left higher education, do not ignore the invitation you may get from the Benefits Agency* to make voluntary Class 3 National Insurance contributions. It is a way of buying back your entitlement to basic state pension (and other benefits) for the years when you were studying.

Pension choices for employees

If you pay National Insurance, entitlement to the basic state pension is automatic, as is entitlement to SERPS (unless you opt out). If you want to make extra provision on top of the state pension, your choice is the same as that for a self-employed person (see page 152) unless you can join an employer's scheme.

At the time of writing you cannot be made to join an employer's scheme, but under the government's pension proposals employers may be allowed to make compulsory membership of their pension scheme a condition of employment, unless employees can prove that they have already made extra provision for a pension on top of what they will get from the state. In fact, 'soft compulsion' already exists: according to the National Association of Pension Funds (NAPF),* nearly half of all private-sector final-salary schemes, and the majority of those in the public sector, automatically enter new employees into pension membership. The number of people choosing to stay in such schemes is rising, as is the number of people who actively choose to join an employer's scheme.

Should you join an employer's scheme?

The short answer is yes. If you have the opportunity to join an employer's pension scheme, it will almost certainly be to your advantage. Paying into an employer's scheme is a relatively cheap way of buying a decent income in retirement, largely because of what your employer will pay in on your behalf and because the employer usually bears the cost of running the scheme. Joining a final-salary scheme will buy you a guaranteed (and inflation-proofed) income in retirement – something it is impossible to buy on the open market. If your employer offers a group personal pension and is prepared to contribute to it, it is likely to cost you less than taking out a personal pension of your own.

Warning

The fact that thousands of people have been compensated for being wrongly advised to leave or not join employers' pension schemes in the great personal pensions mis-selling scandal amply demonstrates the fact that joining an employer's scheme is better than buying a personal pension.

How much will it cost?
If the scheme is 'non-contributory', your employer foots the entire pensions bill and you do not have to pay anything towards your pension (although this is usually taken into account in the salary you are offered). If the scheme is a contributory one (whether final-salary or money-purchase) the amount you contribute is expressed as a percentage of your salary. This is usually anything between 2 and 6 per cent of your salary, and typically 4 per cent, but this is a lot less than what it would cost you to build up the same pension outside your employer's scheme. The way in which your employer pays into your pension depends on whether the scheme is a final-salary scheme or a money-purchase scheme. With a:

- **final-salary scheme** your employer pays enough into the scheme (on top of your contributions) to make sure that the promised pensions will be paid, so what your employer pays in is not directly linked to your salary
- **money-purchase scheme** your employer's contribution to the scheme is expressed as a percentage of your salary – this is typically more than the percentage you are asked to pay (the exact percentage will vary according to the employer). Your combined contributions go into the fund which will be used to provide your pension. For example, if you earn £20,000 and you are asked to pay 3 per cent of your salary, you will pay £50 a month (before tax relief) into your pension. If your employer contributes 6 per cent, a further £100 a month will be paid in.

149

The total £150 which is invested in your pension fund will have cost you less than £50 (after taking tax relief into account – see page 169)

- **hybrid scheme** your employer's contributions will be set at a level to ensure that you will receive the better of either the final-salary scheme or the money-purchase scheme – whichever pays the better pension at the time of your retirement.

Warning

Not joining an employer's scheme is like taking a pay cut. Given that there are no plans to make employers contribute to the proposed stakeholder pension (see page 147) and that employers will seldom pay into a personal pension on your behalf if they already run their own scheme, you could be losing out both on a better pension and a valuable part of your salary package.

Which type of scheme should you join?

Whether you have a choice between a final-salary scheme or a money-purchase scheme depends on your employer; it is very likely that you will not have a choice. However, this should not stop you from joining whichever is on offer. If you do have a choice of schemes, you must balance the portability of a money-purchase scheme (you can take your accumulated fund from one pension scheme to another when you change jobs) against the guarantee of the final-salary scheme. Some enlightened employers are making this choice easier by offering new employees either a hybrid scheme (see above) or the flexible option of a money-purchase scheme for the first few years with the opportunity to join a final-salary scheme for people who end up staying in the job.

What happens if you leave your job?

Changing jobs can reduce the amount of pension you get when you retire, but thinking that you might be likely to change jobs in future should not stop you from joining an employer's pension scheme. If you do leave you will get at least something back, depending on how long you have been in the scheme. If you have been in an employer's scheme for two years or more, you are entitled to:

- **final-salary schemes** You can leave your pension behind as a 'preserved' pension, which will be paid to you when you retire. This is based on your salary when you leave and must be increased annually by the lower of 5 per cent or prices inflation. Alternatively, you can convert your pension entitlement into a lump sum in the form of a 'transfer value' which you use to buy into a new scheme
- **money-purchase schemes** You have the right to either take your accumulated fund with you or leave it to grow in the scheme you are leaving.

In theory, people who leave an employer's scheme with less than two years' membership are entitled only to a refund of their pension contributions (less tax at 20 per cent). Those in non-contributory schemes receive nothing back. In practice, many employers extend the benefits available to people who stay in their scheme for at least two years to people who leave earlier than that (see table below).

What you may get back if you leave an employer's scheme before two years

	Final-salary		Money-purchase
	Private sector	Public sector	
Contribution refund	76%	92%	58%
Preserved pension	31%	15%	n/a
Transfer value	42%	30%	54%
Take your fund with you	n/a	n/a	40%
No benefit [1]	18%	8%	7%

Source: NAPF annual survey of occupational pension schemes 1998.
[1] These are schemes which do not require you to contribute to your pension. Note that employers may offer more than one option (which is why the figures do not add up to 100).

Other benefits
The other main reason for joining an employer's scheme (of whichever type) is the fact that your pension contribution not only buys you a pension at normal retirement age, but may also include a range of other benefits such as:

- a tax-free lump sum when you retire (although you usually have to take a reduced pension if you choose this option)

- a pension if you have to (or want to) retire early
- life insurance
- a pension for your spouse and/or children if you die before or after retirement.

All employers' schemes must also give you the option of making extra contributions towards your pension on top of the contributions you are required to make, in the form of AVCs (see page 146).

Pension choices for the self-employed

If you are self-employed, you have very little choice: if you want an element of guarantee to your pension arrangements, you need to make sure that your National Insurance record is up to scratch. If you want to have more than the basic state pension to live on when you retire, a personal pension is your only option until stakeholder pensions come into being (see page 147). Even then, a personal pension may still be preferable if you want to contribute more than £3,600 a year to your pension (this is the proposed maximum yearly contribution you will be able to make to a stakeholder pension). To work out how much you should be paying into your pension, see pages 157–172.

Choosing a personal pension

When stakeholder pensions are introduced, it is proposed that certain minimum standards will be in place to ensure that as much of your pension contributions as possible are invested in your retirement fund. Personal pensions have no such minimum standards, so it is up to you to ensure that you get the best deal in terms of the main factors which affect the size of your fund at retirement, which are:

- the type of investment (see opposite)
- performance (see page 154)
- charges (see page 154)
- flexibility (see page 155).

Which type of investment?

If you decide to buy a personal pension from a traditional pension provider such as an insurance company, your contributions will typically be invested in a with-profits fund, a unit-linked fund or in a combination of the two types. Both types depend on stock market performance but a with-profits fund carries an element of guarantee because the bonuses which are added to the fund each year cannot be taken away. Whether you choose a with-profits fund or a unit-linked fund will depend on your attitude to risk. In general, the longer you have to go until retirement the more risk you should be prepared to take, while the nearer you are to retirement the more risk-averse you should be. If you choose a plan which combines both with-profits and unit-linked investments, you can balance the risk by splitting your contributions between the two types.

There are no hard-and-fast rules for which type of investment is best, but if you will not want your pension for about 15 years or more, a unit-linked plan is probably the better choice. If you are taking out a pension with fewer than 15 years to go until retirement, you are probably better off taking out a less risky with-profits plan that will be less susceptible to the vagaries of stock markets.

'New investment opportunities with Lisa'

At the beginning of 1999, the government announced a proposal to allow personal pension contributions to be invested directly in unit trusts, investment trusts and shares in open-ended investment companies (see Chapters 20 and 21), with the same tax benefits and rules that apply to investing in one of the more traditional personal pensions offered by life insurance companies. (At the time, despite the government's claims that this proposal was not a new kind of pension, it was given the unofficial nickname LISA – lifetime individual savings account.) The thinking behind this proposal was that these collective investments should be able to provide a personal pension that is transparent, flexible and good value (i.e. with low charges). It was also proposed that if sufficient interest was shown by the kind of companies which offer this sort of pooled investment, regulations enabling them to offer personal pensions could be in place by the end of 1999.

Performance

Unfortunately, there is no way of knowing how well your investments will perform. You can only go on what has happened in the
past, but note that good investment performance in the past is no
guarantee of future performance.

Charges

High charges restrict the performance of your pension fund which
can make a serious dent in your eventual pension. The biggest dent
in the early years is usually commission, which may be paid to the
person selling you the pension. Other charges include an initial
charge on the amount you pay in and an annual management charge
levied as a percentage of the value of your fund. With the most
expensive – and usually least flexible – plans you may also encounter
penalty charges which you will have to pay if you do not keep to the
terms and conditions of the plan. This is particularly true of some
regular premium policies, which is why it is so important to check
how flexible a plan is (see 'Flexibility', opposite). However, it should
be possible to spot a high-charging plan before you commit yourself
because you must be given an 'illustration of benefits' for each plan
you are considering.

All illustrations have to use the same assumptions about how well
your fund will grow but they have to use real charges. When
comparing illustrations:

- check that they have used the same assumptions about your
  retirement date and the amount and type of contributions you are
  going to make to the plan
- look at the projected values of your fund because these will tell
  you which plan has the lower charges: the smaller the projected
  values, the higher the charges
- for a precise idea of how big a dent charges will make on the
  performance of the investment, look for the phrase 'Putting it
  another way, this would have the same effect as bringing the
  investment growth used from 7 per cent a year down to (whatever
  figure is given on the illustration). The closer it is to 7 per cent,
  the lower the charges
- look for the figure given under the heading 'How much will the
  advice cost' which is the amount of commission your adviser is

likely to receive if you take the plan out from a provider that pays commission

- you can see the effect of the cost of advice by looking at the estimated value of the fund at the end of years 1 and 2 with the amount you have paid in. With plans that pay large commissions, it is likely that the estimated value of the fund will be less than your total contributions to date.

Flexibility

The more flexible a personal pension plan is, the better suited it will be to your changing circumstances – a particularly important consideration if you are an employee and may be able to join an employer's scheme in the future, or you may take time out of the workplace (to have a baby, for example, or to travel). Flexibility is also important if you think you might want to transfer to a stakeholder pension but do not want to delay your pension planning. The questions you need to ask are:

- **what can you afford to invest?** Most plans set a minimum amount that you can pay in, with different limits for regular and lump-sum contributions. The maximum will depend on your earnings and Inland Revenue rules (see pages 166–168).
- **how do you want to pay?** You need to decide whether you want to make regular monthly or yearly payments or whether you would prefer to make lump-sum payments of irregular size and frequency. The most flexible plans will let you do both without charging extra
- **do you want to allow for increases?** If you have decided that you want to make regular payments, check that you can increase them and find out whether you can arrange for them to be increased automatically in line with inflation or by a fixed percentage (but check that this does not mean paying extra commission or other charges)
- **is the retirement date flexible?** Most plans will ask you to set a date for retirement when you take the plan out. If you don't know when you want to retire or you think you might change your mind, make sure that you are either not obliged to set a retirement date, or can change it without paying a penalty. Note

that you can usually change to a later date without penalty, but changing to an earlier date can cause problems

- **what happens if you stop making payments?** Make sure that you will not be penalised if you stop paying into the plan. A good plan will let you stop and restart payments without penalty or charges. If you are worried about not being able to keep up payments because of sickness, you could consider paying more for the option of 'premium waiver'. Your contributions are treated as though they are still being paid so your pension continues to build up

- **how long do you have to pay in for?** With some plans, you have to pay in for a certain amount of time before the plan is worth anything to you (which is why it is so important to study any illustrations you are given very carefully and to ask what happens if you stop paying in – see above). Others may reward you with a loyalty bonus if you pay in for a certain amount of time – ten years, for example.

Tip

Personal pensions which require you to make regular contributions can be expensive and inflexible. If you want the discipline of regular saving but do not want to commit yourself to making long-term regular payments into a personal pension plan – your earnings vary from year to year, for example, or your earnings future is not certain – consider making regular payments into a savings account and making lump-sum payments to the pension plan once or twice a year.

Where to buy

A good place to start is by looking at the annual surveys published by *Which?* magazine★ and also *Money Management* magazine★ (you can order a back copy of the edition which includes the pension survey) because they will help you to identify low-charging, flexible plans which have shown consistently good performance in the past. If you feel confident about making your own financial decisions, you can buy direct from whichever provider offers the type of pension that meets your needs – check that it does by asking the questions above. If you would rather get professional help, research conducted by *Which?* has shown that you have the best chance of good advice from an independent financial adviser (IFA) rather than from a financial adviser (or salesperson) tied to giving advice about the products of only one company. You can get a list of independent financial advisers in your area by contacting IFA Promotion★ and/or the Money Management National Register of Fee-based Advisers.★ It would also be worthwhile getting hold of two booklets published by the Financial Services Authority:★ *FSA Guide to Pensions* and *FSA Guide to Financial Advice*.

However you choose to buy your pension, do compare several plans before making your final choice and for each plan make sure you are given a 'Key features' document which outlines the important points about the pension (and which will help you to answer the flexibility questions on pages 155–156). The key features document also includes the illustration which enables you to compare charges (see pages 154–155).

Tip

Don't be shy about asking any financial adviser how much commission he or she will be getting for recommending a particular pension. You are allowed to ask and – unless the 'adviser' is the salesperson for a particular company – you must be told the answer. The amount of commission should be spelled out in the illustration of benefits for your pension plan (see page 154).

Paying into your pension

The amount you pay towards your state pension(s) is decided for you, as is the amount you are required to pay if you join an employer's scheme. It is up to you to decide whether what you are required to pay towards an employer's scheme is enough to provide you with the level of income you want to live on when you retire. With a personal pension you need to work out how much your contributions need to be.

Since pension planning is about buying a future income, you need

157

to have a rough idea of how much you will need to live on in retirement before you can make sensible decisions about how much you ought to be paying into your pension (or, if you are already paying into your pension, whether you are paying enough). What you need to pay in will also depend on:

- when you want to retire (see page 161)
- when you will be allowed to take your pension (see pages 161–162)
- what you will get from your pension (see pages 162–166)
- Inland Revenue limits on what you are allowed to pay in (see pages 166–168).

Tip

The earlier in your working life you start paying into a pension, the better chance you have of achieving your desired retirement income and/or retirement date. Starting early also means that you can be more relaxed about periods when you cannot pay into your pension – you take time out to bring up children, for example, or are left short of funds after buying a home.

How much income will you need?

The government has guaranteed that from April 1999 the minimum income pensioners will have to live on will be £75 a week for single people and £116.60 for couples. However, research carried out for Age Concern suggests that the minimum a pensioner couple needs to maintain a modest lifestyle in retirement is £150 a week. A survey of the incomes of current pensioners conducted by NatWest Life in 1998 found that the average couple had a financially comfortable life on a weekly sum of £175 (around £10,000 a year before tax), while the most affluent pensioners in the survey were content with a pension of £245 a week (£15,000 a year before tax). While none of this tells you how much you will need to live on, it does suggest that the common formula for working out how much pension you will need of 'two-thirds your before-tax salary' bandied about by the pensions industry does not accurately reflect what people really need to live on.

To get a realistic idea of the level of income you will need in retirement, the first step is to look at your current income in terms of its post-retirement spending power. To do this, take the figure after all deductions from your payslip (or a monthly average of what you pay yourself if you are self-employed) and then subtract all your monthly spending on things which you will not have to pay for in retirement such as:

- mortgage repayments and mortgage-related insurance, if your mortgage will be paid off by the time you retire
- rent – if you plan to buy a home and the mortgage will be paid off
- pension contributions (unless you pay into an employer's scheme, in which case these will be included in the after-tax figure on your payslip)
- savings plans which will have matured by the time you retire (so you will not be paying into them)
- child care and other child-related spending such as after-school classes, school fees and university costs
- anything else you will not have to pay for once you have given up work (although you can ignore savings on the costs of going to work because they will probably be cancelled out by the extra costs of being at home).

Add on the monthly costs of having to replace perks from your job such as the costs of running a vehicle if you have a company car, and premiums for private medical insurance or life insurance if you receive free cover from your employer. This will give you a rough idea of the level of after-tax disposable income you would need in order to avoid taking a cut in your standard of living. The nearer you are to retirement, the more exact and detailed you can be (see Chapter 25 for more information on planning your income if you are nearing retirement). To see how this monthly after-tax figure corresponds to an annual before-tax income, see the table overleaf which gives you an annual figure to compare with what you are likely to get from your pension.

How monthly after-tax income corresponds to an annual before-tax pension

Monthly after-tax income	Equivalent annual before-tax pension if you retire:	
	Before age 65	At (or after) age 65
£650	£8,600	£8,150
£700	£9,350	£8,950
£750	£10,150	£9,750
£800	£10,900	£10,500
£850	£11,700	£11,300
£900	£12,500	£12,050
£950	£13,250	£12,850
£1,000	£14,050	£13,600
£1,050	£14,800	£14,400
£1,100	£15,600	£15,200
£1,150	£16,400	£15,950
£1,200	£17,150	£16,750
£1,250	£17,950	£17,650
£1,300	£18,700	£18,550
£1,350	£19,500	£19,450
£1,400	£20,250	£20,250
£1,450	£21,050	£21,050
£1,500	£21,850	£21,850
£1,550	£22,600	£22,600
£1,600	£23,400	£23,400
£1,650	£24,150	£24,150
£1,700	£24,950	£24,950
£1,750	£25,750	£25,750
£1,800	£26,500	£26,500
£1,850	£27,300	£27,300
£1,900	£28,050	£28,050
£1,950	£28,850	£28,850
£2,000	£29,600	£29,600

The figures in the table are for a single person at 1999–2000 tax rates. The before-tax figures are for pension income only and do not allow for income from other sources such as savings. For more on calculating tax, see Chapter 17.

> **Tip**
>
> Buying a home of your own is an indirect way of improving your chances of a comfortable retirement. Homeowners will need less disposable income in retirement than pensioners who have to pay rent – for the obvious reason that a home of your own is rent-free. A home can also be used to provide further income (see Chapter 24).

When do you want to retire?

If you do not want to carry on working until state retirement age you will need to pay more into your pension than someone who does want to soldier on to 65 (60 for women born before 6 April 1950). This is because:

- you are less likely to get the maximum state pension
- the state pension will not be paid to you at the time you retire (you will have to wait until you reach state pension age)
- you have less time in which to build up your pension
- the younger you are at retirement the greater your financial needs are likely to be
- the younger you are, the more expensive it is to buy a pension.

> **Tip**
>
> If you fill in form BR19 from the Retirement Pension Forecasting and Advice Service,* not only will you get a forecast of what your state pension entitlement is likely to be if you carry on to state pension age, but (by ticking the relevant boxes on the form) you can also ask for a forecast of the pension that will eventually be paid if you retire early, and what you will get if you carry on working beyond the age of 65.

When are you allowed to retire?

You can retire at any age you like but if you want to have a pension to live on you will generally have to wait until you are at least 50, if

. you have a personal pension, or until the age at which your employer's scheme allows you to retire. As part of the wider pension reforms, the government has put forward proposals to allow people in employers' schemes to enjoy the same flexibility as people with personal pensions. The government is also looking at the possibility of allowing employees to take the pension built up through extra pension payments (AVCs and FSAVCs) at a different time from the pension from their main employer's scheme. Details of those proposals were due to be announced at the end of April 1999.

What will you get from your pension?

If you belong to an employer's final salary scheme, finding out what your pension will provide is very straightforward: your pension statement will tell you, or you can ask your scheme administrator what the figures are.

If you pay extra pension contributions into a separate scheme from your employer's final-salary scheme or pay into an employer's money purchase scheme or a personal pension, you need to know the value of the fund that your invested contributions have built up. To estimate how much pension your fund will currently buy you, multiply your fund by the annuity rate given in the table below which is appropriate for your gender and the age at which you want to retire. Note that the annuity rates in the table are for an income which remains the same throughout retirement; for an idea of how much a pension increasing by 5 per cent a year would be at the start of retirement, halve the figures given in the table. For more on choosing an annuity on retirement, see Chapter 25.

Annuity rates

Age at retirement	Man	Woman
55	6.9%	6.5%
60	7.6%	6.9%
65	8.6%	7.6%

Level annuity rates in April 1999. Note that you can find up-to-date annuity rates in the personal finance pages of the national press.

Source: The Annuity Bureau.*

162

As well as finding out what your current pension will pay you, you also need to find out what you can expect to receive from pensions you have left behind in previous pension schemes. If these pensions will not be paid until several years after your planned retirement date, you should not include them in your calculations unless you are prepared to alter your retirement date.

Tip

If you do not have up-to-date statements of previous pensions, try to obtain these. The Pensions Schemes Registry* can help you to trace missing pensions you have lost track of.

Will your pension pay you enough?

Once you have worked out roughly how much income you will need to live on and how much you can expect from the current value of your pensions, compare the two figures. If the total of all the pensions available at your chosen retirement date is less than the income you will need, you have three choices:

- accept that you may have less to live on than you would like
- postpone your retirement date (which may be a good idea if waiting until the age at which a pension from a previous employer or the state will be paid can take your anticipated income up to the level you think you will need)
- pay more into your pension.

Warning

If you have a personal pension, do not be lulled into a false sense of security by any projections you may have been given for the pension you can expect at retirement. With the exception of rebate-only personal pensions used to contract out of SERPS (see page 145), projections do not take inflation into account. The pension you are projected to get will have had its purchasing power eroded by the time you retire.

163

How much extra do you need to pay?

If you belong to an employer's final-salary scheme, you may be able to buy extra years of entitlement (this is most likely if you work in the public sector). Check with your employer and then run through the calculations again to see if this will get your pension income up to where it needs to be. If it does not, you may need to find other ways of saving for your retirement (see Chapters 20 and 21).

If you cannot buy added years in this way or you decide not to, the alternative is to make extra pension payments to an additional voluntary contribution (AVC) scheme which runs alongside your main pension and puts your pension on the same footing as the pension from a money-purchase scheme or personal pension. Your pension payments are invested to build up a fund which you then use to buy an annuity.

How to calculate the size of fund that you need to produce extra pension income	
Enter the figure for the before-tax yearly income you require	A
Enter your total expected yearly pension income on your selected retirement age	B
To find the yearly shortfall, subtract B from A and enter the result at C	C
Note that if B is greater than A, your pension is already on track to produce the level of income you need – but you should review the situation every year	
Enter the annuity factor (from the table below) which corresponds to your gender and desired retirement age	D
Divide C by D and enter the result at E	E
The figure at E is the fund you need to produce the extra income you require.	

Annuity factors

Age at retirement	Man	Woman
55	0.069	0.065
60	0.076	0.069
65	0.086	0.076

Making assumptions

Once you know how big a fund you require, you have to take a view about future investment growth and how inflation will eat into it – i.e. what the real rate of return is going to be. The more pessimistic you are, the better protected you will be against adverse investment conditions, rising inflation and falling annuity rates. Using zero per cent means assuming that the rate of inflation and the rate of growth will be exactly the same. If you are more optimistic, subtract your assumed inflation rate from your assumed rate of growth to give the real rate of return. Your assumptions should also be coloured by how near you are to retirement: if you have a long time to go, you can be optimistic about growth but pessimistic about inflation; the reverse is true if you are very near to retirement. The calculator below shows you how to convert the fund you need into the extra monthly contributions that you will need to make in order to bring your pension up to the level of income you think you will need to live on in retirement.

Tip

If you do not want to take a guess, the best way of taking inflation, growth and changes in annuity rates into account is to assume a real rate of return of 0%, and to sit down every year and repeat all the calculations for desired income, expected pension and fund needed. This also makes the sums much simpler because to convert your fund into pension contributions, you divide it by the number of months to retirement (i.e. number of years x 12).

How to convert your required fund into monthly pension contributions	
Enter the figure for your required fund (from the calculator opposite)	E
Enter the fund that a monthly contribution buys you for the real rate of return you are assuming from the table overleaf	F
Divide E by F and enter the result at G	G
Multiply G by 100 and enter the result at H	H
H is the extra monthly pension contribution you need to make.	

The fund that a monthly contribution of £100 buys you

Age now	Years to retirement	assuming a real rate of return of: 0%	0.5%	1%	1.5%
21	44	£52,800	£59,000	£66,300	£74,600
25	40	£48,000	£53,100	£59,000	£65,600
30	35	£42,000	£45,900	£50,300	£55,100
35	30	£36,000	£38,800	£41,900	£45,400
40	25	£30,000	£31,900	£34,100	£36,400
45	20	£24,000	£25,200	£26,500	£28,000
50	15	£18,000	£18,700	£19,400	£20,200
55	10	£12,000	£12,300	£12,600	£12,900
60	5	£6,000	£6,100	£6,150	£6,200

Tip

If you want to know how much extra you can contribute to your pension as a lump sum – you have just received a bonus or have had a win on the Premium Bonds, for example – multiply the figure H in the calculator on page 165 by 12.

How much are you allowed to pay into your pension?

Once you have calculated how much extra you need to save to buy the pension you will require, the next question is whether you will be allowed to pay that much into your pension. This is because the Inland Revenue puts limits both on how much you can pay into a pension each tax year and – if you belong to an employer's scheme – how much you can take out. To find out whether you are within the limits, fill in the calculator opposite.

Note that if the monthly amount that you are allowed to save (figure H from the calculator opposite) is smaller than the monthly amount that you need to save (figure H from the calculator on page 165), you will not be able to achieve the level of income that you require at your chosen retirement date from your pension alone – unless you have a personal pension (see 'Extra payments for personal pensions' on page 170). You will either need to find some other way of saving towards your retirement (see Chapters 20 and 21) or you will have to change your hoped-for retirement age.

Are your extra contributions within the Inland Revenue limits?	
Enter your annual before-tax pay including overtime, commission and bonuses or, if you are self-employed, your taxable business profits less capital allowances and losses	A
Enter the taxable value of all your perks (you can get these figures from your P11D which your employer gives you)	B
Add A to B and enter the result at C	C
Note that if the figure at C is greater than £90,600 (in the 1999–2000 tax year) and you are paying into a personal pension or an employer's scheme which you joined after 31 May 1989, you should enter £90,600 at C.	
Enter 15% (if you belong to an employer's scheme) or the relevant percentage for your age from the table below if you are paying into a personal pension	D
Multiply C by the percentage at D and enter the result at E	E
Enter the yearly amount of pension contributions (including AVCs or FSAVCs) that you are already paying	F
Subtract F from E and enter the result at G	G
Divide G by 12 and enter the result at H	H
The figure at H is the extra monthly contribution you are allowed to contribute – but if you belong to an employer's scheme, see 'Limits on what you can take out', overleaf.	

How much can you pay into a personal pension?

Maximum percentage you can pay into a:	Age at the start of the tax year (6 April)						
	35 or under	36 to 45	46 to 50	51 to 55	56 to 60	61 to 74	75 or over
Personal pension plan [1]	17.5%	20%	25%	30%	35%	40%	0%
Retirement annuity contract [2]	17.5%	17.5%	17.5%	20%	22.5%	27.5%	0%

[1] For personal pensions, the amount of earnings to which the maximum percentage can be applied is capped at £90,600 for the 1999–2000 tax year.

[2] Retirement annuity contracts are personal pension plans taken out on or before 30 June 1988.

Note: if you have both sorts of plan, the overall limit is the same as the limit for a personal pension although the carry forward rules become more complex.

Limits on what you can take out

If you pay into a personal pension, there are no limits on what you can take as a pension when you retire, although there are limits on what you can take as a lump sum. But, if you belong to an employer's scheme the most you can take as pension is broadly two-thirds of your earnings (including the taxable value of perks such as a company car) at retirement.

However, according to figures published by the National Association of Pension Funds currently only 1 per cent of people in employers' schemes are in danger of going over this limit.

You are most likely to be caught by the limits if you earn £90,600 or more and you joined an employer's scheme after May 1989. You will also be close to the limits if you belong to an employer's final-salary scheme which pays a pension of one-thirtieth of all your taxable earnings for each year that you are in the scheme, and you will have 20 years' membership by the time you retire – however, few schemes are so generous.

If you belong to a money-purchase scheme, you will exceed the limits only if your fund is sufficiently large – for a man retiring on a final salary of £45,000, for example, that could mean a fund of around £700,000; however, a woman would need more. If you are worried about going over the limits, talk to your pension scheme administrator who will also be able to calculate whether the extra you want to pay into your pension scheme will take you over Inland Revenue limits.

Note that the limits on what you can take as a pension from an employer's scheme are reduced if you take a lump sum in cash from your pension. For more details, see Chapter 25.

Under the limit

The £50 a month that Matthew pays into his employer's final salary scheme falls well short of the £291.25 he is allowed to pay according to Inland Revenue rules. The 4 per cent that his employer requires him to pay is based on his basic salary and does not include the perk of private medical insurance or his end-of-year bonus.

AVC or FSAVC?

You do not have to pay your extra pension contributions into the AVC scheme that your employer offers; you could choose to pay extra into a 'free-standing' AVC scheme (FSAVC) from a commercial provider instead. But you will nearly always be better off staying with what your employer offers because your employer is likely to meet some – or all – of the charges for running the scheme. An FSAVC will nearly always cost more. Whichever type of AVC scheme you choose, your employer has to monitor what you are paying in to make sure that you do not go over the Inland Revenue limits. The Financial Services Authority* publishes a useful booklet, *FSA Guide to Boosting your Occupational Pension*, which tells you what to ask when comparing an AVC scheme with an FSAVC scheme.

How much will your extra contributions cost?

The other limiting factor on how much extra you can pay into your pension is the amount of surplus cash which you have available to make the necessary extra payments.

However, the actual cost of making extra contributions is less than the amount that needs to be invested in your fund because of tax relief. For every £100 that goes into your fund, the Inland Revenue chips in a minimum of £23.

To work out what your extra contributions will cost you, multiply the monthly figure by 0.77 (if you are a basic-rate taxpayer); by 0.6 if you pay tax at the higher rate. If you do not know what your highest rate of tax is, see Chapter 17. How you get the tax relief depends on your employment status and the type of pension you are paying into:

- if you pay into an employer's pension scheme, all the tax relief is automatically included when working out your after-tax pay
- if you are an employee who pays into a personal pension plan, you get basic-rate tax relief by paying reduced contributions to the pension provider (so if you want £100 to go into your pension, you hand over only £77); higher-rate tax relief (if

applicable) is given through your tax code provided you tell your tax office about your pension contributions (see Chapter 17)

- if you are self-employed you have to pay the full amount of your contributions to the pension provider and get tax relief in the form of a lower tax bill.

Extra payments for personal pensions

If you have a personal pension and the extra you want to pay in is more than you are allowed to contribute for this tax year (see page 166–167), you may still be able to pay the extra by making use of the rules which let you look back to years where you could have paid into your pension but did not, or did not pay as much as you could have. If you have not paid in the maximum allowed by the Inland Revenue in previous years, there are two ways you can make use of the rules.

The first is to ask your tax office to pretend that a contribution you made this tax year was actually made last tax year (called 'carry back'), or the tax year before last if you did not have any earnings last year. So if you could have paid £3,000 last year, but paid only £2,000, you can allocate £1,000 of this year's contributions to last year. If you get a tax return but you have not yet filed it, you can do this by filling in the relevant boxes on your tax return. Alternatively, ask your tax office for form 43 or form PP43. You get tax relief at last year's rate, which can be useful if your rates of tax have gone down.

The second method (called 'carry forward') goes further back in time. You have to pay the maximum allowed in the current tax year but can then add any unused contributions you could have made from up to six years earlier (seven if you combine carry back with carry forward), starting with the year furthest away. This method is particularly useful if you have a lump sum that you want to pay into your pension. Although the amount you can contribute is based on earnings, the actual pension payment can be made with any sort of income – a legacy, for example, or the proceeds from a maturing life policy. Ask your tax office for help sheet IR330: *Pension Payments* and, if you have already filed your tax return, form PP42. Your tax office should also be able to help with the calculations.

Making up for lost time

Jane did not start paying into a personal pension until the birth of her daughter six years ago. When she took her pension out, she paid in a lump sum of £5,000 which she was able to do because she had unused contributions from the years she was earning but making no pension provision. Since then she has paid a regular monthly contribution of £100 (after tax relief) but this is £3,000 less each year than the maximum 17.5 per cent of her £24,000 taxable earnings (including the taxable value of her company car) that the tax rules allow her to contribute, so she still has unused contributions. When she turns 36 in March, the total amount she will be allowed to contribute in the tax year following her birthday will go up to £4,800 because she will be able to pay 20 per cent of her earnings (see table on page 167).

Keeping track of your pension

If you want to make sure that your pension will provide you with the income you will need at retirement, you should review its progress every year to take account of changing circumstances – both your own and those over which you have no control such as inflation, investment performance and annuity rates. If you do not get them automatically, make sure that you get hold of up-to-date statements of all your pensions from various sources every year.

If government proposals go ahead, keeping track of your pension will be much easier in the future because it is planned that you will get a 'combined pension forecast' which will show the pension you have built up to date from all sources (state, employer's scheme, personal pension) and what you could expect to receive if you carry on until state retirement age. It is also proposed that this combined forecast will tell you how much extra pension you would get by increasing your contributions. An example of what this sort of combined statement could look like is shown overleaf.

Combined pension forecast: illustrative summary

Name:	A Smith
Age:	58
The contributions you have made so far have built up the following pension entitlements	
State pension	
Your basic pension	£55.00
Your State Second Pension	£12.50
Occupational/personal/stakeholder pension	£62.30
Total current pension earned so far	**£129.80 a week**
If you stay in your present job your pension at age 65 is forecast to be:	
State pension	
Your basic pension	£64.70
Your State Second Pension	£12.50
Occupational/personal/stakeholder pension	£85.70
Forecast pension	**£162.90 a week**
If you increased your pension contributions by 5 per cent of your earnings from 1 January your forecast pension would increase to:	£170.20 a week

Source: *A new contract for welfare: PARTNERSHIP IN PENSIONS*

Should you switch?

If you have changed jobs frequently in the past and have several different pensions which you have left behind with previous employers, there may be a case for rationalising them. Whether this is a sensible thing to do depends on the type of scheme(s) you have left behind. Generally, you should *not* think about switching if:

- you have pension rights in a public sector scheme – you were a teacher, worked for the NHS or local government, for example
- your scheme was part of an industry-wide arrangement and you still work, or may return to work, in that industry
- your ex-employer's scheme offered particularly good benefits such as an inflation-proofed pension after retirement.

Even if none of the above apply to you, it may still be better to leave your old pension well alone if switching would mean that you lose benefits you would get by leaving it where it was. Before making any sort of transfer, you should get advice. For more information on transfers, contact the FSA public enquiries helpline.★

If you have a personal pension, switching may be worthwhile if you can increase the rate at which the fund builds up. This is likely to be possible if:

- you can switch to a less costly provider
- you can transfer the fund to an employer's money-purchase scheme
- you can transfer your fund to a stakeholder pension – depending on the final form of the government's proposals (see page 147)
- your current pension plan does not penalise you for switching.

Part 3

Saving money on your finances

Chapter 9

Renting a home

At the beginning of the twentieth century, the majority of people in England lived in a rented home; at the century's close people who rent are in the minority. However, for most people, renting somewhere to live is still the first step in becoming an independent householder. But renting can also be necessary as a temporary measure – if your job takes you away from home during the week, for example, or if you need somewhere to live between selling and buying a home or you have split up with your partner. For an increasing number of people, renting a home also provides a relatively cheap way of getting on to the first rung of the property ladder.

This chapter looks at the price of renting, the different ways in which you can rent a home, and how you can keep costs to a minimum. Advice is given on how to get the best from a letting agent, together with an explanation of your rights and responsibilities as a tenant. To find out more about how renting can provide a low-cost way of buying a home turn to pages 184–185 – and see Chapter 10 for details of how to finance the purchase.

What renting costs

The main factors that affect the amount of rent you pay are the size, condition and location of the property and more generally the part of the country in which you want to live. Renting a room as a lodger in the north of England, for example, could cost £200 a month including bills while a four-bedroomed house in an expensive part of London could cost thousands. Another important factor in determining the price you pay and also what rights you have as a tenant is whether you choose to rent from:

- a private landlord (see below)
- a social landlord (see pages 183–185).

What it costs to rent

	Average weekly rent	average monthly rent
Private landlords	£87	£375
Housing associations	£52	£225
local authority housing	£38	£165

Source: Government Housing Statistics 1998

Renting privately

One of the simplest – and cheapest – ways to rent somewhere to live is by becoming someone's lodger. A good starting point is to ask friends, colleagues and neighbours if they know anyone who is interested in letting out a room in their home (prime targets are single people who have just bought their first home and who are beginning to think that a little extra financial help with the mortgage might not go amiss). Other good searching grounds are office notice-boards, cards in newsagents' and small ads in local newspapers.

Newspapers are also a good source of accommodation to let if you want to find somewhere that is more than just a room plus shared facilities. However, as soon as you start to consider self-contained accommodation with an absentee landlord, you will probably find

---

Warning

If a landlord is unable to show you proof of an annual gas safety check, do not rent the property. By law, landlords must have the property's gas appliances safety-checked by a Council for Registered Gas Installers (CORGI) installer every 12 months. Landlords are legally obliged to provide you with written proof of this yearly check plus records of any repairs.

---

that your choice is limited unless you use a specialist letting agent, or an estate agency which also handles rented accommodation (see 'Using a letting agency' on pages 182–183).

What it costs

If you rent directly from a landlord, you will usually be required to pay one month's rent in advance. If you rent a self-contained property (rather than a room in someone's house), you may have to pay a deposit as well. This is usually between four and six weeks' rent and it covers any damage you may inflict on the property or non-payment of rent. It should be returned to you in full when you leave provided the property is still in the same condition as when you moved in and you have paid all the rent due.

Tip

Before you hand over any money for a deposit, make sure you are given an accurate inventory of all the furniture and other items that belong to the property and details of their condition before you move in. If the landlord has not prepared an inventory, do one yourself and get him or her to sign it. You should also check that the money will be held in an interest-paying account and that the interest will be repaid to you when your deposit is returned – ask for the tenancy agreement (see pages 180–181) to include a clause to this effect.

As well as paying rent, you will also have to meet the costs of the bills. The rent may include council tax and water rates (check the tenancy agreement see pages 180–181) but it is unlikely to cover the costs of gas, electricity and telephone calls (see Chapter 11 for more on the most cost-effective way to pay your bills).

You also need to consider buying insurance for your belongings. Although the landlord will usually be responsible for insuring the property and the items in it that do not belong to you, the possessions that you bring with you are unlikely to be covered. Since most contents policies (see Chapter 10) are aimed at homeowners, it may be worthwhile using an insurance broker (or other insurance inter-mediary), who can find a specialist policy aimed specifically at people who rent.

Your rights as a tenant

If you rent a room, either as a lodger where you share a property with the owner or in a shared flat or house with other people (whether you know them or not) you have little legal protection, and the landlord can put up the rent or ask you to leave at any time. However, you should be given 'reasonable' notice – a month, for example – so that you have time to find somewhere else to live.

If you rent a self-contained property, you should have a tenancy agreement, which gives you certain rights under the Housing Act of 1996. Unless your landlord specifies otherwise (which is very unlikely), most tenancy agreements are 'assured shorthold tenancies' (short assured tenancies in Scotland), which are for a fixed term and which usually last for a minimum of six months. Provided you keep to the terms of the agreement, you will have the right to live in the property for at least six months. After that the landlord has to give you two months' notice if he or she wants you to leave.

The tenancy agreement

Assured shorthold tenancies can be granted verbally but from a tenant's point of view it is better to get the agreement in writing. If your landlord does not provide this information within 28 days of your asking, he or she is committing a criminal offence and could be fined. The tenancy agreement should state:

- the landlord's name
- your name
- the address of the property
- the length of the tenancy (if it is for a fixed term)
- the notice period (if there is no fixed date when the tenancy comes to an end)
- the date the tenancy starts
- the amount of rent payable
- when the rent will be increased (if it is not a fixed-term tenancy)

- when the rent is due (the day of the week if you pay weekly or the date if you pay monthly) and whether it is payable in advance
- whether the rent includes council tax and/or water rates
- when the first rent payment has to be made (usually on signing the agreement)
- the type of tenancy agreement it is – for example, assured shorthold
- what the tenancy includes – usually with reference to an attached inventory
- the amount of the deposit, what it is for, whether it will be held in an interest-paying account and when you will get it back
- your responsibilities as a tenant – for example: to keep the property in a good condition, pay your fuel bills, TV licence, not to sub-let, not to keep animals, not to annoy the neighbours, to look after the garden (with a definition of what constitutes 'looking after')
- the obligations of the landlord – for example to keep the property in a good state of repair.

Note that unless the tenancy agreement specifically states the circumstances in which the rent can be increased, the landlord cannot put up the rent until the tenancy has come to an end or without following a procedure laid down in the 1988 Housing Act.

Tip

If you think that you might want to move out of the property before the end of the fixed-term, make sure that the agreement contains what is called a 'break clause', which allows you to do this. Otherwise, you may be liable to pay the rent up to the date when the agreement expires.

The right to reduce the rent

In the first six months of an assured shorthold tenancy, you have the right to apply to have the rent assessed by the local rent assessment committee. However, the rent can be assessed only if the rent you are being asked to pay is significantly higher than that for other similar properties in the area and there are enough similar properties to be able to make a comparison. If the rent assessment committee decides that the rent should be reduced, it has to remain at the reduced level for at least 12 months from the date of the assessment or until the tenancy comes to an end (whichever is later). Note that you can apply to have the rent assessed only once – even if your tenancy agreement is renewed.

New rules for existing fair-rent tenants

If you are entitled to have your rent registered by an independent rent officer under the Rent Act 1977 (broadly, you entered into your tenancy agreement before 15 January 1989 and you have long-term security of tenure), any future increases in your rent will be capped. Since the beginning of 1999, if an application is made to have your rent re-registered, the rent officer cannot agree to an increase of more than prices inflation plus 7.5 per cent; for subsequent re-registrations, the limit is prices inflation plus 5 per cent. A leaflet, 'A change to the fair rent rules', which explains the new rules in detail is available from the Department of the Environment, Transport and the Regions (DETR).* Note that these changes do not apply to the assured shorthold tenancies described in this chapter. For more information on the different types of tenancies, consult The *Which? Guide to Renting and Letting* also published by Which? Books.*

Using a letting agency

If you cannot find a suitable home to rent directly from a landlord, you may need to extend your search by using a letting agency. However, be prepared to pay more than just advance rent and a deposit. It is illegal for letting agents to charge you simply for registering your details or giving you information (if they try, report them to the local Trading Standards Office). If you decide to rent one of the properties the agent has offered, you may find that you have to pay a 'holding deposit' of between £50 and £200 as a way of demonstrating your firm interest in the property. If the property becomes unavailable, you will get the deposit back but if *you* pull out (or in some cases, if your references are not satisfactory) it may not be returned to you. Usually, if the rental goes ahead, the holding deposit is put towards the first month's rent but with a limited number of agents, you may not get it back at all.

Although some letting agents do not charge tenants when they go ahead with the rental, others may charge a fee of anything between £25 and £150 for:

- general administration involved in finding you the property
- taking up references
- drawing up and witnessing the tenancy agreement
- checking you into the property (which includes handing over the keys and giving you the inventory to check through and sign off)
- returning the deposit at the end of the tenancy.

Choosing a letting agent

Because a letting agent will be responsible for looking after your money in the form of deposits and sending the rent paid on to the landlord, it makes sense to choose a well-established agency which has professional indemnity insurance (this offers some protection for your deposit if the agent goes bust). The agent will have the necessary insurance if it belongs to one of the following trade bodies:

- Association of Residential Letting Agents (ARLA)★
- Incorporated Society of Valuers and Auctioneers (ISVA)★
- Royal Institution of Chartered Surveyors (RICS)★.

Some members of the National Association of Estate Agents (NAEA)★ also have professional indemnity insurance. Members of ARLA and RICS also have extra insurance in the form of a bonding scheme which protects your money from fraudulent letting agents.

As well as checking that an agent is reputable and has insurance in place to protect your money, you should make sure that you ask about all the charges that may be involved in the renting process.

Renting from a social landlord

The main differences between renting privately and renting from a social landlord – which includes local authorities, councils and registered housing associations – are that you have the right to live in your home for as long as you like (subject to a one-year probationary period) and the rent tends to be lower than in the public sector. You also have the right to buy your home provided certain conditions are met (see below).

If you want to rent from a council or registered housing association, you have to apply to be put on the waiting list. In some areas, the council and local housing associations operate a joint waiting list so you have to register only once for both types of housing. However, both councils and housing associations set their own rules for who gets priority when homes become available so unless you meet their published criteria (you can ask for a copy), you may have a long wait.

The right to buy

Most council tenants of two years' standing have the right to buy the home they rent, with the exception of sheltered housing and homes particularly suited to elderly people. People who have been tenants of a registered housing association for a minimum of two years have the same right to buy provided the property was built or purchased with public money and it has remained in the public sector ever since. Ex-council tenants whose landlord is now a registered housing association have the same rights as council tenants in the form of a 'preserved' right to buy.

Rent-to-buy discounts

Apart from not having to go through the cost and trauma of moving home, the main appeal of the right-to-buy scheme is the discount on the purchase price of the home. The minimum discount for a house is 32 per cent of its market value plus an extra 1 per cent for every extra year the person has been a tenant beyond the two-year qualifying period. The maximum is 60 per cent. For flats the discounts are 44 per cent minimum, 2 per cent for each extra year, up to a maximum of 70 per cent. In both cases there is a cash limit on what the discount can be; this (since February 1999) depends on where in England you live. These cash limits range from £38,000 in London and the South East of England to £22,000 in the North East of England. Your local council will be able to tell you the cash limit that applies to your area – ask for the leaflet 'Your right to Buy Your Home'.

Rent-to-mortgage

Rent-to-mortgage gives council tenants who have the right to buy their home, but who cannot afford to take out a mortgage (see Chapter 10), the ability to turn rent payments into loan repayments of exactly the same amount on an interest-free loan from the landlord. The tenant makes a small down-payment to gain legal ownership of the home but does not own the home outright until the loan is paid off. Details of this scheme are available in the leaflet 'How to Buy Your Own Home ... At a Price You can Afford' from the local council.

Cash incentives

Some councils (mostly those where demand for social housing is high) offer cash payments to tenants to help them buy a property privately under the Cash Incentive Scheme. The maximum grant is 80 per cent of the average 'Right-to-Buy' discount in their area up to the same cash maximum.

Shared ownership schemes

Shared ownership schemes – which are mostly available from housing associations – provide a halfway house between renting and buying and they offer an option to people who cannot afford to buy outright but who want to gain a foothold in the property market. Shared ownership means that to start with, you buy only a part of the home and pay rent on the rest, with the option of buying a bigger share as and when you can afford to.

Most shared-ownership schemes are for homes in new or renovated developments run by housing associations and housing trusts. For people who want to make their own choice of home on the open market, there is also a 'homebuy scheme', where you buy a 75 per cent share in a property and pay a subsidised rent on the rest. This scheme was set to replace the 'do-it-yourself shared-ownership scheme' (where you could buy a share of between 25 and 75 per cent) in April 1999. You can get more information on the shared-ownership schemes available in your area by contacting the Shared Ownership Advice Line* or the Housing Corporation.*

Chapter 10

Buying your home

Buying a home is not something to be taken lightly: it is expensive and the process of purchasing a property can be long and drawn out. If you do not plan to stay in the same place for at least two years, you are probably better off renting (see Chapter 9), although it would be a good idea to start saving for the time when you do eventually decide to settle somewhere (see Chapter 21). However, if you have already got to this stage, buying a property will not only give you somewhere to live, but by the time you have paid for your home (with modest help from the Inland Revenue – see page 197), you will have acquired a substantial financial asset. Having your own home can give you a relatively cheap way of borrowing (see Chapter 13) and it can also boost your finances in retirement: you will need a lower pension (see Chapter 8) than someone who rents, and the property itself can be used to raise cash (see Chapter 25).

This chapter takes you through the costs involved in buying – and selling – property, and looks in detail at the main way of raising the finance in the form of a mortgage. There is advice on working out how much to borrow and how to choose the best mortgage, together with tips on keeping the monthly cost of buying a house to the absolute minimum. If you already have a mortgage but you are not sure that you are getting the best deal, turn to the calculator on page 213 which will help you work out whether switching mortgages will be worthwhile. If you are interested in speeding up the process of paying off your mortgage, turn to pages 204–205. For information on how you can get on to the property ladder by renting a home, turn back to Chapter 9.

Can you afford to buy?

Whether you are thinking about buying a home for the first time or you have decided that it is time to move on from a property you already own, you need a rough idea of whether this is an affordable option, which means:

- finding out the price you will have to pay for the kind of property you want (see below)
- knowing how much you can borrow (see pages 188–191)
- estimating what the costs involved in buying the property will be (see pages 191–195)
- calculating how much cash you will need to put towards the purchase (see page 195)
- working out whether you will be able to manage the monthly costs of paying for your home (see pages 196–197).

You may find it useful to fill in the calculator on page 195. This will help you to work out in detail whether buying a property is affordable, how much you will be able to borrow and how much cash you will need.

The cost of property

The biggest single cost of buying your home will be the price of the property itself. The value of the property (which is not necessarily the same thing as the purchase price – see page 190) will also have a bearing on the amount of money you will be able to borrow. The best way to get an idea of how much you will have to pay for the kind of property you want is to look in estate agents' windows or check out the property advertisements in local newspapers. If you are thinking of buying in a different part of the country this may not be practical; you could however look at the web sites of estate agents with branches nationwide.

The table overleaf gives an idea of average house prices around the UK, while the map on page 189 gives details of average prices broken down by the type of property. Average prices are higher for movers than for first-time buyers because they are trading up.

The cost of property

	Average prices in fourth quarter of 1998		
	First-time buyers	Movers	All properties
Scotland	£43,584	£66,760	£59,115
Northern England	£35,977	£57,809	£48,532
Yorkshire and Humberside	£39,897	£61,013	£52,645
East Midlands	£44,138	£64,725	£56,485
East Anglia	£51,159	£122,760	£66,387
Greater London	£90,721	£131,169	£107,464
Outer Metropolitan Area	£76,258	£122,760	£103,322
Outer South East	£58,240	£89,916	£77,318
South West	£55,347	£79,609	£70,179
West Midlands	£48,920	£76,132	£64,135
Wales	£41,295	£62,579	£53,218
North West	£43,367	£67,010	£57,271
Northern Ireland	£51,273	£65,450	£57,984

Source: *Nationwide Quarterly Housing Review*, January 1999.

How much will you be able to borrow?

Unless you have the resources to buy a property outright, you will need to borrow the money by taking out a mortgage. Although usually used to refer to the loan you get if you need to borrow to buy your home, a mortgage is the legal document which gives your lender the right to the repossess the property if you fail to repay the loan (the borrower is known as the 'mortgagor' and the lender is known as the 'mortgagee'). How much you can borrow depends on three main factors:

- your income
- the valuation your lender puts on the property
- the lender's lending limits.

House prices in the UK

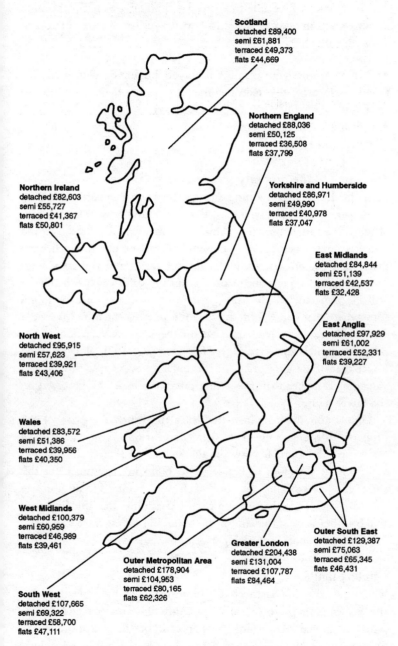

Scotland
detached £89,400
semi £61,881
terraced £49,373
flats £44,669

Northern England
detached £88,036
semi £50,125
terraced £36,508
flats £37,799

Northern Ireland
detached £82,603
semi £55,727
terraced £41,367
flats £50,801

Yorkshire and Humberside
detached £86,971
semi £49,990
terraced £40,978
flats £37,047

East Midlands
detached £84,844
semi £51,139
terraced £42,537
flats £32,428

North West
detached £95,915
semi £57,623
terraced £39,921
flats £43,406

East Anglia
detached £97,929
semi £61,002
terraced £52,331
flats £39,227

Wales
detached £83,572
semi £51,386
terraced £39,956
flats £40,350

West Midlands
detached £100,379
semi £60,959
terraced £46,989
flats £39,461

Outer South East
detached £129,387
semi £75,063
terraced £65,345
flats £46,431

Outer Metropolitan Area
detached £178,904
semi £104,953
terraced £80,165
flats £62,326

Greater London
detached £204,438
semi £131,004
terraced £107,787
flats £84,464

South West
detached £107,665
semi £69,322
terraced £58,700
flats £47,111

Source: *Nationwide Quarterly Housing Review, January 1999*

189

Your income

The most you will be able to borrow – although this is not the same as what you can sensibly afford to borrow – is based on a multiple of your annual income and is usually:

- 3 to 3.25 times your earnings if you are buying on your own
- 3 to 3.25 times the main income plus 1 times the second income if you are buying with another person; *or*
- 2.5 to 2.75 times the total of your joint earnings if you are buying with another person.

The value of the property

Some lenders will give a mortgage 'promise' or 'guarantee' based on an assessment of your earnings so that you know how much you can afford to pay for a property. This is a firm offer of a mortgage and you may get a certificate – a useful document to show sellers to prove that you are serious. However, the maximum you are able to borrow in relation to your income is not the same as what the lender will be prepared to 'advance' (i.e. lend you) once you have found somewhere that you want to buy. This is because the most the lender will be prepared to lend is based on the lender's valuation of the property (which you have to pay for – see page 192), which may be lower than the asking price. In the unlikely event that the lender's valuation is higher than the asking price, the loan will be based on the lower figure.

Unless you can convince the seller to reduce the price of the property to the amount of the lender's valuation, you will need to make up any shortfall between the selling price and the lender's valuation. It therefore makes sense to build in an estimate of this shortfall when working out how much cash you need to put towards the purchase. The calculator on page 195 assumes that the difference will be 2 per cent of the cost of the house but if you want to be ultra cautious, you could assume 5 per cent.

Lending limits

The other limiting factor is the percentage of the valuation that the lender is prepared to lend you. Although you can find lenders who are prepared to lend 100 per cent of the valuation of the property (sometimes 105 per cent when house prices are rising), most lenders will not lend more than 90 to 95 per cent of the valuation. However, if you borrow this much, you may face a higher interest rate and/or you will have to pay a mortgage indemnity guarantee (MIG). This is a one-off lump-sum fee of several hundred pounds (usually added to the loan) paid to buy an insurance policy that protects the lender from the risk of not being able to recover the full amount of the loan if house prices fall (and you fail to keep to repayments). The fee is typically 7.5 to 8 per cent of the difference between the amount you borrow and 75 per cent of the valuation. However, you may not realise what you are being charged for because lenders use different terms to describe a MIG, such as: high loan-to-value fee; high percentage loan fee; high lending fee; mortgage risk fee; additional security fee; increased risk advantage.

Buying costs

As well as finding money to pay for the difference between what the property costs and the amount you can borrow, you will also need to find cash to pay for:

- legal fees
- valuation and survey fees
- the costs of moving in.

Legal fees

A major cost of buying a home is made up of the fees involved in the legal process of transferring the ownership – or 'title' – of property (called 'conveyancing'), for which you will have to pay:

- **legal fees** of a solicitor or licensed conveyancer to undertake the legal mechanics for you. As well as the conveyancing work, these fees usually include the cost of creating the mortgage document (unless your lender does not agree to this – most do, but it is worth checking). Expect to pay around 1 per cent of the purchase price (plus VAT at 17.5 per cent). You may be able to get the legal work done for a fixed fee. If you are selling as well as buying, you have to pay two sets of legal fees because the transfer of ownership occurs twice

191

- **the Land Registry fee** which is a flat fee based on the purchase price of the property (see table below)
- **local authority search fees** to pay for information provided by the local authority about planning etc. Expect to pay around £60 (£100 in London boroughs) but a nominal fee in Scotland
- **other search fees** which you will not necessarily have to pay for, but which cover general checks on information from other sources that may affect your eventual ownership of the property. Allow about £70 for these extra fees
- **stamp duty** which you will have to pay only if the whole price of the property is more than £60,000. The rates are 1 per cent if the purchase price of the property is over £60,000 but less than £250,000; 2.5 per cent for properties costing over £250,000 but less than £500,000; and 3.5 per cent for properties over £500,000 (for purchases taking place in the 1999–2000 tax year).

You will save money if you can get the price of the property down to just £1 below the nearest threshold. If you cannot persuade your sellers to drop the price but you have agreed to buy some of their belongings (such as carpets and curtains) as part of the deal, and the cost of these items is tipping the total over the threshold, then try to get the sellers' agreement to pay for these separately. Because stamp duty is charged only on the price of the property, you could find yourself saving up to £600, £3,750 or £5,000 in tax.

Land Registry fees

Cost of property		Fee
From	to	
£0	£40,000	£40
£40,001	£60,000	£70
£60,001	£80,000	£100
£80,001	£100,000	£150
£100,001	£200,000	£200
£200,001	£500,000	£300
£500,001	£1,000,000	£500
£1,000,001	£5,000,000	£800
£5,000,001	and over	£1,200

The cost of transferring ownership

Purchase price of property	Legal fees [1]	Land Registry fee	Local authority searches [2]	Other search fees [3]	Stamp duty	Total [4]
£30,000	£360	£40	£60	£70	n/a	**£530**
£40,000	£470	£40	£60	£70	n/a	**£640**
£50,000	£590	£70	£60	£70	n/a	**£790**
£60,000	£710	£70	£60	£70	£600	**£1,510**
£70,000	£830	£100	£60	£70	£700	**£1,760**
£80,000	£940	£100	£60	£70	£800	**£1,970**
£90,000	£1,060	£150	£60	£70	£900	**£2,240**
£100,000	£1,180	£150	£60	£70	£1,000	**£2,460**
£110,000	£1,300	£200	£60	£70	£1,100	**£2,730**
£120,000	£1,410	£200	£60	£70	£1,200	**£2,940**
£130,000	£1,530	£200	£60	£70	£1,300	**£3,160**
£140,000	£1,650	£200	£60	£70	£1,400	**£3,380**
£150,000	£1,770	£200	£60	£70	£1,500	**£3,600**
£160,000	£1,880	£200	£60	£70	£1,600	**£3,810**
£170,000	£2,000	£200	£60	£70	£1,700	**£4,030**
£180,000	£2,120	£200	£60	£70	£1,800	**£4,250**
£190,000	£2,240	£200	£60	£70	£1,900	**£4,470**
£200,000	£2,350	£200	£60	£70	£2,000	**£4,680**
£210,000	£2,470	£300	£60	£70	£2,100	**£5,000**
£220,000	£2,590	£300	£60	£70	£2,200	**£5,220**
£230,000	£2,710	£300	£60	£70	£2,300	**£5,440**
£240,000	£2,820	£300	£60	£70	£2,400	**£5,650**
£250,000	£2,940	£300	£60	£70	£6,250	**£9,620**

[1] Assumes 1% of purchase price plus VAT at 17.5%; figures have been rounded up to the nearest £10.

[2] Minimum most people should allow; likely to be more in London boroughs but less in Scotland.

[3] For average house purchase.

[4] If you are selling as well as buying add another set of legal fees to this total.

Valuation and survey fees

If you arrange a mortgage, you will have to pay a valuation fee for the lender's mortgage valuation. This fee (plus VAT) is based on the price of the house and varies according to the lender's arrangements with the valuers. Fees range from around £100 to £140 for a property valued at £50,000 and between £230 and £270 for one valued at £250,000. As an incentive for you to take out a mortgage with them, some lenders do not charge a valuation fee, or promise to refund it if the mortgage goes ahead. Most lenders will encourage you to combine the mortgage valuation with a survey of your own, of which there are two types:

- **a homebuyer's report** which provides comments on the general condition of the parts of the property which are visible or readily accessible and makes recommendations for further investigations which may be needed to check up on possible defects. The fee is linked to the price of the property – for example, £150 for a property costing £35,000; £330 for a £100,000 house
- **a full structural survey** which is a detailed assessment of the structure of the property. This is essential for many older properties and for those which are particularly large or unusually designed. Expect to pay between £250 and £1,000 (plus VAT).

The costs of moving in

You also need to budget for the cost of moving your belongings into your new home, letting people know that your address has changed, getting services and appliances connected, and attending to various minor repairs which may need fixing. Allow from a minimum of £300 to over £1,000, depending on whether you will do your own removal or get professional help. The greater the distance and the more stuff you have to move, the more it will cost.

Tip

You can save money if you combine your own survey with the mortgage valuation which your lender will require, by getting the lender's valuer to perform your own homebuyer's report or full structural survey.

Calculating how much cash you need

If you are a first-time buyer, the cash you need to put towards the purchase will have to come from savings. If you are moving, you will also have the proceeds from selling your current home after deducting estate agent's fees of 1.5 to 2.5 per cent of the selling price (plus VAT). To get an estimate of the amount of cash you will need to put towards the purchase of your new home, fill in the calculator, below.

How much cash do you need to raise?	
Enter an estimate of the cost of the property	A
To estimate the lender's valuation, multiply A by 0.98 (or 0.95 if you feel ultra cautious – see page 190) and enter the result at B	B
Enter the maximum percentage of the valuation your lender is prepared to lend, or 95% if you do not know	C
To find out the most you can borrow based on the value of the property, multiply B by the percentage at C and enter the result at D	D
Enter the most you can borrow based on your salary (see page 190)	E
If E is greater than D, the most you can borrow is the figure at D. If E is less than D, the most you can borrow is the figure at E.	
Subtract the most you can borrow (D or E) from A and enter the result at F	F
Enter an estimate of your total buying costs (see pages 191–194) including any mortgage indemnity guarantee (see page 191) if this will not be added to the loan	G
Add F to G and enter the result at H	H
The figure at H is the amount of cash you will need to put towards the purchase of the property.	
Enter the amount of cash you have available	I
If you are selling, enter an estimate of your sale proceeds less estate agent's fees	J
Add I to J and enter the result at K	K
Subtract H from K and enter the result at L	L
If L is a plus figure, you have more than enough cash to pay for the purchase. If L is a minus figure, you do not have enough cash to buy your chosen property.	

Can you manage the monthly mortgage costs?

Every mortgage advertisement has to carry a warning that your home will be at risk if you do not keep up your repayments. If you do not meet your monthly mortgage payments, the lender will force you to sell your home and at best you will be back to where you started before you bought it – at worst you will be homeless, have a bad credit record and may still owe the lender money because of the costs involved in repossessing. So as well as working out the most you can borrow, you need to consider how your monthly budget will stand the mortgage repayments (see table below).

The cost of monthly mortgage payments

	if the interest rate is:					
Size of mortgage	5%	6%	7%	8%	9%	10%
£30,000	£175	£195	£210	£230	£250	£275
£35,000	£205	£225	£250	£270	£295	£320
£40,000	£235	£260	£285	£310	£335	£365
£45,000	£265	£290	£320	£350	£380	£410
£50,000	£290	£325	£355	£385	£420	£455
£55,000	£320	£355	£390	£425	£460	£500
£60,000	£350	£385	£425	£465	£505	£545
£65,000	£380	£420	£460	£500	£545	£590
£70,000	£410	£450	£495	£540	£585	£635
£75,000	£440	£485	£530	£580	£630	£680
£80,000	£470	£515	£565	£615	£670	£725
£85,000	£495	£550	£600	£655	£715	£770
£90,000	£525	£580	£635	£695	£755	£820
£95,000	£555	£610	£670	£735	£800	£865
£100,000	£585	£645	£705	£770	£840	£910

Figures do not include tax relief, are rounded to the nearest £5 and are based on a repayment mortgage paid back over 25 years.

As well as the monthly cost of the mortgage, you also need to take into account the other costs of being a homeowner such as:

- buildings insurance (which your lender will insist that you take out)
- life insurance (if you have dependants or a joint mortgage)

- contents insurance (if you do not already have this)
- gas and electricity bills
- council tax and water rates
- ground rent and service charges if you buy a flat
- general house maintenance costs.

Tip

If you are currently renting and you are not sure how you would cope with more expensive mortgage repayments, consider putting aside the difference between what your mortgage would cost and what you are currently paying in rent. This will not only give you a feel for how you would cope with the extra costs but you will also be building up cash to put towards the purchase.

Tax point

You get a subsidy on the interest you pay on the first £30,000 of a mortgage in the form of mortgage interest tax relief. In the 1999–2000 tax year the subsidy is worth 10 per cent. However, tax relief on mortgage interest will be abolished altogether from 6 April 2000. For this reason, the figures in the table opposite do not include the tax relief although any quotations you get from a mortgage lender will include it. You get the tax relief through MIRAS (mortgage interest relief at source), which means that you make lower payments to your lender.

Choosing a mortgage

For most people, the priority when choosing a mortgage is to find a lender prepared to lend the amount of money needed. However, the other things you need to think about when choosing a mortgage are:

- how long you want the mortgage to last (see below)
- how you want to repay the loan (see below)
- how you want to pay the interest (see pages 202–203)

- what the penalties are if you repay early (see page 203)
- how the lender calculates interest (see page 204)
- how flexible you want the terms of the mortgage to be (see pages 204–205).

How long do you want the mortgage to last?

Most mortgages are arranged over 25 years but you can arrange for different mortgage terms. The advantage of extending the term to 30 years, say, is that your monthly repayments will be lower than for a 25-year term. The major downside is that the overall cost of interest goes up. The reverse is true if you arrange to repay your loan over a shorter term – see table (below).

How the mortgage term affects the cost

Term	Monthly cost	Total cost of interest
20 years	£390	£43,000
25 years	£355	£56,000
30 years	£335	£70,000

Figures are for a £50,000 mortgage at an interest rate of 7 per cent.

How do you want to repay the loan?

Deciding how you will repay your mortgage loan is probably the most important decision you have to make because it affects the overall cost of the loan and what you will have to pay for your mortgage each month. There two options for repaying your mortgage:

- with a **repayment mortgage** you pay back the loan little by little and your monthly mortgage payments are a combination of interest and capital (i.e. the money you have borrowed) – although to start off with, you pay mostly interest (see the example opposite). Provided you keep up the repayments the loan is guaranteed to be paid back at the end of the term. If you have dependants, you need to take out life insurance in the form of a mortgage protection policy to ensure the loan will be paid off if you die

Example of a repayment mortgage of £30,000 over 25 years

	Mortgage outstanding at the beginning of the year	Yearly mortgage Payments	Amount of payment used for interest	Amount of payment used to pay back the loan	Percentage of loan paid off at the end of each year
Year 1	30000.00	2663.04	2214.00	449.04	1%
Year 2	29550.96	2663.04	2180.86	482.18	3%
Year 3	29068.78	2663.04	2145.28	517.76	5%
Year 4	28551.02	2663.04	2107.07	555.97	7%
Year 5	27995.04	2663.04	2066.03	597.01	9%
Year 6	27398.04	2663.04	2021.98	641.06	11%
Year 7	26756.97	2663.04	1974.66	688.38	13%
Year 8	26068.60	2663.04	1923.86	739.18	16%
Year 9	25329.42	2663.04	1869.31	793.73	18%
Year 10	24535.69	2663.04	1810.73	852.31	21%
Year 11	23683.38	2663.04	1747.83	915.21	24%
Year 12	22768.18	2663.04	1680.29	982.75	27%
Year 13	21785.43	2663.04	1607.76	1055.28	31%
Year 14	20730.15	2663.04	1529.89	1133.15	35%
Year 15	19597.00	2663.04	1446.26	1216.78	39%
Year 16	18380.22	2663.04	1356.46	1306.58	43%
Year 17	17073.64	2663.04	1260.03	1403.01	48%
Year 18	15670.63	2663.04	1156.49	1506.55	53%
Year 19	14164.08	2663.04	1045.31	1617.73	58%
Year 20	12546.35	2663.04	925.92	1737.12	64%
Year 21	10809.23	2663.04	797.72	1865.32	70%
Year 22	8943.91	2663.04	660.06	2002.98	77%
Year 23	6940.94	2663.04	512.24	2150.80	84%
Year 24	4790.14	2663.04	353.51	2309.53	92%
Year 25	2480.61	2663.04	183.07	2479.97	100%

- with an **interest-only mortgage** you pay back the loan all in one go at the end of the mortgage term, and the whole of your monthly payments are made up of interest. To build up a sufficiently large lump sum to be able to pay back the loan, you make separate payments into some form of investment (see below for the different investment options). There is no guarantee that the loan will be repaid. Depending on which investment you choose to back up the loan, you may need to buy life insurance if you have dependants.

A repayment or interest-only mortgage?

If you do not want to take a risk with your mortgage, a repayment mortgage is the better option and it can also work out cheaper in the long run. A repayment mortgage also has the advantage of being more flexible if you cannot make repayments for a while – you are made redundant, for example. You may be able to reduce your monthly repayments by extending the term of the mortgage, or you can negotiate to pay interest only for a time. Neither of these options is available with an interest-only mortgage.

If you are happy to take a risk with your mortgage and you like the idea of mixing long-term investment with the process of buying your home, an interest-only mortgage could be worth considering. You run the risk that your investments will not provide the lump sum to pay off the loan, but you may end up with more than you need if your investments do particularly well. You also have to be disciplined about paying enough into the investment you choose to run alongside your mortgage: lenders make it very clear that this is your responsibility. The table opposite gives you an idea of how much you will have to save (on top of the interest you pay your lender) to build up the lump sum you will need, using different assumptions about investment growth and different tax treatments. To work out what your monthly interest payments will be, multiply the mortgage amount by the interest rate and divide by 12.

Which type of investment?

If you decide to go down the interest-only route, you need to decide which type of investment you will use to back up the loan. The traditional investment vehicle is an endowment policy – either with-profits or unit-linked – which is a life insurance policy with an investment element built in (for more on how these work, see Chapter 20). The people who sell these are paid commission – which can be as much as all the money you pay into the policy in the first two years.

The main drawback of this sort of investment is that for the policy to be worthwhile, you have to keep it going to the end of the mortgage term. In recent years, a lot of people taking out this sort of policy have been asked to increase their savings or risk a shortfall. For most people endowment mortgages are not suitable and are best avoided if you do not need life insurance, for example if you are single and have no dependants. You should also think twice if you would like to be able to cash in your investment in the future – if you want to repay part of the loan, for example, or you want to stop saving and switch to a repayment mortgage. However, endowment mortgages used to be a good idea for some people when the cost of this sort of life insurance was subsidised by the Inland Revenue (before 1984), and the subsidy on mortgage interest was over a quarter of the monthly interest payments. These tax subsidies have all but vanished now.

The main alternative to insurance-based investments is to save in an individual savings account (ISA), which has the advantage of being tax-free and flexible. Unlike insurance-based investments, you should be able to get at your savings whenever you want so you will not have to wait until the end of the mortgage term if you decide to use part of your savings to pay off some of the loan. For more on ISAs, see Chapters 20 and 21.

How much you need to save alongside an interest-only mortgage for 25 years

Minimum amount you will need to save each month	Lump sum you may build up if the investment is:					
	Tax-free ISAs and personal pensions			Taxed Endowment policies		
	5%	7%	9%	4%	6%	8%
£50	£30,000	£40,000	£55,000	£26,000	£35,000	£47,000
£100	£60,000	£81,000	£110,000	£52,000	£69,000	£94,000
£150	£90,000	£121,000	£165,000	£78,000	£104,000	£141,000
£200	£120,000	£161,000	£220,000	£104,000	£139,000	£188,000
£250	£150,000	£202,000	£275,000	£130,000	£174,000	£235,000

Figures have been rounded to the nearest 1,000. Investment assumptions are those used for standard projections for investment products set by the Personal Investment Authority.

Another tax-free alternative if you have a personal pension (see Chapter 8) is to use the part of your fund that you can take as a lump sum when you retire – but your fund will need to be worth at least four times the size of your mortgage. You also need to bear in mind that if you have more than 25 years to go to retirement, you will have to keep paying the mortgage interest for longer than with a conventional mortgage. You also need to ensure that the fund you build up in your pension is sufficiently large to both give you the pension income you need and provide the lump sum. If you are not paying enough into your pension to provide your future income, you should not link your pension fund to your mortgage.

How do you want to pay the interest?

Once you have chosen the method you want to use for repaying the loan, you need to decide how you want to pay the interest. This has a direct effect on your monthly payments and it can also affect how tied you are to staying with the same lender. If the interest rate is:

- **variable** your monthly payments will go up and down in line with interest rates generally (although some lenders are quicker to change their rates than others). If your budget can cope with fluctuations in what you have to pay (see table on page 196 for an idea of how a change in interest rates affects your monthly payment), choosing a variable rate often means that the mortgage is more flexible

- **variable with cash back** you pay the lender's standard variable rate but get a percentage of the mortgage – typically around 5 per cent – back as a cash payment shortly after the loan starts. However, in exchange for the cash you have to stay with the lender for up to six years unless you are prepared to return the cash

- **fixed** you pay the same interest rate for a fixed period (of two, three, five or ten years) regardless of fluctuations in interest rates generally. At the end of the period, you go back to your lender's variable rate. Fixed rates are ideal if you want the security of stable repayments and would find it hard to cope with interest-rate rises. However, if interest rates fall, you end up paying over the odds for your mortgage

- **capped** you get a semi-fixed rate in that it is guaranteed not to go above a certain level during the capped period, but if the lender's variable rate goes down, so too do your monthly payments
- **capped and collared** the interest rate is variable between an upper and a lower fixed rate
- **discounted** you pay a lower-than-normal variable rate for a certain number of years. Some deals keep the same discount for the period while others gradually reduce the discount each year. A discounted rate is worth considering if you do not need the security of stable payments that you get with a fixed rate but you like the idea of paying less for your loan to begin with. Some discounted deals also offer a modest amount of cash if you proceed with the loan.

What are the penalties if you repay early?

When choosing a mortgage, it is always worth asking what the penalties will be if you want to repay the loan early – which includes repaying the loan when you move house – or if you want to switch your mortgage regularly to take advantage of better terms from other lenders. It is unlikely that you will face penalties if you choose to pay a variable rate of interest with no special deals attached (but it is worth asking all the same). However, if you choose any of the special methods of charging interest described above, it is more than likely that you will face penalties if you want to pull out of the deal early. Note that the penalty may be waived if you move house but take out your new mortgage with the same lender.

Penalties can involve repaying all the benefits from a special deal (such as the cash with a cash-back deal) or paying up to nine months' interest. The worst penalties are from lenders who tie you in beyond the period of the special deal – for example, some five-year fixed-rate deals have penalty periods of seven years.

These extended penalties mean that after the special deal finishes, you are tied to paying the lender's standard variable rate, which may be higher than a similar rate on offer from another lender. However, not all special deals carry an extended penalty, so if you are arranging a new mortgage, look for a deal which does not tie you in for a long period.

How does the lender calculate interest?

The way in which your lender calculates interest is most important if you have decided you want a repayment mortgage or if you are thinking about repaying some of your loan before the end of the term. Most lenders adjust the amount of the outstanding loan on which you pay interest at the end of each year. If you have a repayment loan, part of your monthly payments includes a repayment of your debt. However, if interest is adjusted annually, these monthly repayments do not get taken into account for the purposes of calculating interest until the beginning of the following year. So if you owe £35,000 at the beginning of the year, but pay back £1,500 during the course of the year, interest will be charged on £35,000 until the beginning of the following year when the outstanding amount will be reduced to £33,500.

With lenders which calculate interest on a daily or monthly basis, you pay less interest because any repayment of debt reduces the outstanding balance of your loan when it is made. In the example given above, the outstanding balance would fall to £34,875 after the first month and would carry on reducing each month.

How flexible do you want your mortgage to be?

Flexible mortgages do not have to be called 'flexible' to be flexible and when it comes to being able to pay off your mortgage more quickly, many variable-rate mortgages offer the same flexibility as specially packaged deals. As well as looking for a lender which calculates interest daily and does not charge an early redemption penalty, if you want to make early repayments, ask if you can repay your loan by increasing your monthly payments or, if you have a lump sum, whether there is a minimum amount you have to pay.

Where the newer flexible mortgages (some of which are linked to a current account) do offer greater flexibility is that in addition to being able to pay more you can also:

- borrow back overpayments
- make underpayments in months when money is tight
- take payment holidays subject to certain limits on the number of full monthly payments you have made

- spread your payments over ten months rather than twelve
- borrow more money at mortgage rates with a loan 'draw-down' facility (a cheque book can be supplied for this purpose) – which can be a cheap way of borrowing for other large purchases such as a car or home improvements.

If you have irregular earnings or spending patterns, a flexible mortgage could be worth considering. However, you need to be very disciplined about your finances since the flexibility that this sort of mortgage offers could mean that you end up borrowing more than you can really afford to.

Mortgages sans frontières

Until the UK joins the euro, do not be tempted to take out a mortgage in euros. Although interest rates in the rest of Europe (at the time of going to press) are much lower than those in the UK, borrowing in euros carries the same risks as borrowing in any foreign currency: the danger of fluctuations in the exchange rate on top of ups and downs in interest rates. This does not simply mean that your monthly payments will rise and fall; it also means that the amount you borrow does, too. So, if you take out the euro-equivalent of a £100,000 mortgage and the value of the pound falls against the euro by, say, 10 per cent, the amount you owe would go up to £110,000 – and your monthly payments would also rise. However, if the pound gains in strength, the amount you owe (and your monthly payments) would go down. Unless you are paid in euros, the losses you make on the currency exchange are almost certain to wipe out any gains from having a lower interest rate.

Getting advice

If you want help selecting the right mortgage you may consider asking a lender or other mortgage adviser. However, research carried out by *Which?* magazine* has consistently found that unless you are very lucky, you cannot rely on advisers to give you good advice. *Which?* has also found that there is an unjustified bias towards endowment mortgages, even though a repayment mortgage is a better deal for most people.

The Mortgage Code

In 1997, the Council of Mortgage Lenders* launched the Mortgage Code – a voluntary code of practice for lenders and mortgage intermediaries – in an attempt to improve the quality of advice given to borrowers (and to persuade the government that statutory regulation of mortgages was unnecessary). The Code covers the relationship between lenders and customers, including advice given to potential borrowers. By subscribing to the Code, lenders promise to act fairly and reasonably, help customers to understand how the mortgage works and aid them to choose a mortgage which will fit their needs. There are three levels of service that can be provided:

- **advice and a recommendation** as to the most suitable deal. Before giving advice, a lender must ask questions about your plans and circumstances and should select a deal most suited to your needs. The lender must then give you a letter summarising the advice and the reasons behind it
- **information on different mortgages** but no specific advice on the different types of deal available. This is to enable you to make an informed choice from the range of products available from your chosen lender
- **information on only one mortgage deal** if you have already made up your mind about which type of mortgage you want.

Advisers must tell you which levels of service are available so that you can choose the one you want (most big lenders say that they offer all three levels). The Code also says that people who have been badly advised can seek redress. But when lenders give information rather than advice, your rights to redress are more limited. So it is important you are clear whether the lender gives advice or information. Since 30 April 1999, lenders have been required to refer to the Mortgage Code and the levels of service they offer in their marketing literature. Lenders and other advisers must also give every prospective borrower a copy of the leaflet 'You and Your Mortgage' as early on in the buying process as possible. The leaflet explains your rights under the Code.

Mortgage intermediaries

About half of all new mortgages are arranged through an intermediary such as an estate agent or independent financial adviser. Since May 1998, lenders subscribing to the Code have accepted business only from intermediaries who also sign up to the Code. On top of requirements about levels of service, the Code requires the interme- diary to tell you if he or she is searching the whole market, giving advice on mortgages offered by a restricted panel of lenders or using one particular lender. Intermediaries should disclose any commission that lenders pay them and any fees they may charge you.

What you should be told

Whichever level of advice you are offered and whoever you get it from, the Code says you must be given the following information:

- the length of the loan
- the repayment method
- the financial consequences of repaying your mortgage early – i.e. whether there are early redemption penalties
- whether the interest rate is variable, fixed or discounted
- what the repayments will be after any fixed or discounted period
- whether you need to take out insurance (such as buildings insurance) with your mortgage and whether you are tied to taking the product offered by the lender
- the general costs which are involved with taking out the mortgage such as valuation fees, arrangement fees, legal fees and so on
- whether your selected mortgage terms can be continued if you move house
- an explanation of mortgage interest tax relief
- whether you will have to pay a high percentage lending fee.

If you are not given this information or you think that you have been given bad advice, or the lender does not give you the leaflet 'Your and Your Mortgage', inform the Independent Review Body for the Banking and Mortgage Codes★ if it is a lender, and the Mortgage Code Register of Intermediaries★ if it is a broker. If you feel you have been pressured into taking out an endowment mortgage instead of a repayment mortgage, your local Trading Standards office may also be interested in knowing.

Tip

When getting advice, ask for quotes for both the repayment option and (if you want to mix buying your home with long-term investment) the interest-only option, together with projections for the investment vehicle which will go with it. You should also ask what the cash-in value of any investment will be at the end of two, five and ten years. Compare this with what you would have saved in the investment vehicle and also with how much of your loan you would have paid off with the repayment option (you can ask for an illustration of the repayment schedule over the full life of the loan, which will look something like the example on page 199). If the figures for the cash-in value of the investment are much lower than what you would have paid in (or the amount of the loan you would have paid off), you are unlikely to be getting a good deal from the interest-only option.

Applying for a mortgage

Once you have decided on a mortgage and a lender, you will need to fill in an application form. If you apply for a mortgage before you have found a property and you can obtain a mortgage offer 'in principle' based on your earnings, you will be able to proceed with the purchase much more quickly and feel less pressured when deciding what kind of mortgage you want. Mortgage application forms are lengthy and can be time-consuming to complete due to the supporting documentation you need to provide. This includes all of the following which apply to you:

- National Insurance number and tax reference
- payslips and P60 (which you get at the end of the tax year)
- contract of employment details
- your accounts or tax statements if you are self-employed
- rent book

- mortgage statements
- bank statements
- loan or hire purchase agreements
- life insurance policy documents
- pension details
- some form of personal identification such as a driving licence
- proof of your current address such as a council tax or utility bill.

Do you need insurance?

You may also be encouraged to apply for life insurance (see Chapter 7), mortgage payment protection insurance (see Chapter 6), buildings insurance and contents insurance, although the only insurance you definitely need is buildings insurance. This covers damage to your home and is designed to pay out for the cost of rebuilding it completely. However, unless the mortgage deal you have chosen ties you to buying the buildings insurance offered by your lender, you will probably save money by buying your own policy – check the regular reports published in *Which?* magazine*. Note that you need to have buildings insurance in place as soon as you have 'exchanged contracts' – the point at which you enter into a legally binding agreement to buy the property – which is usually several weeks before you 'complete' the purchase and move in.

The mortgage offer

One of the reasons that it is better to apply for the mortgage before you have found a property is the amount of time it can take to get your mortgage offer. This can often be several weeks. As part of wider proposals to speed up the process of buying and selling property under the title 'The key to easier home buying and selling', the government has asked mortgage lenders who do not already do so to develop the idea of making 'in principle' mortgage offers to give buyers accurate information on what they can really afford and to help reassure sellers that an offer is genuine. In addition, the government would like lenders to make faster mortgage offers, with a target of making 80 per cent of offers within two days of receiving the relevant information. If the proposals go ahead it should mean that

. the process of applying for a mortgage will be much faster and less stressful than it has been in the past.

The lender will not make the final mortgage offer until you have found a property, made a firm offer and the mortgage valuation has been done (see page 193). You will then be told how much you can borrow based on the valuation. If this is not enough, you will have to renegotiate on price with the seller, or, if he or she will not budge, find somewhere else – which means paying another valuation fee to your lender. If the mortgage offer is acceptable, you can go ahead with the purchase. For what to do if your mortgage application is turned down, see Chapter 15.

Warning

If you get an 'in principle' mortgage offer, do not offer this amount when you find a property to buy. The final mortgage offer will be based on the lender's valuation of the property and the percentage of that figure which the lender is prepared to lend – for more details, see page 190.

Keeping track of your mortgage

After your loan has come through, make sure that the payment details match those quoted on your mortgage offer. You should also check the arrangement for paying your first monthly repayment: it may be larger than the monthly repayment figure quoted in the mortgage offer if it includes interest for the period between the mortgage being advanced and the normal monthly payment date (if the lender fixes this date). If you have bought insurance from your lender, you should also check that payments for the premiums have been set up correctly.

Warning

Some lenders add insurance premiums to the mortgage loan which means you pay interest on them. If this has happened to you, ask your lender if you can pay the premiums separately.

Keeping up repayments

Most lenders offer you the opportunity to make your mortgage payments by standing order or direct debit – which you should take, since it means that you will always pay your mortgage on time (unless the payments are bounced because there is not enough money in your bank account). If you do not pay your mortgage on time, you may face arrears charges and you risk losing your home.

Tip

If you are having difficulty making your mortgage repayments, get in contact with your lender as soon as possible. Your lender should deal with the problem sympathetically as lenders prefer not to have to go to the trouble of repossessing properties unless there is no other alternative. For more on what to do if you get into serious debt, see Chapter 16.

Making overpayments

There are two ways in which you can make overpayments (depending on how flexible your mortgage is – see pages 204–205): monthly, by increasing your regular mortgage payment; or in a lump sum. It is usually unwise to increase your monthly payment unless your lender calculates interest daily.

If your lender calculates interest on a yearly basis, consider instead making regular savings into a savings account and then using the savings to pay a lump sum. When you make a lump sum payment, the lender will adjust the balance immediately.

If making a lump sum payment, make it clear to your lender (in a letter) that you are paying off part of the loan rather than paying interest. When you get your mortgage statement, check that the outstanding loan balance has been reduced and that the interest charge has also dropped. If not, contact your lender and ask for the mistake to be put right.

Switching mortgages

Repaying some of your mortgage – whether on a regular basis or as a lump sum – will save you money on interest, but you can also save money by switching. You are most likely to benefit from switching mortgages – or 're-mortgaging' – if you are paying a variable rate of interest, you are not tied into the mortgage by penalties for paying the loan off early, and you can find a better deal.

You may even save money without switching lenders if your own lender is prepared to offer you better terms – which may happen if your lender does not want to lose your custom. If your lender cannot come up with a better offer, you need to weigh up the potential monthly savings against the costs of switching (although some of these are often met by the new lender). Switching also gives you the opportunity to change to a more flexible lender.

When switching may not be worthwhile

You should not switch if the costs of doing so far outweigh the potential monthly savings. You should also think twice about switching if either of the following apply:

- you have a mortgage in joint – but unmarried – names dating from before August 1988, because you may lose tax relief (this is given at a low rate now, but it is still worth doing the sums).
- you took your mortgage out before October 1995. The help you will get from the state with your mortgage interest if you cannot work because of sickness or redundancy is made available more quickly than for mortgages taken out after that date. However, whether you will get this help at all depends on what other arrangements you have in place for coping (see Chapters 5 and 6).

How to switch

If another lender can give you a quote for lower monthly payments, fill in the calculator opposite to see how much you can save. Before you do this, you need to find out how much your current lender will charge you for redeeming your loan. This includes:

- redemption penalty
- charges for deeds administration and sealing fee
- interest you may be charged after you have switched (if your lender charges until the end of the month in which you redeem).

You then need to find out what your new lender will charge for arranging the new loan. Some lenders will pay some of the following fees as an incentive for you to switch, while others may offer a cash incentive:

- valuation fee
- arrangement or booking fee (mostly for fixed-rate deals)
- mortgage indemnity guarantee (see page 191)
- legal fees.

You should also review the cost of your house-related insurance to see if you can make further savings by switching insurers.

Will you save by switching?

Calculate the monthly savings	
Enter your current monthly payments	A
Enter the monthly payments from the new lender	B
Subtract B from A and enter the result at C	C
Multiply C by 12 and enter the result at D	D
Calculate the cost of switching	
Enter the total cost of redeeming your loan	E
Enter the costs of taking out the new loan (excluding costs which the new lender will meet)	F
Add E to F and enter the result at G	G
Enter the amount of any cash incentives	H
Subtract H from G and enter the result at I	I
Should you switch?	
Subtract I from D and enter the result at J	J

If J is a plus figure, you will recoup the cost of switching through the savings you make in the first year.
If J is a minus figure, you should think twice before switching because it will take longer than a year to recoup your costs from the monthly savings. To find out how many months it will take to recoup the costs, divide I by C.

Chapter 11

Paying bills

If you do not pay your household bills on time, you risk having the service you are paying for cut off. This applies not only to heating, lighting, water and local services but also to essential insurance cover protecting your home and belongings. Even if you always pay your bills on time, the nasty habit they have of arriving all at once can mean that your finances suffer severe dents at certain times of the year.

This chapter looks at how you can save money on this essential but dull aspect of your finances, with advice on how to cut your costs by changing the way you pay. If you want help with the financial dips that bills can cause, you can work out your own bill-paying budget, which will help to smooth their effect on your bank balance. For advice on how to cope with large, unexpected bills, see pages 221–225.

How to pay your bills

As a general rule the best way to pay for bills is in full by whichever current-account payment method (see Chapter 2) you find most convenient. The reason for this is that with most utility bills (gas, electricity, water and telephone) you pay in arrears, so in effect, you are getting a free loan. You may also save money if your utility company gives a discount for prompt payment. With bills that you have to pay in advance – such as premiums for insurance, for example – paying the bill in full is also the best option. The exceptions to the pay-in-full rule are where you are offered the opportunity to:

- pay in free instalments, which is both a way of spreading the cost of the bill and getting a free loan

- claim a discount, rebate or cheaper price in return for paying by regular direct debit, which can be either monthly or quarterly. Some companies also give a discount if you pay by regular standing order but this is relatively rare.

If you like to pay your bills with cash or by cheque over the counter at a bank or post office but face a charge for doing so (either because you are unable to use a branch of your own bank, for example, or the company you are paying does not have an arrangement to have the fee waived), the alternative is to use PayPoint. This is a scheme that lets you pay your bills for free at local shops: you simply take your cash (or cheque) together with a special swipe card or bar-coded bill to a local outlet displaying the PayPoint logo (where you will also be able to get details of the scheme).

Regular savings

Carol used to pay her electricity bills in full when they arrived each quarter. However, when her electricity company offered her the chance to cut her annual bill of £150 by about 5 per cent if she paid by monthly direct debit, she took it. Carol has saved about £7.50 a year by changing the way she pays.

How not to pay your bills

It is in your interest to spread the cost of your bills in a way that costs you nothing or which gets you a reduction in the amount you have to pay. However, you should avoid:

- **budget plans** Most utility companies are keen for you to pay your bills by monthly direct debit because it is a way of getting you to pay in advance. If it is not financially advantageous to do so, you should think twice before agreeing to pay in this way. Although the attraction is being able to spread the cost of your bills (which you can arrange for yourself – see page 217–218), the monthly payment may be more than is necessary to cover your bill. Unless the monthly amount that you have to pay is adjusted regularly to take account of any overpayments, you end up paying out more each quarter than you would have if you had waited to receive the bill (you can ask to be reimbursed for this amount at the end of the year, or else the money can be rolled over to cover the next year's bills). If the monthly payment is set too low, you may face an extra bill at the end of the year to make up for your underpayments

- **charges for paying in instalments** If you are given the chance to pay for other bills in instalments, you should make sure that you are not charged for doing so. For example, some insurers charge you up to 10 per cent more than they would have done if you made a one-off payment

- **extra mortgage interest** If you are tied to buying buildings insurance from your lender as part of a special mortgage deal (see Chapter 10), the lender may add the cost of the insurance on to your mortgage loan, which means that you have to pay interest on the insurance premium. If your lender does this, ask if you can arrange to pay the insurance premium separately from your mortgage

- **savings stamps** Budget plans which involve you buying savings stamps are also an expensive way to budget for your bills. Not only do you not get interest on the money you set aside by buying the stamps, but if you lose them, you cannot get a refund. Your money will be more secure in a savings account, where it can earn interest

- **prepayment meters** Prepayment via a meter is the most expensive way to pay your gas and electricity bills. This is because the standing charges and the cost per unit of gas or electricity tend to be higher. However, prepayment may be your only option if the utility company will not allow you to pay your bills in arrears – i.e. will not give you credit. If this happens and you think you have been turned down for credit unfairly, see Chapter 15. If you have to prepay your bills, you may save money if you can arrange to pay them by making cash prepayments using PayPoint (see opposite) rather than by using a prepayment meter. Check with your gas or electricity company.

Save by switching

As well as being able to save money by changing the way you pay your bill, you may also be able to save money by changing the company that sends it. Increased competition in the telephone, gas and electricity markets means that, depending on where you live, you can make substantial savings by changing suppliers. You can get further information on the suppliers in your area from Ofgas★ (for gas companies) and Offer★ (for electricity companies).

Tip

The simplest way to save money on your heating bills is to turn your thermostat down by 1°C. You are unlikely to notice the difference and you could cut your bills by up to 10 per cent. For free advice on other ways of saving money on your bills, contact the Energy Saving Trust,* which has set up Energy Efficiency Advice Centres across the UK.

Every little helps

You can save money on your shopping if you sign up for loyalty cards, offered by an increasing number of retailers. Every time you go shopping, you present your card and you are awarded with a number of points for every £1 spent (although you may not earn points against spending on certain items such as stamps or tobacco). Shops sometimes give extra points to encourage you to buy their special offers. When you have earned enough points, you can swap them for money off your bill or – depending on the shop's scheme – discounts on other products and services. How much you save depends on how much you spend and on how susceptible you are to the special offers that earn you extra points.

How to budget for your bills

You can avoid costly budget plans and sharp dips in your current account balance when bills arrive simultaneously by working out your own bill-paying budget. You work out the regular monthly amount that you need to set aside to cover all your bills for the year, set up a standing order to an account (the bill-paying account), which is separate from your current account, and pay all your bills from that. You could do this by adding up all your bills for the year and dividing by 12. However, you need to know whether there will be months when your bills will exceed the amount that will be in the bill-paying account. You can do this by filling in the calculator on page 220. This will also help you to decide which sort of account to use for paying your bills. To fill in the calculator, you need to:

- decide when your new bill-paying regime is going to begin – it is likely to be most convenient to have each monthly period coinciding with pay-day
- add up your total bills for each monthly period
- add up the yearly total
- divide the yearly total by 12 to get the amount you need to transfer to your bill-paying account each month.

Tip

As well as your regular bills, you can include your mortgage payments, gym membership, car insurance, car tax and so on. The more you pay into the bill-paying account, the less likely it is to dip below zero.

Ryan works out his bill-paying budget

After an unpleasant letter from his bank manager, Ryan decides to do something about the bills which are dragging his current account into the red every month. The worst months are those when his electricity, gas and telephone bills all come in at once. February and March are not too bad because these are the months when he doesn't have to pay any council tax (this is paid in ten free monthly instalments). However, by paying £200 a month into a separate current account, which gives him an interest-only overdraft, he can keep his main account in credit while knowing that he has the money he needs to pay his bills.

Ryan works out his bill-paying budget

Months	Total monthly bills	Total yearly bills divided by 12	Running total
October	£337	£200	-£137
November	£217	£200	-£154
December	£47	£200	-£1
January	£352	£200	-£153
February	£147	£200	-£100
March	£112	£200	-£12
April	£297	£200	-£109
May	£217	£200	-£126
June	£112	£200	-£38
July	£312	£200	-£150
August	£112	£200	-£62
September	£112	£200	£26
Total bills for the year	£2,374		

Choosing an account for your bills

Once you have worked out your bill-paying budget, you need to decide which sort of account you are going to use to operate it. The most convenient options are:

- **a completely separate current account** The advantage of this option is that you get the full range of payment methods (see Chapter 2) and – by having a completely separate account – you will be less tempted to spend your bill-paying money on other things. This is probably the best option if you are setting up a bill-paying account jointly with your partner or flat mates. If your bill-paying budget shows that your monthly running total is mostly negative, you will either need to choose an account with a free or cheap overdraft or you will need to pay in an extra amount of money to cover the biggest deficit. Unless you are particularly keen to pay your bills in cash, having a convenient branch or cash

How to calculate your bill-paying budget

Step 1: Enter the months starting with the month in which your budgeting will begin	Step 2: For each monthly period, enter your total monthly bills at A	Step 4: To calculate the monthly payment you need to make, divide B by 12 (round it up to the nearest round figure if you want) then enter it at C for each monthly period	Step 5: For the first month subtract A from C and enter the result at D. For subsequent months, start with D from the previous month, subtract A and add C. This gives you the running total for each month.
Month 1	A	C	D
Month 2	A	C	D
Month 3	A	C	D
Month 4	A	C	D
Month 5	A	C	D
Month 6	A	C	D
Month 7	A	C	D
Month 8	A	C	D
Month 9	A	C	D
Month 10	A	C	D
Month 11	A	C	D
Month 12	A	C	D
Step 3: Total all the monthly figures at A and enter the result at B	B	The total of all the figures in this column should be the same as B (unless you rounded them)	Figure D at the end of the last month should not be less than zero

machine is less important than it is when choosing your main current account

- **a savings account linked to your current account** If you already have savings in an instant-access or no-notice account (see Chapter 4) and you can transfer money between your savings account and your current account quite easily – by phone, for example, or you have home-banking via computer – you can use the savings account to receive your monthly bill-paying money. Each time a bill arrives, you transfer money back from the savings account to your current account, which is what you use to pay the bill. The advantage of this is that the money will earn more interest and your existing savings will act as a buffer against the months when your running total is negative. However, if this all sounds too much like hard work, you are better off with a separate current account.

How to pay for large bills

The best defence against some of the occasional bills which you may face on top of your regular household bills is to have enough money set aside in an emergency fund (see Chapter 4). If you do not have an emergency fund, you will have to borrow (see Chapter 13), which can add quite considerably to the cost. Another way of paying for large and unexpected bills is to buy insurance. Whether you should buy insurance depends on three main factors:

- the likelihood that there will be a bill to meet – insurance pays out only against the unexpected and unpredictable
- the seriousness of the financial consequences of having to pay the bill yourself
- the price you have to pay for 'peace of mind'.

In some cases, buying insurance is well worthwhile; in others, however, the limitations on what the insurance will and will not pay out for can mean that you spend more on the insurance than you would have spent by paying the bill yourself. The main thing to remember with any kind of insurance is it will pay out only if the item you are claiming for is covered by the policy. It is always worth asking specific questions about the things you are particularly worried about before you buy any insurance so that you can be clear about what the policy will and will not cover. The main types of insurance designed to cover unexpected bills are:

- buildings insurance (see below)
- contents insurance (see opposite)
- appliance insurance (see opposite)
- private medical insurance (see page 224)
- pet insurance (see page 225).

Buildings insurance

Buildings insurance covers the fabric of your home (the bricks and mortar, windows, roof and so on) as well as fixtures and fittings (such as kitchen units and central heating boilers). Buildings insurance is not a maintenance contract: it is intended to pay out for specific damage or loss as a result of specific occurrences and not to pay for your running repairs. It is a condition of buildings insurance that you keep your property in good condition and take reasonable steps to avoid damage to it.

If you want the policy to pay out for accidental damage – your drill slipping while putting up a shelf, for example – you will need specific accidental damage cover but this costs extra.

Because the financial consequences of losing your home due to unforeseen disaster are so great, you should definitely buy buildings insurance. If you have a mortgage your lender will insist that you do.

Other buildings-related insurance

You can also buy insurance or service contracts, which aim to pay out for repairs to your plumbing and/or central heating system. With plumbing policies, in particular, you need to check very carefully that such policies do not duplicate the cover you get from a buildings policy – some do and some do not. Service contracts for central heating which include an annual service and which provide free repairs whatever the cause of the problem could be worth considering. Your boiler will be well-maintained, and you can avoid the expense of calling an emergency plumber.

Contents insurance

Where buildings insurance covers the fabric of your home, contents insurance pays out if you unexpectedly lose or damage the things in it. You need to buy extra cover if you want your belongings covered against accidental damage or if you want to have them covered when outside the home (this kind of cover is sometimes referred to as 'all risks'). Contents policies often include legal expenses and pay out for legal bills if you are involved in a dispute. This type of cover can also be bought as a stand-alone policy.

If you could not afford to pay to replace any or all of your possessions if they are lost, damaged or stolen, you need to buy contents insurance. If you opt for all risks cover, your belongings should also be covered when you take them abroad, so you can save money on holiday insurance (see Chapter 12).

Other insurance for your belongings

Although you can buy separate insurance policies to cover special belongings, such as mobile phones, contact lenses, musical instruments, sports equipment, small boats and caravans, it is usually cheaper to ask your insurer to cover them on your contents policy.

Appliance insurance

This type of insurance – also called 'extended warranty' insurance – is usually sold rather than actively bought. It covers the cost of repairs to domestic appliances – up to a point because it pays out only for unexpected electrical and mechanical breakdown. You do not need it in the first year of buying an appliance (or other electrical goods) because you are covered by the manufacturer's own free warranty. It is also likely that you will not need it in subsequent years. Research conducted by *Which?* magazine★ consistently finds that the cost of paying for repairs as they occur is nearly always cheaper than buying appliance insurance. If you are convinced that you will be one of the unlucky few, a multi-appliance policy (which covers more than one appliance) bought direct from an insurer will be cheaper than buying separate policies for each item. This also has the advantage that you can wait until the manufacturer's warranty has expired before having to pay for the insurance.

Private medical insurance

You may already have this sort of insurance as a perk with your job, but whether it is worth buying for yourself, if you do not, is a question of personal choice. Private medical insurance buys you the option of paying for private medical treatment if you do not want to wait for treatment under the NHS, if you want to be able to choose when and by whom you are treated and you are attracted by the idea of a well-furnished private room. The insurance lasts for a year at a time and, provided you pay the premiums, most insurers will automatically renew the policy − and put up the premiums − each year. If and when you need treatment, the policy pays out − provided your illness is covered.

Private medical insurance is designed to pay the bills for private treatment of 'acute' conditions, which means short-term and curable disorders. In general, policies do not cover the treatment of long-term illnesses that cannot be cured such as asthma, diabetes and multiple sclerosis − conditions commonly referred to as 'chronic'. Because private medical insurance covers the unforeseen, you cannot take out a policy to get treatment for something which has arisen recently. And it will not cover all your health needs.

Private medical insurance policies always have some sort of clause covering claims for pre-existing conditions. Most will pay out for the treatment of existing (or foreseeable) conditions only if the insurer agrees to cover them when you take out the policy. Some will cover existing conditions on a 'moratorium basis', which means that any illness or condition that has occurred in the five years before taking out the policy will not be covered for a specified period − usually two years.

Dental insurance

You cannot take out stand-alone dental insurance if you are treated under the NHS. If you pay for private dental treatment, whether dental insurance is worth buying depends on the state of your teeth and the fees your dentist charges. If you rarely have to pay for treatment it is unlikely that your dental charges are high enough to warrant buying insurance. If you have private medical insurance − either as a perk from your job or which you pay for yourself − you might already be covered, although what the policy will pay out for dental costs is limited. An increasing number of employers are offering dental insurance as part of a job package: if you are eligible to join an employer's scheme, it will almost certainly be cheaper than paying for dental insurance yourself.

Pet insurance

There is no NHS for animals so you have to meet the cost of vets' bills in full out of your income unless you take out insurance. However, just like private medical insurance for humans, pet insurance will not cover all treatment or all pets (you may not be able to buy cover for ten-year-old cats and dogs, for example). Even where treatment is covered, what will be paid out is limited. Pet insurance differs from private medical insurance in that it provides cover against the damage your pet might do to another person or their belongings – although you might be able to extend the 'liability' cover you get with your contents insurance.

Chapter 12

Holiday money

You do not need to change your spending habits if you plan to take your holiday in the UK. However, if you are going abroad, how you organise your holiday money will depend to a large extent on where you are going. This is because the destination will dictate which payment methods will be the most convenient for you to use. The other main factor in choosing your holiday money is cost, which depends on two things: the exchange rate and the way you choose to pay. While you cannot do anything about exchange rate fluctuations, you can take steps to minimise the costs of your holiday money – although it is unlikely that you will be able to save a large amount. Where you *can* make substantial savings is in your choice of holiday insurance – especially if you are planning more than one trip abroad each year.

This chapter looks at the costs involved in buying holiday money, examines the options available for spending money abroad and gives practical advice on pre-holiday preparations. But however you choose to organise your foreign spending, you cannot do without insurance, and on pages 232–237 you will find advice on choosing the right policy, together with tips on how you can save money on this holiday essential.

The cost of holiday money

How much your foreign transactions cost will depend to a large extent on the type of payment method you use. But whichever type you choose, there will usually be some form of:

- **commission**, which is usually a set percentage of the amount of the transaction, although you usually have to pay a fixed minimum charge

- **exchange-rate loading**, which is the difference between the exchange rate you get and the rate at which the bank or bureau de change buys or sells the currency – the rate you get is never as good as the market rate that the bank gets. In the case of buying foreign currency in the form of hard cash, the loading also takes into account the costs of storing, transporting and insuring the cash.

Warning

Low commission is not always a good indication of a low-cost deal. Low commission can mean a poor exchange rate, so always look at the two things together when calculating the cost.

Holiday money options

Before you can decide which option will suit you best, you need to find out which forms of payment are most widely accepted and what the availability of cash machines is likely to be at your chosen destination(s). Your bank should be able to help, as should your holiday company or the tourist office of the country you are visiting. You also need to consider what you would do if your preferred method of payment lets you down – your purse or wallet is stolen, for example, or the foreign cash machine swallows your debit card. If you are travelling with someone else, that person may be willing to act as your back-up. If you are travelling alone, you may want to organise your own fallback position by taking several different types of payment method.

Buying foreign currency

The main thing you need to decide is how you will pay for foreign currency once you reach your destination. However, although buying foreign currency in the UK tends to be more expensive than buying it abroad, you will have to buy some before you leave to meet your expenses on arrival (and also if your travels will take you a long way from financial civilisation). It is not wise to take more currency than you absolutely have to, and you certainly should not take more than the limit given in your travel insurance policy (see pages 232–233).

You can buy foreign currency from banks, building societies, bureaux de change and major travel agents using any of the usual current-account payment methods. Expect to pay 1 to 3 per cent in commission (with a minimum charge of £1 to £3). If you buy foreign currency with a credit card and some Visa debit cards at a different bank from your own you may be charged more than if you pay by cheque or with cash. For buying foreign currency and paying for purchases abroad, the main options are:

- credit card (see below)
- debit card (see pages 229–230)
- disposable cash cards (see page 230)
- travellers' cheques (see pages 230–231)
- eurocheques (see pages 231–323).

Tip

If you buy currency before you set off, leave the receipt for it at home. If you lose your money while on holiday, you will need proof that you bought the currency if you claim on your travel insurance.

Credit cards

You can use credit cards (and charge cards) to pay for purchases and to get cash from banks and any cash machines that display your card's logo – provided you know your PIN. They can also be useful for unexpected emergencies – it may be worth asking for a temporary increase in your credit limit if yours is on the low side.

You usually have to pay a 1.5 per cent handling fee for cash withdrawals, and, depending on your card issuer, you may also face interest charges. Both cash withdrawals and purchases are also subject to a loading charge, which is incorporated into the exchange rate used to convert your foreign transactions into sterling. However, even taking this charge into account, the exchange rate is usually more favourable than normal tourist rates so it will usually be cheaper to use your card for purchases than to pay in foreign currency. Some cards use a higher loading charge than others for foreign transactions, so it is worth checking the terms and conditions of your current card well in advance of your holiday – especially if you are charged interest as well as a handling fee on cash withdrawals. This should give you time to apply for a card with better terms for foreign transactions before you go (see Chapter 3 for what to look out for in the terms and conditions).

Another advantage of using a credit card is that it gives you the protection of the Consumer Credit Act, which should extend to problems you have with purchases you made abroad (see Chapter 3), so always keep receipts. This is not the case if you use a charge card.

Tip

It is a good idea to use your credit card to buy your holiday because of the extra protection you will get from the Consumer Credit Act. If something goes wrong and the travel company is uncooperative, you can claim compensation from your card issuer. However, some travel companies will make you pay a surcharge if you pay for your holiday by credit card. If you want to have the protection but keep the surcharge to a minimum, the answer is to pay at least £100 of the holiday cost by credit card and the rest of the cost by some other means.

Debit cards

Debit cards can be used to obtain cash from foreign cash machines and to make purchases. Because the money comes straight out of

---

Tip

If you plan to rely on debit cards (see below) and credit cards as your main source of holiday money, always make sure that they will not expire while you are away and check the cards for damage. If the daily limit for cash withdrawals is low, ask for it to be increased. If you have more than one credit card, it is worth taking them all so that you have back-up.

---

your current account, you need to make sure you have enough money in it to cover your holiday spending. You will be able to use your debit card for all foreign transactions abroad but only if the card has either the Visa symbol or both the Cirrus and Maestro symbols. As with credit cards, the exchange rate will include a charge, and most banks charge a commission or handling fee on cash withdrawals.

Disposable cash cards

If you want to be able to use cash machines but you do not have a credit or debit card, you could choose a disposable cash card (available from a few outlets), which you 'charge up' in the UK before you leave and then use to withdraw money from cash machines when you are on holiday. Any money left on the card when you get home is refunded without a charge. You can put between £10 and £5,000 on the card, and the costs are about the same as for buying foreign currency and travellers' cheques.

Travellers' cheques

Travellers' cheques are useful in places where plastic cards are not widely accepted but they can be expensive because you pay commission to buy the cheques and sometimes when you use them as well. However, it is easy to get a quick refund or replacements if they are lost or stolen, and you will generally get a better rate of exchange than you would if you use cash to buy foreign currency. Like foreign currency, travellers' cheques are available from banks, building societies and bureaux de change. They are sold in fixed denominations, and you have a choice of:

- **sterling travellers' cheques**, which can be used to buy foreign currency abroad, attract commission (of between 1 and 3 per cent) when you buy them in the UK and may attract commission when you use them to purchase currency abroad. If you have sterling cheques left over at the end of your holiday, you can pay them into your bank account at no extra cost
- **dollar travellers' cheques** can be used like sterling travellers' cheques outside the USA because the dollar is such a widely recognised currency. However, if you have any left over, you may face a charge if you return them. If you use them in the USA,

you should not have to pay commission and they are widely accepted as a method of payment

- **foreign currency travellers' cheques** are made out in the currency of the country you are going to – ask a bank or tourist office whether it would be better to take foreign currency travellers' cheques. The advantage is that you are able to use them for purchases as well as for getting cash. The disadvantage is that you may have to pay to convert them back into sterling when you get home
- **euro travellers' cheques** are foreign currency cheques made out in euros, which can be used to get cash in 'euroland', so they can be useful if you are visiting one or more country where the euro is used. You may also be able to use them to make purchases but do not rely on this because not all retailers will accept them.

Euroland

Until 2002, the only difference you will see when travelling in Euroland countries will be the fact that the prices are displayed in both the existing local currency and the euro. Cash spending will still be done in the local currencies – euro notes and coins are not scheduled to be introduced until 1 January 2002. However, spending on a debit card or credit card may be done either in local currency or in the euro depending on the retailer. Which currency the retailer chooses makes no difference to the sterling equivalent because the amount you will be charged will be exactly the same. If you travel to several countries, changing currencies should be cheaper because all the currencies are fixed at the same value so you will not have to pay exchange commission, although there may be a small administrative charge. The exception to this is if you are travelling between euro and non-euro countries, Denmark, Greece, Sweden and the UK.

Eurocheques

You can use eurocheques in the same way as you would use a normal cheque: you write out cheques in the local currency and the money is converted into sterling and taken off your current account. The eurocheque card guarantees cheques up to the equivalent of £100;

you may also be able to use the card for getting cash from cash machines.

You can have eurocheques only if you have a current account but they are an expensive option because you pay an annual fee for the card, a handling fee each time you write a cheque as well as foreign exchange commission and a loading charge. Most banks issue euro-cheques but you can use them only in Europe and they are not widely accepted. Some banks are phasing them out.

Travel insurance

If you are taking a holiday in the UK, it is unlikely that you need travel insurance because the insurance you already have should cover you. However, you definitely need it if you are travelling abroad. Travel insurance is many different types of insurance rolled into one, with each type covering different potential mishaps:

- **medical expenses** covers the potentially very expensive bill for emergency medical treatment should you become ill or injured, and also a flight home by air ambulance, if necessary. You should aim for minimum cover from your travel insurance policy of at least £1 million
- **personal liability** (also known as public liability) covers you if you are legally liable to pay compensation because you have injured someone or damaged his or her property. You should aim for minimum cover from your travel insurance of £1 million (£2 million if you are travelling in the USA)
- **cancellation and curtailment** makes sure that you are not out of pocket as a result of having to cancel your holiday after paying for it. Cover for 'curtailment' ensures that you get part of the cost of the holiday back if you have cut your holiday short. You should make certain that you have enough cover for the full cost of your holiday but note that you cannot cancel or cut your holiday short without good reason – it has to be something unexpected and out of your control, such as sudden illness or having to do jury service, for example
- **belongings and money** covers stolen, lost or damaged possessions – aim for a minimum overall limit of £1,500. Note that there is usually a limit of £300 for single items within the overall

limit. If you have an all-risks extension to your contents policy (see Chapter 11), which covers your belongings abroad, you do not need this cover but check that your contents policy will cover you for the number of days you plan to be away

- **delayed baggage** is a modest allowance that is paid if you have to replace essential items – washing things and underwear, for example – while you wait for your luggage to catch up with you. Most policies that offer this sort of cover will pay out if your baggage is delayed by more than 12 hours, although some make you wait for 24 hours
- **personal accident** pays out a lump sum, say, £10,000, which is supposed to compensate you (or your heirs) if you are disabled (or die) as a result of an accident
- **legal expenses** covers the legal costs of pursuing claims for compensation and/or damages if you are killed, injured or become ill while on holiday
- **delayed departure** covers you for expenses – such as food and accommodation – you may incur because your plane or boat is late leaving. Most policies will pay out a small allowance only after you have been delayed for 12 hours followed by a lower amount for subsequent 12-hour delay periods
- **missed departure** pays out if you miss your plane or boat (due to reasons beyond your control) and you incur extra expenses because you have to make other arrangements to get to your holiday destination.

Insurance for skiing holidays

If you are going skiing, you need to buy special insurance (and pay more for it) to cover you against the greater likelihood and cost of your claim and also for particular expenses related to a skiing trip. So, as well as the kind of cover you get with a standard travel insurance policy, you should also ensure that the insurance covers you for the following, unless they are not relevant to you – for example, if you are a beginner you will not need cover for off-piste skiing:

- mountain rescue, if you have an accident and are too badly hurt to get off the mountain unaided
- the cost of refunding 'pre-paid expenses' (such as ski pass, ski and

boot hire and lessons) if you have to cancel your holiday or injury prevents you from skiing
- loss or theft of your ski pass
- loss, theft or damage of *hired* ski equipment – if your policy covers the full cost of the equipment you are hiring, you do not need to buy the insurance offered by the hire shop
- extra expenses you incur as a result of being held up by an avalanche on the way to the resort
- the cost of having to hire skis and boots while you wait for your own to turn up
- the cost of being transported to another resort if there is no snow at yours
- piste closure – although this usually means all lifts being closed for more than 24 hours, which is very unlikely
- snowboarding, racing, mono-skiing, tobogganing, skiing off-piste, heli-skiing.

Insurance for other hazardous sports

If you are going on any other kind of activity holiday – or you are planning to take part in some of the activities on offer at your destination – you need to make sure that your travel insurance will cover you. Not all policies list what they consider to be hazardous or not hazardous so it is always worth checking before you buy. Insurers generally regard the following as hazardous:

- football (if playing in an organised team, but not a friendly knock-about on the beach)
- mountaineering with ropes or guides
- water-ski jumping
- white-water rafting
- aquaplaning
- paragliding
- sub-aqua diving
- scuba diving below a certain depth
- pot-holing
- hang-gliding
- motorcycling
- motor racing

- professional sports
- parachuting
- ballooning
- flying
- gliding.

Buying travel insurance

The most important consideration when buying travel insurance is to make sure that the policy you are buying gives you the cover you need, especially if you are planning to take part in activities that insurers regard as dangerous. The second most important consideration is price. If you buy a package holiday from a tour operator or through a travel agent, it will usually be a condition of the booking that you have adequate travel insurance, and the company will be keen to sell you its policy. However, this is very unlikely to be a good deal, not least because it can be difficult to find out whether you are getting the cover you need. Ringing round insurers will be a better bet, and some of the best deals are from independent travel insurance specialists and other direct insurers, who will also be able to explain the cover to you.

Sneaky tricks

Travel agents and tour operators have been banned from selling compulsory travel insurance since November 1998 but many are getting round the ban. One tactic is to refuse to take your booking unless you can prove that you already have insurance that is as good as the policy they are offering. This may be difficult if the agent's policy has artificially high levels of cover. Another tactic is to inflate the cost of the holiday and include 'free' insurance but to offer a discount if you have already made your own arrangements. The most worrying tactic is for an agent to offer what looks like a cheap policy but which is 'cheap' only because the levels of cover are low.

The other reason for not buying insurance from a travel agent or tour operator is that you will be offered insurance only for a single trip.

If you plan more than one holiday abroad each year, you will save a substantial amount of money if you buy an annual policy, which covers all your foreign travel for a whole year. As well as including cover for winter sports and other types of activity holiday, many annual policies also include cancellation cover for pre-booked holiday accommodation in the UK. If you are buying insurance for more than one person – whether as a couple or a family – you will also save money if you buy a joint policy rather than separate policies for each individual.

What to ask before you buy

Whether you choose a single-trip policy or an annual policy, you should check that it gives the cover you need for the type of holiday you are going on. If you have decided to buy an annual policy:

- make sure that the maximum duration of each trip is long enough. Thirty-one days should be sufficient for most people but may not be enough if you are planning an extended visit to relatives in far away places

- if you want the policy to cover skiing holidays, make sure that the limit does not apply to just one trip if you are a frequent skier
- if you are planning an energetic holiday such as scuba diving or white-water rafting, check the 'hazardous sports' exclusions
- make sure that your chosen destinations are covered. This will not be a problem if you buy a worldwide policy, but you need to check the details if you are considering a Europe-only policy. Insurers differ in their definition of Europe
- if you are buying a joint policy, check that each person named on the policy is covered for individual travel. Some policies cover only the first named person if he or she is travelling alone, and not the second
- if you are buying a family policy, check what the insurer means by 'child'. Some policies will cover children only up to the age of 18; others will class offspring as children up to the age of 23 if they are in full-time education; some policies will cover your children's friends
- if you want to be covered for business trips, check that this is possible

- ask about discounts – some insurers will give up to 25 per cent off if you exclude cover for baggage and personal belongings, which is worth doing if you already have these covered under an all-risks extension on your contents policy. You may also be able to exclude cancellation cover. This is worth doing if you do not tend to pre-pay your holidays or if you buy flexible travel tickets.

Holiday money checklist

Taking a few precautions before you set off on your travels can save you both money and time and can help to avoid problems if you have to claim on your insurance:

- make a note of the details of debit and credit cards (and travellers' cheques if you are taking them) and keep it separate from the cards and cheques
- take the emergency telephone numbers for all your cards (which are usually on the back of your statement)
- check what the limit for cash is in your insurance policy and do not take more than that. You should also check the definition of 'cash' since it may include other things such as travel tickets
- take a photocopy of your insurance policy with you on holiday so that you know what to do if you have to claim (there will be certain steps you have to take while abroad – such as reporting loss or theft to the police within 24 hours – which cannot wait until you get home)
- make arrangements to pay your credit-card bill if it will arrive while you are away
- consider paying money into your current account to cover your holiday spending if you plan to use your debit card
- find out how your card issuer will replace cards and/or provide emergency cash if your cards are lost or stolen
- try to avoid changing too much money towards the end of your holiday or you could end up paying a second lot of commission to change it back into sterling when you get home
- check the expiry date of your passport because it will be expensive if you need to replace it while you are away.

Part 4

Borrowing

Chapter 13

Loans

If you are contemplating making a major purchase, borrowing will take the waiting out of wanting – a concept not lost on the people who dream up the advertisements for loans, with their tantalising pictures of faraway beaches, glamorous kitchens, sumptuous sofas and invitations to spend, spend, spend. With the notable exception of borrowing to buy your own home (see Chapter 10) taking out a loan can push up the price of your potential purchase quite considerably. If you have to pay to borrow, waiting will be worthwhile – but if waiting while you save up is not a practical solution, there are steps you can take to keep the cost of borrowing to a minimum.

This chapter looks at the types of loan that are suitable for making major purchases where a bank overdraft (which is repayable on demand) is not suitable. It examines the loan options that may be open to you, explains the pros and cons of each and gives practical advice on comparing the cost of different types of loan. If you need to borrow to buy your own home, see Chapter 10. The kind of finance deals available for car purchase are dealt with in Chapter 14.

How much can you afford to borrow?

The most important thing to consider when borrowing money is how much you can afford to repay each month because the consequences of not repaying a loan can be serious (see Chapter 16). Working out how much you can afford to repay will also tell you how quickly you can pay off the loan: the longer it takes to repay the loan, the higher the total cost of the loan is likely to be (because you pay more interest).

Warning

If the length of time it will take you to repay the loan far exceeds the useful life of whatever you bought with it – which will certainly be the case if you borrow to pay for a holiday, for example – think hard about how you will feel if you are still paying for something you no longer have. You should seriously consider waiting until you have saved up enough to pay for your purchase (see Chapter 20).

What is on offer

If you have decided that you definitely cannot wait to save up the money and you know how much you can afford to repay each month, you need to find the cheapest way to borrow the money you require to make your purchase. The route map on pages 243–244 will help you decide which of the following options are right for you:

- a loan from your employer (see page 245)
- 0% finance deals (see pages 245–246)
- borrowing from your savings (see page 246)
- borrowing from a cash-rich relative or friend (see page 247)
- a loan from a credit union (see pages 247–248)
- borrowing against a life insurance policy (see page 248)
- a credit card (see page 249)
- credit cheques (see page 249)
- a personal loan (see pages 249–250)
- credit from a shop (see page 250)
- a season ticket loan (see page 251)
- hire purchase (see page 251)
- flexible mortgage (see page 251)
- extending your mortgage (see pages 251–252).

Deciding how to borrow

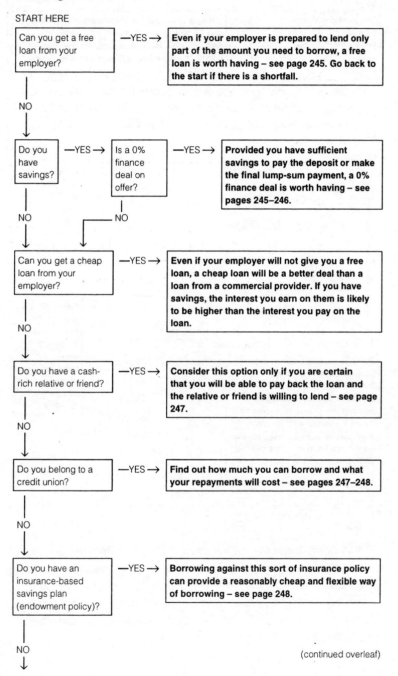

START HERE

Can you get a free loan from your employer?	—YES→	**Even if your employer is prepared to lend only part of the amount you need to borrow, a free loan is worth having – see page 245. Go back to the start if there is a shortfall.**

NO

Do you have savings?	—YES→	Is a 0% finance deal on offer?	—YES→	**Provided you have sufficient savings to pay the deposit or make the final lump-sum payment, a 0% finance deal is worth having – see pages 245–246.**

NO   NO

Can you get a cheap loan from your employer?	—YES→	**Even if your employer will not give you a free loan, a cheap loan will be a better deal than a loan from a commercial provider. If you have savings, the interest you earn on them is likely to be higher than the interest you pay on the loan.**

NO

Do you have a cash-rich relative or friend?	—YES→	**Consider this option only if you are certain that you will be able to pay back the loan and the relative or friend is willing to lend – see page 247.**

NO

Do you belong to a credit union?	—YES→	**Find out how much you can borrow and what your repayments will cost – see pages 247–248.**

NO

Do you have an insurance-based savings plan (endowment policy)?	—YES→	**Borrowing against this sort of insurance policy can provide a reasonably cheap and flexible way of borrowing – see page 248.**

NO

(continued overleaf)

243

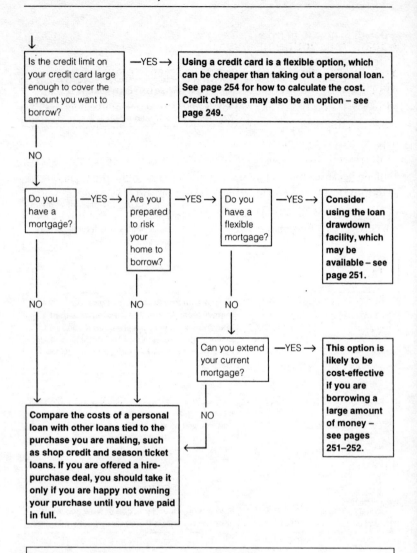

↓

Is the credit limit on your credit card large enough to cover the amount you want to borrow? —YES→ **Using a credit card is a flexible option, which can be cheaper than taking out a personal loan. See page 254 for how to calculate the cost. Credit cheques may also be an option – see page 249.**

NO
↓

Do you have a mortgage? —YES→ Are you prepared to risk your home to borrow? —YES→ Do you have a flexible mortgage? —YES→ **Consider using the loan drawdown facility, which may be available – see page 251.**

NO | NO | NO

Can you extend your current mortgage? —YES→ **This option is likely to be cost-effective if you are borrowing a large amount of money – see pages 251–252.**

NO

Compare the costs of a personal loan with other loans tied to the purchase you are making, such as shop credit and season ticket loans. If you are offered a hire-purchase deal, you should take it only if you are happy not owning your purchase until you have paid in full.

Tip

If you cannot borrow the full amount you need from one source, do not automatically discount it. You can use one type of loan to fund part of the purchase and another sort of loan to pay for the remainder. However, make sure the total of the various monthly repayments is not more than the amount you can afford to repay each month.

A loan from your employer

Your employer may be prepared to give you a free or cheap loan, particularly if you are borrowing to buy something work-related, such as a season ticket or a car or you are moving house because of work commitments. The cost of borrowing from your employer will depend on your employer.

Borrowing from your employer is likely to be cheap and convenient because your repayments will come straight off your salary each month. However, this is not a good option if you are thinking of changing jobs because you will usually have to pay the outstanding repayments as a lump sum.

Tax point

If you borrow more than £5,000 in total from your employer, you have to pay tax on the difference between the interest you would have paid if you had been charged interest at the 'official' rate of interest (you can get this by phoning your tax office) and the interest you actually paid. However, even if you go over the £5,000 limit, the cost of borrowing is still likely to be cheaper than taking out a loan from a commercial provider.

0% finance deals

Many shops offer 0% finance deals to tempt you to buy their goods. Whether or not these are a suitable option depends on whether you can meet the repayment terms and on whether the price of the goods in question is competitive. You can be offered 0% finance in three ways:

- **interest-free credit** You pay a deposit of about 10 or 20 per cent, for example, followed by equal monthly instalments. These repay the remainder of the purchase price over an agreed period of time, which can be anything from six months to two years. This is a good way of spreading the cost of a large purchase without paying to borrow. However, it is not an option if you cannot pay the deposit

- **limited interest-free credit** You pay a deposit and a series of small monthly instalments for a limited interest-free period of about nine months, say. At the end of this period, you can pay off the outstanding balance as a lump sum or you can continue to spread the repayments over a longer period. The catch is that if you do not repay the balance at the end of the limited interest-free period, you have to pay interest on the remaining repayments. This option is worth considering only if you can repay the lump sum at the end of the interest-free period. If you cannot, it is an expensive way to borrow

- **buy now, pay later** Rather than putting down a deposit and making monthly repayments, you pay nothing for the first few months and then pay the full purchase price at the end of the given period, and no interest will be charged. However, you will be asked to sign a credit agreement when you buy the item, which usually gives you the option to extend the credit period (at extra cost) if you cannot repay the full amount (or you forget to pay the full amount). The credit company may not remind you to pay because it would rather you paid the interest. This sort of deal is best avoided if you cannot or are likely to forget to repay the amount in full at the end of the free period.

Warning

Always check exactly how an interest-free deal works – it may not be made obvious that you will have to pay interest if you do not pay off the full amount at the end of a limited period.

Borrowing from your savings

Unless you can borrow cheaply from your employer or you are offered an interest-free credit deal, it is better to use savings (if you have any) to make your purchase. Doing this will always be better than borrowing, provided that you do not wipe out an emergency fund (see Chapter 4). It is highly unlikely that you will find a loan that charges interest at a lower rate than the interest you earn on your savings. You should aim to pay back your savings in the same way that you would pay back a loan.

Borrowing from a cash-rich relative or friend

You should consider this option only if you are certain that you will be able to repay the loan. The advantage for the person lending you the money is that he or she can charge an interest rate that is as good as the best savings rate available. The advantage for you is that the interest will still be lower than that on a loan from a commercial provider. You will need to agree – preferably in writing – how much interest you will pay, how you are going to make repayments and how long the loan will last. To ensure that the loan will be repaid regularly, you should set up a standing order directly to the lender's bank account. This is not a good option if there is the remotest chance that you will not be able to repay the loan and your relationship with the lender would suffer as a result.

Tax point

If you borrow money from another person, the interest you pay on the loan is taxable so the lender should declare it to his or her tax office.

A loan from a credit union

Credit unions are mutual savings and loans organisations, which can be set up by any group of people with a 'common bond' (for example, they live, work or worship together). Members pay a small fee to join, contribute regular savings and elect a committee to run the union's affairs. If you are a saving member, credit unions are an excellent way to borrow up to about £5,000. Because credit unions are run in the interests of their members, the interest rate is low (a maximum of 1 per cent per month) and repayment schedules can be tailored to the borrower.

Borrowing from a credit union is only an option if you are already a saving member of one. However, in future, it may be easier to find a credit union to join if government proposals go ahead. These proposals (which were still being discussed at the time of writing) aim to relax the rules governing credit unions to encourage more of them to be set up. If you want to join a credit union or start one yourself, contact the Association of British Credit Unions.★

Tip

Even if you are not a member of a credit union, you may be able to borrow cheaply if you belong to a certain profession (you are a teacher or lecturer, for example) or a trade union. Some professional associations and unions arrange cheap deals for their members so it is worth checking whether this applies to you.

Borrowing against a life insurance policy

If you have an endowment policy (an insurance-based savings plan) that is not linked to your mortgage, you may be able to borrow against it – provided you are still paying the premiums. In comparison with loans from other commercial lenders, interest rates tends to be lower and the options for repaying the loan are flexible. Most endowment policies allow you to make repayments as and when you are able, and if you can repay the loan using the lump sum you will get when the savings plan comes to an end, you usually have the option to pay interest only.

The amount you can borrow depends on the policy you have got and the length of time you have had it. If you think you have a policy that is suitable, look at the policy details and contact your insurer. You need to ask:

- **how much you can borrow** The most you can borrow is usually about 75–90 per cent of the current value of your policy (i.e. what you would get if you cashed it in)
- **what interest rate you will be charged** This depends entirely on the insurer and on the size of the loan
- **how you will have to repay the loan** If you can repay the loan with the proceeds of the policy when it comes to an end, you pay interest only, so your monthly repayments will be lower than if you have to pay back the loan as well as paying interest. Depending on your insurer, repayments may be very flexible or you will have to pay a fixed amount monthly, quarterly or yearly.

Credit cards

Provided your credit-card limit is large enough to cover the cost of your purchase, using a credit card is a very flexible way of borrowing. However, to make a credit card a reasonably cheap deal, you need to have one that charges a sufficiently low rate of interest (for more details, see pages 253–254), and you have to be disciplined enough gradually to repay the loan. Shop cards, which work like credit cards, are unlikely to be a good deal because the interest they charge tends to be high (see Chapter 3).

Credit cheques

Some credit cards issue you with 'credit-card cheques', which enable you to borrow on your card account by writing a cheque (see Chapter 3). You can also find standalone 'credit cheque accounts', which are similar to credit-card cheques except that you get only a cheque book. As with a credit card, you are given a credit limit and you repay as much of the loan as you want or the minimum amount required by the card or cheque issuer. However, instead of writing the cheque to the person you want to pay, you pay the credit cheque into your current account and access the money from there. This method of borrowing is flexible but whether it is an option depends on whether the credit limit is sufficient to cover your purchase and on whether the interest rate compares favourably with other forms of borrowing.

The main disadvantage of using credit cheques rather than a credit card is that you lose the protection of the Consumer Credit Act if something goes wrong with your purchase (see Chapter 3).

Personal loans

The virtue of a personal loan is convenience coupled with certainty. You decide how much you want to borrow and for how long. The repayments are then fixed for the duration of the loan so you know exactly how much you need to repay each month. However, if you want to repay some of the loan early, you may face penalties, although a handful of lenders will not charge you an early repayment penalty – always check before you take out a loan.

Variations on the personal loan theme include allowing you to put off making repayments for the first few months or to take repayment holidays. However, this pushes up the price because interest is still charged on the loan in the months when you are not making repayments.

The interest charged on personal loans varies enormously but the lowest rates can compare favourably with rates on credit cards, especially if you want to borrow more than £3,000. If you want the security of knowing what your monthly repayments will be, a personal loan can be a good choice (if none of the cheaper borrowing options are open to you). However, if you want to repay some or all of the money before the end of the duration of the loan, a cheap credit card may be better – unless you can find a loan for which there is no early repayment charge.

Note that if you can find a low-charging credit card (see Chapter 3) with a sufficiently high credit limit, the credit-card option will invariably be the better deal.

Tip

Do not automatically take out the personal loan offered by your current-account provider: it is unlikely to be the best deal available unless you can negotiate an ordinary bank loan. Not all banks offer ordinary bank loans and those that do tend not to advertise the fact, although it is always worth asking.

Shop credit

Loans you are offered by a shop – often called 'extended credit' – work very much like personal loans except that you usually have to pay a deposit of about 10 per cent of the purchase price. If you are intending to make a large purchase from a shop, you should find out the monthly cost of other borrowing options before you go shopping. This will enable you to make an informed decision about whether the shop's credit offer is worth having. If the shop is unable to give you written details of the length of the loan and the size of the monthly repayments, avoid the loan.

Season ticket loans

If you are a regular commuter and you cannot get a loan from your employer to buy an annual season ticket, you could take up an offer of a season ticket loan from your rail network. This is worth doing if the total cost of the loan is lower than that of 12 monthly season tickets and lower than the cost of borrowing from another source.

Hire purchase

Hire-purchase arrangements are not very common these days except for car purchase (see Chapter 14). As with personal loans, you make equal monthly repayments to clear the borrowing, but unlike personal loans, you usually have to pay a deposit, and the goods you buy do not belong to you until you have repaid the full amount. If you fail to make repayments, the goods can be repossessed, although if you have paid at least 30 per cent of the loan, the finance company has to obtain a court order to do this.

Flexible mortgage

If you have one of the newer flexible mortgages (see Chapter 10), which has a 'loan drawdown facility', you have access to a fast and convenient way of borrowing to make large purchases. This kind of borrowing is also cheap because you pay mortgage rates on the loan. Whether you can borrow in this way depends not only on having this sort of mortgage but also on the overall borrowing limit set by your lender. This, in turn, depends on the value of your property and the size of your existing mortgage. With some lenders, loan drawdown is available only if you have built up a reserve of mortgage overpayments.

Extending your mortgage

If you do not have a flexible mortgage, you may still be able to borrow extra money against the value of your home by extending your existing mortgage. However, your lender may be prepared to do this only if the loan is to finance home improvements. The alternative to borrowing more from your existing lender is to use the value of your home to get a separate secured personal loan from another lender — although the interest you will be charged is likely to be higher than it would be if you simply extended your mortgage. In both cases, you usually have to pay legal fees and a fee to have your home valued. Neither of these options will be available if you do not have a mortgage or if your mortgage is already over a certain percentage of the value of your home.

Warning

With any kind of mortgage-related borrowing, you offer your home as security for the loan. This means that if you do not keep up your repayments, your lender can repossess your home and sell it to pay off the loan. You cannot be made homeless if you fail to repay an unsecured loan (i.e. all the other types of borrowing described in this chapter) but you will get a bad credit record.

Comparing the cost

Once you have identified what your borrowing options are, you need to compare the cost of loans from different lenders. The first thing to check is that the monthly repayment is within your budget. Even if you are able to borrow for nothing from your employer, for example, if the amount you have to repay each month is more than

---

Tip

When looking at the monthly repayment costs, make sure that you are comparing like with like: a loan repaid over 24 months is always going to look more expensive (in monthly terms) than a loan repaid over 36 months. For example, if you borrowed £3,000 and paid it back over 24 months, the monthly repayments could be £143.99 compared with £102.48 if you paid it back over 36 months. However, the total cost of credit for the shorter loan would be £3,445.76 compared with £3,689.28 for the longer loan.

---

you can afford, it will not be the best option. The other things to look at when comparing the cost are the APR (annual percentage rate of charge) and the total cost of credit.

APR

The APR is not an interest rate; it represents the total charge for credit expressed as a percentage and enables you to compare the cost of loans of the same type. The APR takes into account not only the interest you pay but also:

- any fees and charges you have to pay for arranging the loan
- any *compulsory* insurance or maintenance contracts you have to take out
- the amount and frequency of the loan repayments
- the length of the loan.

Although the APR helps you to whittle down your choice of loans it does not tell the whole story because different assumptions are used when calculating the APR for different types of credit. This is not a problem if you are comparing two loans of exactly the same type with exactly the same duration and repayment schedule – you are comparing one personal loan with another, for example. However, if you want to compare the cost of a personal loan with the cost of a credit card, the APR will not help. This is because the APR for a personal loan takes into account the fact that the amount you owe gradually goes down as you make your monthly repayments. With a credit card, the APR is calculated by assuming that the amount you borrow stays the same until you pay it in full and that you pay only interest throughout the duration of the loan.

This difference in assumptions can have the effect of making a personal loan that charges the same rate of interest as a credit card look cheaper than using a credit card and gradually paying off the loan each month. However, as a guide, if the credit card APR is the same as or lower than the APR for the personal loan, the credit card will give you the better deal provided you gradually pay off the loan.

The table below shows the monthly repayments you would need to make if you used a credit card to borrow £1,000 over various periods of time. The table is set out in the same way as illustrations used in personal loan advertising literature so you can use it to compare the monthly repayment figures using a credit card with those for a personal loan. To find out the monthly cost for a loan larger than £1,000, divide the size of loan you want by 1,000 and multiply the result by the monthly repayment figure given in the table. Note that the table also shows the annual rate of interest charged so you can use it to compare the cost of other sorts of borrowing as well.

Monthly repayments for £1,000 borrowed on a credit card

Credit card APR	annual rate of interest	12 months	24 months	36 months	48 months	60 months
10.4%	10%	£87.50	£46	£32	£25	£21
11.5%	11%	£88	£46.50	£32.50	£25.50	£21.50
12.6%	12%	£88.50	£47	£33	£26	£22
13.8%	13%	£89	£47	£33.50	£26.50	£22.50
14.9%	14%	£89.50	£47.50	£34	£27	£23
16%	15%	£90	£48	£34	£27.50	£23.50
17.2%	16%	£90	£48.50	£34.63	£28	£24
18.3%	17%	£90.50	£49	£35	£28	£24
19.5%	18%	£91	£49	£35.50	£28.50	£24.50
20.7%	19%	£91.50	£49.50	£36	£29	£25
21.9%	20%	£92	£50	£36.50	£29.50	£25.50

Monthly repayment figures have been rounded to the nearest 50p

The total cost of credit

As well as comparing the APR and monthly repayments for a loan, you should also look at the 'total cost of credit' or 'total amount payable', which has to be included on all advertisements (including marketing literature) for personal loans – but not credit cards. This tells you the total amount you will have paid out by the time you have finished paying off the loan.

Warning

When looking at the monthly repayment figures for personal loans, watch out for the extra cost of loan insurance. This sort of insurance is usually quite restrictive when it comes to paying out and can push up the cost of borrowing quite considerably. Common ploys used in personal loan literature are to: make the repayments with insurance look far more attractive than those without it; or to make the repayments without insurance hard to read; or to hide the details of repayments without insurance over the page. For more details of the limitations of loan payment protection insurance, see Chapter 6.

Chapter 14

Car finance

Buying a car is a major financial commitment: not only will you have to find a substantial lump sum to make the purchase but you will also have to find the funds to meet the ongoing costs involved in putting the car on the road as well as insuring it, fuelling it and generally looking after it. Unless you are one of the fortunate few who can meet the whole cost with cash, you will also usually need to add on the monthly cost of borrowing to finance your purchase.

This chapter looks at the cost of buying and running a car, examines the pros and cons of new versus second-hand and looks in detail at the main ways of raising car finance. Advice is given on the best way to insure your car, together with tips on keeping the cost to a minimum. If you drive a company car and you want to know whether switching to having a car of your own would save you money, you will find the answer on page 269.

The costs of car ownership

Personal taste, your individual requirements, the size of the car and your budget will all play a significant part in determining how much your car will cost you. Other, equally important, factors are:

- the potential resale value of the car (see page 257)
- reliability (see page 258)
- fuel consumption (see page 258)
- the cost of car insurance (see pages 258–262)
- other motoring costs (see pages 262–263).

The resale value of the car

One of the biggest costs involved with owning and running a car is depreciation – i.e. the reduction in its value over time. This is particularly true of new cars: simply driving a new car out of the showroom can reduce its value by 12 per cent; and in the first two years a car can lose nearly 45 per cent of its value. As a car ages, the rate of depreciation slows down, but over the first six years a new car can lose about 75 per cent of its value.

The type of new car will also affect the rate at which it loses its value: models that are popular with company car fleets are prone to rapid depreciation, whereas some small cars (especially those with power steering and those made by manufacturers such as Audi, BMW and Mercedes-Benz) tend to hold their resale value better. Depreciation also tends to be less rapid with mid-range models – so avoid the most basic and the most expensive models in a range. You should also think twice before choosing a 'special edition' or 'exclusive' car because you may pay over the odds for what are often only cosmetic differences.

New versus second-hand

Although depreciation contributes substantially to the cost of private motoring, it does not have a *direct* effect on running costs, and you cannot calculate its exact cost until you come to sell your car (although you can get a rough idea by consulting the various price guides published in specialist motoring magazines). However, one of the best ways of minimising the effects of depreciation is to buy a second-hand car instead of a brand new one so that you do not bear the costs of the spectacular fall in value in the early years. You could also consider the 'nearly-new' option.

Nearly-new cars (which are typically ex-company, lease or demonstration cars) are usually less than a year old and cost much less than they would to buy new. If you choose a car with a manufacturer's warranty still left to run, you might also be able to get any problems with the car repaired for free (provided it has been properly serviced).

Reliability

Generally, the more reliable a car is, the less you will have to spend on repairs but however reliable it is, it will still need regular maintenance. Making sure that your car is regularly serviced (and that you keep a full service record) will help to maximise the car's resale value (and so minimise depreciation). The table, below, gives average service and repair costs for different types and ages of car. You can find out which makes and models of car tend to be the most reliable by consulting the reliability data in *Which? Car* published annually in June. A good indicator of reliability is the length of the manufacturer's warranty on a new car: those with a three-year warranty, for example, tend to be the most reliable.

Annual service and repair costs

	Age of car		
Type of car	Less than 2 years old	3 to 5 years old	6 to 8 years old
Supermini	£150	£300	£340
Small family car	£180	£380	£390
Large family car	£230	£430	£490
Executive car	£270	£590	£690

Source: *Which?* Annual motoring survey 1997

Economy

How much fuel a car uses obviously affects its running cost as does your annual mileage and the conditions in which you tend to drive. Buying a car with low fuel consumption will not only be better for the environment but it will also save you money. But unless you do a high annual mileage, the savings will be fairly modest compared with other motoring costs. Doing 10,000 miles a year in a car that uses fuel at a rate of 35mpg (miles per gallon) will cost about £800 in fuel compared with about £550 for a 50-mpg car.

Car insurance

Car (or motor) insurance adds significantly to the cost of running a car but if you want to drive a car, motorcycle or any other motor vehicle on a public road, you have to have it. The two main types most commonly sold are:

- **third party, fire and theft**, which covers you if you (or your passengers) injure someone or damage their property. It also covers you if your car is damaged by fire or is stolen
- **comprehensive**, which covers you against the same things as a policy for third party, fire and theft but also provides cover for accidental damage to your car, some cover for personal possessions left in the car – usually up to a limit of £100 – and medical expenses which you have to pay as a result of an accident involving your car. Comprehensive policies also provide limited personal accident benefit, which pays out a specified lump sum of about £5,000 if you (and sometimes another person insured by the policy) die or suffer certain specific injuries – typically loss of sight or a limb – in a car accident. A comprehensive policy will generally cover you for damage to your windscreen and other glass and it may also provide a courtesy car if your own car is too badly damaged to drive after an accident or while your car is being repaired. For most people comprehensive cover is the best choice.

What car insurance costs
The type of policy you choose affects the cost of your car insurance because the higher the level of cover, the higher premiums you will pay. The other factors that affect the cost of car insurance are:

- **type of car** Insurers class cars using a group rating system of 20 groups, which are based on: the probability of the car being stolen; likely costs of repairs and parts; repair times; new car prices; the availability of the basic frame of the car; and performance in terms of the car's top speed and acceleration capabilities. The higher the rating, the more expensive the car is to insure. Your annual mileage will also affect the cost of your insurance
- **age of driver** Your age can have a dramatic effect on the price you pay. In general, older drivers pay less – although the price may rise if you are over 70 years of age. The price will also take into account the ages of all the drivers who are insured on the policy – not just the main driver

How insurance costs can vary

Insurance group of car	High-risk		Low risk	
	Low	high	Low	high
2	£300	£550	£110	£170
3	£335	£605	£120	£180
4	£385	£635	£130	£190
5	£410	£645	£140	£205
6	£420	£670	£145	£215
7	£440	£705	£155	£220
8	£480	£800	£180	£240
9	£530	£840	£195	£260
10	£650	£930	£210	£290
11	£670	£980	£220	£310
12	£700	£1,000	£225	£330
13	£740	£1,010	£240	£350
14	£850	£1,110	£280	£380
15	£870	£1,150	£300	£400
16	£890	£1,200	£320	£420

Figures are an indication only: all car insurance costs depend on personal circumstances

- **occupation** Your job may also affect how much you pay. People considered to be in low-risk occupations, such as teachers and civil servants, generally pay less than people in what insurers view as high-risk occupations, including actors, journalists and pub landlords. However, insurers are gradually realising that such blanket classifications do not give an accurate picture and are beginning to assess each risk on an individual basis
- **sex of driver** Generally, young men pay higher premiums than young women because they are considered to be a higher risk. However, there tends to be little or no difference in the price paid by older men and older women
- **claims record** If you have a bad claims record or you have been convicted of motoring offences, you will pay more for your insurance
- **number of drivers** The more drivers who are insured on a

policy, the more expensive it will be. The most expensive option is an 'any driver' policy, where anyone (with a valid licence) who has your permission to drive your car is insured to do so

- **where you live** The price you pay will also be affected by where you live – based on your post code. Insurance claims are more frequent in urban areas so motorists in cities usually pay more than motorists in rural areas
- **where you keep your car** You may pay less if you keep your car in a garage overnight rather than parked in a drive or on the street. The price may also be different if you usually keep your car somewhere other than your home address
- **how you use your car** Most private car insurance policies give you cover for 'social, domestic and pleasure' use, which usually includes driving to and from your place of work. If you intend to use your car for business-related travel – you will be visiting clients in it, for example – your insurers will need to know, otherwise it will not be insured.

How to cut the cost

You cannot cut the cost of insurance by being untruthful about your circumstances (it is a criminal offence to obtain motor insurance by deception) but there are several legitimate ways in which you can keep the cost to a minimum:

- **do not take the first quote you are offered** Although car insurance is pretty standard, prices are not (see table opposite). Research by *Which?* magazine* has shown that by phoning round to get several different quotes, you can almost halve the cost
- **change to an insurer you have not used before** Many insurers offer start-up discounts to new customers
- **volunteer to pay more towards any claim** If you agree to pay more than the 'compulsory excess' towards any claim – £250 rather than £100, for example – you could save about 10 per cent a year on the cost of your policy
- **tell the insurer who you work for** Some insurers offer special schemes to people in certain low-risk occupations (although these are not always the best deal) but if you work for a large company, you may find that your employer has negotiated a discount that you can take advantage of. You may also be offered a discount if

you belong to a union, are a member of the AA or RAC or other organisations such as the National Trust

- **tell the insurer about any security measures** Your insurance should cost less if you have fitted an ABI-approved immobiliser or car alarm, for example, or you have had your car registration number etched on to all your car windows. The insurer will be able to tell you which types of security measures will help to cut the cost
- **take an advanced-driving course** If you are a newly qualified driver, some insurers will give you a one-year no-claims discount (see below) if you take an intensive advanced-driving course
- **combine your insurance** If you are insuring more than one car and several drivers, you can save money by putting them all on one policy
- **haggle** A lot of insurers will reduce the price they quote if you tell them you have found a cheaper quote elsewhere (provided this is true, of course). Even if they will not reduce the price, they may offer extra cover at no extra cost
- **do not claim** All insurers offer big discounts if you do not claim on your policy. Typically this 'no-claims discount' will be 30 per cent after one year building up to a maximum of 60, 65 or 70 per cent after four to six years, depending on your insurer. You can keep your no-claims discount even if you change insurer.

Other motoring costs

The other cost you cannot avoid if you want to drive on a public road is Vehicle Excise Duty – more commonly known as the tax disc. This costs £100 a year for cars with an engine size of up to 1,100 cc and £155 a year for cars with engines over 1,100 cc. If you have to park on the road, you may also need to buy a resident's parking permit but how much you will be charged depends on your local authority.

Roadside rescue
If you want the security of knowing that someone will come to your rescue if you break down (which includes running out of petrol, punctures and a flat battery), you also need to include the fee for belonging to a breakdown recovery service in your car running costs.

Typically, this will be £75 a year if you choose the basic service, rising to about £125 for a policy that covers extras such as home cover (where a mechanic will come to your home if you cannot start the car).

Warning

Do not confuse breakdown recovery insurance with 'mechanical breakdown' insurance – more commonly referred to as an 'extended' car warranty. This aims to cover you for a limited list of possible repairs to your car after the manufacturer's warranty has run out. However, if you are offered this sort of insurance at no extra cost as part of the deal when you buy a second-hand car, you might as well take it.

Car finance

The best way of paying for a car is with savings you already have: this will put you in a better position to negotiate on price, and you will not have to add the cost of borrowing to your monthly running costs. Having savings also means that you can take advantage of 0% finance deals. These usually require you to pay a sizeable deposit – anything from 35 to 50 per cent of the purchase price – but you do not have to pay extra to spread the cost of the car by paying for it in monthly instalments.

If you do not have savings or if the amount you have saved is not enough to cover the cost of your chosen car, you will need to look at other ways of financing your purchase. The most important thing to consider with any kind of borrowing is whether you can afford the monthly repayments, but when borrowing to buy a car you also need to take into account whether you can afford the monthly repayments combined with all of the car running costs. The length of the loan also matters more because you should aim to have paid off the loan by the time you will want to change your car.

How you choose to finance your purchase will be limited by two main factors: whether you have enough money to put down as a deposit and whether you want to own the car from the outset. The options include:

- a personal loan (see below)
- a car loan (see below)
- hire purchase (see page 264)
- personal contract purchase schemes (see pages 265–266)
- personal leasing plans (see page 266).

Personal loans

A personal loan is your only option if you want to own the car from the outset. It is also likely to be the only option if you do not have money to put down as a deposit. Taking out a personal loan has the advantage of giving you the same bargaining power as someone who has cash. You pay a fixed rate of interest over a fixed period of time; monthly repayments are the same throughout the life of the loan (for more details, see Chapter 13). The personal loan market is quite competitive so it is always worth getting quotes (and, if possible, an in-principle agreement that the lender will lend you the money) before you go car shopping so that you can compare the cost with finance deals offered by car dealers.

Car loans

Most car loans from high-street lenders are personal loans with car-related frills tacked on; these might be discounts on break-down recovery insurance, free pre-purchase vehicle inspection and the chance for your lender to sell you car insurance. Do not be taken in by the frills if you could get cheaper credit on a plain personal loan: a low annual percentage rate (APR), see pages 253–254, and no early repayment penalties are the best indicator of good value.

You may also come across car loans with names like 'car purchase plan' or 'car loan package with upgrade option'. With these sorts of car loans, you put off repaying a chunk of the loan (typically 30 to 60 per cent of the car's value) until the end of the loan. The theory is that the end of the loan will coincide with your selling the car – the proceeds from which will help to pay off the rest of the loan.

The main advantage is that the monthly repayments tend to be lower than with a personal loan. However, you take the risk that the proceeds from selling your car will not be enough to meet the final repayment.

Hire purchase

This is the kind of finance deal you are most likely to be offered by a car dealer, who usually arranges the finance through the car manufacturer's own finance company. You usually have to pay a deposit of between 10 and 40 per cent of the cost of the car – although part-exchanging your old car can also act as a deposit. You then pay off the balance of the loan over a period of one to five years. A one-off administration fee is usually added to the first monthly repayment. As you would expect, the more you pay up front, the lower your monthly repayments will be, and the longer you take to pay, the higher the overall cost.

The main disadvantage of hire purchase (HP) is that, as the name suggests, you are hiring the car with a view to purchasing it at the end of the repayment period, when you will finally own the car. If you fail to keep up repayments under the HP agreement, the finance company can repossess the car. If, on the other hand, you want to pay for the car in full earlier than planned, you may have to pay a penalty. Finally, because the finance company owns the car until you have finished paying for it, you cannot sell it without its permission.

Tip

If you choose to arrange car finance through a dealer, do not just haggle over the price of the car, haggle over the cost of the finance deal too.

Personal contract plans

Introduced as a way of making the purchase of a new car more affordable, personal contract plans are designed for people who want to change their car every two to four years. These schemes are similar to HP (because you do not own the car until it is finally paid off), but instead of paying off the whole cost of the car during the repayment period, part of it is deferred. This part is known as the minimum guaranteed future value (MGFV), and the amount is fixed when you enter into the finance agreement. You also have to agree a maximum mileage that you will do during the period of the contract.

You usually have to pay a deposit of between 10 and 40 per cent of the car price, and then pay monthly instalments over the following two to three years. Because these do not include paying off the MGFV, they are lower than the repayments with a conventional loan but the overall cost of the loan is higher because you are paying interest on the MGFV. When you have paid all the monthly instalments you have to pay the lump sum that was deferred at the beginning – i.e. the MGFV. You either trade the car in to raise the cash to pay this back or you pay it off and keep the car. You also have the option of returning the car but doing this makes this kind of deal an expensive way to rent a car.

Long-term rental

A personal leasing plan (PLP) is a way of renting a car for two to three years – so you never actually own the car. Instead, you pay an initial deposit made up of an administration charge and three to six months' rental, followed by regular monthly payments until you give the car back. The monthly payments usually include the charge for borrowing the car plus the majority of your other motoring costs, including servicing, repairs, your road fund licence (tax disc) and membership of a breakdown service. PLPs vary from manufacturer to manufacturer, and the payments depend on the type of car you hire and also on the mileage you do.

Should you switch from a company car?

Changes in the way company cars are taxed – with further changes linking company-car taxation to carbon dioxide emissions from the 2003–04 tax year – have prompted an increasing number of people to give up their company cars – so should you join them?

In purely financial terms, relinquishing your company car should be well worthwhile if the tax (and whatever you pay your employer for personal use of the car) comes to more than the cost of buying and running your own car. The figures look even better if your employer offers you extra pay in place of your lost perk.

How much does a company car cost?

If you are tempted to give up the perk of a company car, you need to work out how much it is costing you in tax and how much it would cost to run your own car. The calculator overleaf will help you to do the sums. But before you can fill it in you will need:

- details of the list price (plus accessories) of your car when you got it (this will be shown on your P11D, which your employer should give you in July each year)
- details of the number of miles you travel on business each tax year
- the yearly figure for what you pay your employer for private use of the car, which, if appropriate, should also appear on your P11D
- your top rate of tax – if you do not know, see Chapter 17
- the tax cost of free fuel provided by your employer for private use (if applicable), which is given in the table on page 269
- an estimate of the yearly costs (including finance costs if appropriate) of running your own car (include fuel only if you would relinquish free fuel provided by an employer)
- the yearly amount of pay you will receive for relinquishing your company car (if applicable).

National Insurance on extra pay

If you earn less than £26,000 you will have to pay National Insurance on the amount of extra pay you get that takes you up to the £26,000 limit. So if you earn £25,000 and will get £2,400 of extra pay, you will pay National Insurance on £1,000. The rates are 10 per cent, or 8.4 per cent if you are contracted-out through an employer's pension scheme.

Will you save by switching from your company car?

Enter the list price of the car (plus accessories) when you first got it	A
The figure to enter at B depends on how many business miles you travel each tax year. If your business miles are: • more than 18,000, enter 0.15 • more than 2,500 but less than 18,000, enter 0.25 • less than 2,500, enter 0.35	B
Multiply A by B and enter the result at C	C
If your car is more than four years old, multiply C by 0.75 and enter the result at D	D
Enter the yearly amount you pay your employer for private use of the car (if applicable); otherwise enter zero	E
Subtract E from D and enter the result at F If D is blank, subtract E from C and enter the result at F	F
The figure at F is the taxable value of your company car	
If you pay tax at the higher rate, enter 0.4 If you pay tax at the basic rate, enter 0.23	G
Multiply F by G and enter the result at H	H
Enter the tax cost of free petrol or diesel for private use provided by your employer (if applicable); otherwise enter zero	I
Add H to E and I and enter the result at J	J
The figure at J is the yearly cost of running a company car	
Enter the yearly pay you will receive if you give up your company car. Enter zero if you will not get any extra pay	K
If you are a higher-rate taxpayer, multiply K by 0.6 If you are a basic-rate taxpayer, multiply K by 0.77	L
If you earn more than £26,000 enter zero. If you earn less than £26,000, enter the cost of National Insurance on your extra pay – see page 267.	M
Enter your estimate of the yearly costs of running your own car (see pages 256–263 for what this should include)	N
Add N to M and enter the result at O	O
Subtract O from L and enter the result at P	P
The figure at P is the net cost (or benefit) of running your own car If P is a plus figure, you will definitely save by switching from a company car If P is a minus figure, compare the amount (ignoring the minus) with the figure at J If J is greater than P, you will save money by running your own car. If J is less than P, keeping you company car may be cheaper than running your own car – see 'The full picture' opposite.	

The full picture

If the calculator shows that it may be cheaper to keep your company car, but future costs of running your own car would be different after the first year (you would pay off a car loan after a couple of years, for example), you need to go through the calculator for each of the years that you would be expected to keep the equivalent company car and total the figures for this period. If you will probably pay cash for a car of your own, doing these calculations will also give you an idea of how long it will take you to replenish the savings you used to buy the car.

Tax cost of free fuel 1999–2000

Engine size of car		Tax cost if you pay tax at:	
		23%	40%
Petrol 0–1,400cc	£1,210	£278.30	£484
1,401–2,000cc	£1,540	£354.20	£616
2,001cc and over	£2,270	£522.10	£908
Diesel 0–2,000cc	£1,540	£354.20	£616
2,001cc	£2,270	£522.10	£908
No cylinder capacity	£2,270	£522.10	£908

Should you switch?

If the cost of running a company car is much higher than the cost of running your own car, it is fairly obvious that you will save money by switching. If the company car looks as though it is a cheaper deal, you have to balance the lower running costs against the fact that you will not own the car after paying to drive it. If the two running cost figures are about the same, whether or not you swap depends on how much you could realistically expect your chosen car to be worth in a few years' time. You should also take into account the fact that the amount you will no longer have to pay for your company car can be offset against the costs of running your own car. So if the net effect of this looks reasonable and your own car will be worth something when you decide to trade it in, switching could be worthwhile.

Tax point

If you do decide to get rid of your company car, you do not have to wait until you fill in a tax return to get the benefit of the tax saving and you do not even have to write a letter. You can get your tax code changed simply by ringing your tax office. Depending on how efficient both your tax office and your employer are, you should see the difference in your payslip within a month or two (it will be back-dated to the time you stopped having the company car).

Caroline counts the cost

When the time came for Caroline to change her company car, she decided to work out whether she could save money by buying a car of her own. She worked out that the company car would cost £2,131.50 a year, made up of the tax cost of £931.50 plus the £100 a month she would have to pay her employer for private use of the car.

She thinks that if she bought a car of her own she would go for the nearly-new option and could buy a similar car to the one she would give up for £10,000, although she would need to take out a loan to do this. She estimates that her yearly running costs would be £3,943, made up of £260.25 a month to pay back a four-year loan, £400 a year for insurance and £420 to cover her tax disc, maintenance and repairs. She does not include petrol because she already pays for this herself so the cost is the same whether she chooses to run her own car or the company car.

If she gives up the company car she will get £200 a month in extra pay – after basic-rate tax this is worth £1,848 a year. The net cost of running a car of her own – after taking into account the extra pay she will get – is £2,095. So she will save about £36.50 a year. However, after four years, which is the length of time she would have to keep a company car, she would have nothing to show for the money spent on a company car. If she chose to run a car of her own, after four years she would own a car that she thinks would be worth about £5,000.

Will Caroline save by switching?		
List price of new company car	A	£15,000
Caroline travels fewer than 2,500 miles on business	B	0.35
A x B = C	C	£5,250
The car would be less than 4 years old so she leaves this blank	D	
She would pay her employer £100 a month for private use of the car	E	£1,200
The **taxable value** of the car is C minus E	F	£4,050
Caroline pays tax at the basic rate	G	0.23
The tax cost of the car is F multiplied by G	H	£931.50
Caroline does not get free fuel	I	£0
The yearly cost of running the company car is the tax cost plus the amount she would pay her employer for private use of the car	J	**£2,131.50**
If she gave up her company car, her employer would pay her an extra £200 a month	K	£2,400
Caroline works out what this extra pay would be worth after basic-rate tax	L	£1,848
She would not pay National Insurance on her extra pay	M	£0
Caroline enters her estimate of the costs of running her own car	N	£3,943
M + N = O	O	£3,943
Caroline calculates the net cost of running her own car after taking into account the extra pay she will get	P	**£2,095**

Chapter 15

What to do if you are turned down for credit

You could be turned down for credit for one of three reasons: you are under 18 (so you are not old enough to enter into a credit agreement); you are not the kind of customer the lender is looking for; or you are not considered to be a good credit risk. If you are refused credit because of your age or customer 'profile', you cannot do very much about it. However, if on applying for a current account, a credit card, or any other sort of loan – which includes regular bills that you pay in arrears – you are turned down because you are considered to be a bad risk, you *can* do something about it by discovering the reasons for the refusal. You should remember, though, that no one has the right to credit, and if the lender has turned you down because it seems unlikely that you will be able to repay the loan, it suggests that you are asking for too much credit.

This chapter looks at how lenders assess your application for credit and how their judgement is affected by information gleaned from a credit reference agency. It tells you how to find out why your application was rejected, how to appeal against a lender's refusal and how you can get the information held about you by a credit reference

---

Tip

You do not have to wait until you are turned down for credit to find out what information is held about you by a credit reference agency. Finding out whether your credit file is correct (and getting it corrected if it is not) could save you time and avoid inconvenience if you plan to apply for credit in the future.

---

agency changed. If you are simply curious about what is on your credit file, turn to pages 275–283.

Are you a good credit risk?

Lenders are not obliged to give you credit and if they think that there is a risk that you will not repay their money – i.e. that you are a bad credit risk – your application is likely to be rejected. The lender may turn you down because:

- **credit scoring** was used and you did not score enough (see below), or
- **a credit reference agency** was used and its file on you contained adverse information (see page 274).

Credit scoring

The most common method used to assess applications for credit is a statistical technique called 'credit scoring'. This has the advantage of being objective and – because it is easily computerised – quick (which is why it is possible to apply for a loan over the phone). Each of the answers you give when you apply for credit is given a score. If your application scores more than the lender's pass-mark, you will get the credit; if it scores less than the pass-mark, you will not (although borderline cases may be assessed individually). Because credit scoring is based on the statistical analysis of a lender's past experiences, different lenders use different scoring systems and pass-marks. The scoring systems generally reflect common sense: if you are tied to your home by your mortgage, have a steady job and a good history of repaying your debts, for example, you will probably score more highly than if you live in a rented flat, have a temporary job and have never had credit before.

Credit scoring is not used simply to accept or reject your application: it may also be used to decide the rate of interest you pay and/or how much you can borrow. Your credit score will also be affected by the information the lender gets from a credit reference agency.

Don't give up if you are refused credit

When Margaret applied for a store card, she was turned down flat because she had lived at more than two addresses in the previous three years – a fact that lowered her credit score quite considerably. She wrote to the store and explained that she had credit cards and paid her bills on time. The store relented and gave her a card.

Credit reference agencies

Lenders use credit reference agencies to share information on how much credit you have applied for and on how good you are at making repayments. Contrary to popular opinion, these agencies do not keep blacklists nor do they give an opinion on your credit-worthiness – it is up to the lender to decide whether the details supplied make you a good or bad credit risk. The two main credit reference agencies are Experian★ and Equifax★ and the kind of information they keep about you includes:

- your entry on the electoral roll
- records of county court judgements (decrees in Scotland) for non-payment of debt
- bankruptcies
- details of your other loans and credit cards – both current and those you have had in the past
- how often you have applied for credit
- how well you have kept up your repayments and whether you have defaulted on any credit agreements in the past
- records about other people who live at the same address as you and/or who are financially connected to you.

Appealing against a rejection

If you think that the lender has rejected your application without good reason, you can ask why. Although it is unlikely that the lender will give precise details of what its reasons were, you should at least be told whether it was your credit score that let you down or whether you were rejected as a result of information supplied by a credit reference agency.

Provided you write to the lender within 28 days of having your application turned down you are legally entitled to ask whether a credit reference agency was used and which one (see Example letter, below). The lender *must* give you this information (although it does not have to tell you what the agency said about you).

Example of a letter appealing against a rejection

[Your address]

[Lending company's name]
[Address]
[Date]

Dear Ms Lender

Your reference: 5559asl

Following your letter of [date] rejecting my application for a personal loan of [amount], I am writing to ask why my application has been turned down.

If a credit reference agency was used in considering my application, please send me the name and address of the agency you used in accordance with my rights under section 157 of the Consumer Credit Act 1974.

I expect a reply within seven working days of your receiving this letter.

Yours sincerely
V Disgruntled

How to get hold of your credit file

If ask the lender the name of the credit reference agency it used (see Example, above), you should get a reply from the lender naming the agency within seven days of getting your letter. To get hold of a copy of your credit file, you need to write to the credit reference agency enclosing a cheque or postal order for £2 (see Example, below).

Note that when the Data Protection Act 1998 comes into force (which is scheduled to happen sometime in mid-1999), you will be able to pay a small fee to receive information just on your financial standing or a full fee for all information held on you. To find out what the fees are, you should contact the credit reference agency before writing. Whatever level of detail you want, your letter should include:

- your full name and address including post code
- the length of time that you have lived at your current address
- details of any other addresses at which you have lived in the past six years
- if you are self-employed as a sole trader, the same details as above for your business.

Example of letter asking for a copy of your credit file

[Your address]

[Equifax/Experian]
[Address]

[Date]

Dear Equifax/Experian

In accordance with my rights under section 158(1) of the Consumer Credit Act 1974, I am writing to request a copy of my file and I enclose a cheque for £2.

My full name is [name] and I have lived at the address above since [date]. Before that date, my address was [address].

Please reply to this letter within seven days of receiving it.

Yours faithfully
David Borrower

What to do when you get the file

Unless the agency replies asking you for more details to help trace your file, you should receive a copy of your file seven working days after your letter reached the agency. The copy of your file will be divided into different sections covering:

- **electoral roll information**, which details your address and the time you have lived at it. The names of previous occupants of the property will also be shown, which is not a problem unless the file contains financial information about them (see page 278)
- **a record of inquiries** about your file which the agency has received in the last one to two years (depending on the agency) showing the type of inquiry and who made it
- **court information** which shows whether you have any county court judgements or administration orders against you for non-payment of debt. Debts you were ordered to pay by a court which you paid within one month should not appear; debts repaid after one month may be marked 'satisfied' but stay on your file for six years
- **public record information** from sources other than court records – such as official gazettes and the insolvency service – may also appear
- **insight account information**, which is the information provided by lenders on a monthly basis. This is where you will find your current credit details and whether your repayments are up to date. This may be shown as a series of codes in reverse date order: 0 means you paid on time; 1 that a payment is one month late; 2 that it is two months late and so on. S means that you have settled the loan. Some lenders supply only default information, so if you have an immaculate record of paying your debts, this section may not contain anything
- **financial information about other people**, which should appear only if the people concerned have a similar name to yours (members of your family, for example), have lived with you at your current or previous address, or are 'financially connected' to you (have a joint loan with you, for example). Agencies must not give the financial information of other people who have no

277

financial connection with you or of people who have not lived with you at your current (or previous) address (even if they have lived with you in the past). If they do give this information, you can ask the Data Protection Commissioner★ to investigate

- **Credit Industry Fraud Avoidance System information**, which could appear if a fraudster has attempted to use your name and address to get credit.

What to do if the file is wrong

As well as a copy of the file itself, you should receive a statement which sets out your rights under the Consumer Credit Act 1974 and (when it comes into force) the Data Protection Act 1998. This sets out what you are legally entitled to do if there is a wrong entry on your file. The steps you should follow to get your file corrected depend on whether you want to:

- **disassociate** yourself from a member of your current (or previous) household because you have no financial connection with him or her (see below)
- **correct** your file because it is factually incorrect or because the file is factually correct but could create a misleading impression without further explanation (see page 280).

Disassociating yourself

If your file contains financial information about another person which is allowed to be in your file but which you do not want there because you have no financial connection with him or her – you are divorced, for example, or you are no longer financially responsible for the person – you can write to the agency asking to remove his or her financial details.

This is worth doing if you do not want the other person to be able to see your financial details (which he or she will be able to do if he or she gets hold of his or her own credit file, because your details will appear on it) or if the other person has a bad credit record which could affect your chances of getting credit. To do this, you should write to the agency asking to be disassociated from the person on your file (see Example letter, below). As well as your full name and address, your letter should include:

- the reference number of your file
- the full name and address of the person(s) you want to have taken off your file
- details of your relationship with the person(s) concerned
- the reason why they are not financially connected to you.

The credit reference agency may want to check that what you say is true but unless it can find a good reason for refusing your request, it must remove the financial information about the person in question from your file and also the financial information about you from the other person's credit file. If the agency refuses to make the necessary changes, you can ask the Data Protection Commissioner to look into the matter (see Example letter overleaf).

Example of letter requesting a disassociation

[Your address]

[Equifax/Experian]
[Address]
[Date]

Dear Equifax/Experian

File reference: 987654321/1234

I am writing to inform you that I no longer have any financial connection with [name] since my divorce from him on [date]. His current address is [address].

Please remove his financial information from my file and information about me from his file. Please send written confirmation that you have created this disassociation within 28 days of receiving this letter.

Yours faithfully
Alexandra Ferguson

Example of letter asking for help if your disassociation request is refused

[Your address]

[Data Protection Commissioner]
[Address]

[Date]

Dear Data Protection Commissioner

I am writing to you concerning the refusal by Equifax/Experian to create a disassociation between me and my ex-husband, [name], to whom I have not been financially connected since our divorce in [date].

I am enclosing copies of all the correspondence I have had with the agency concerned and, as you will see, they are refusing to remove information about him from my file.

I should be very grateful if you would look into this matter for me.

Your faithfully
Alexandra Ferguson

Correcting your file

If you think that an entry on your file is wrong and you believe that you will suffer as a result of the mistake, you are legally entitled to get the file corrected. Write to the agency explaining why you think that the entry is wrong and what you want the agency to do about it (see Example opposite). If you have documents which will support your view, it may help to streamline the correction process if you enclose copies of them.

The agency should reply to your letter within 28 days of receiving it. The reply should tell you whether the entry has been corrected (in which case you will receive a copy of the correction) or removed or whether the agency has done nothing.

Example of letter asking for a file to be corrected

[Your address]

[Equifax/Experian]
[Address]
[Date]

Dear Equifax/Experian

File reference: 987654321/1234

I am writing to ask you to make two corrections to my file in accordance with my rights under section 159 of the Consumer Credit Act 1974.

1. The county court judgement of [date] for non-payment of a debt of [amount] was not against me but against my cousin [name], who was living with me at the time but who now lives at [address]. Please remove this item from my file.

2. The file states that I am three months behind with my ABC personal loan repayments, which is not the case. I enclose a copy of the letter from ABC Finance Company confirming that all my repayments have been paid on time. Please amend the information on my file to reflect this fact.

I look forward to hearing from you within 28 days from the date you receive this letter.

Yours faithfully
Peter Neville

Adding a note of correction

If you are not happy with the correction or the agency tells you that it has done nothing or if it does not reply within 28 days of getting your letter, you have the right to compose your own 'note of correction'. This should be no longer than 200 words long and it should give a clear and accurate explanation of why you think an entry is incorrect. You can also write a note of correction if an entry on your file is factually correct but could be misleading without further explanation (see Example overleaf). If you need to do this, you should write to the agency within 28 days of its reply to your first letter (or the deadline for its reply if you did not get one). Your letter should tell the agency to add your note of correction to your file and to include a copy of it whenever information included on the uncorrected entry is given out.

Once the agency has received your note of correction, it has 28 days in which to let you know whether it will add it to your file or not accept it.

Example of a letter sending a note of correction

[Your address]

[Equifax/Experian]
[Address]
[Date]

Dear Equifax/Experian

File reference: 987633331/1897

Thank you for your letter dated [date] telling me that you do not propose to make the correction I asked for in my letter dated [date].

Please add the following note of correction to my file and ensure that a copy of it is attached to the entry on my file whenever you provide anyone with information included in the entry or any information based on it.

Note of correction

I, [name], of [address], would like it to be known that the county court judgement recorded against me for [amount] concerns a credit-card bill which I was unable to pay because I was made redundant in [month and year]. I paid the bill in full after returning to work in [month and year]. Since then, I have paid all my bills on time (as I did before losing my job) and I would ask anyone searching this file to take account of these facts.

Please confirm that the note of correction given above has been added to my file within 28 days of the date on which you receive this letter.

Yours faithfully
Myfanwy Williams

If your note is accepted

If the agency accepts the note of correction, it must send a copy of the note to any lender who has asked for a credit reference in the six months immediately before you asked to see your file. If the note of correction relates to the judgement or decree of a court, the agency should pass your correction on so that the public records can be updated. The correction then goes on to the other credit reference agency (i.e. Experian if you have been dealing with Equifax, and vice versa). If your note relates to something not held in public records, it can be a good idea to check that the records of the other agency have been updated and also that lenders have been informed. Note that amendments to your file which the agency agrees to without the need for a note of correction should also be passed on in the same way.

If your note is rejected

The agency can decide not to accept your note of correction if it thinks that the note is incorrect, defamatory, frivolous or scandalous. In such a case the agency will refer your note to the Data Protection Commissioner for a ruling. Within 14 days of receiving the agency's request, the Commissioner will ask for your comments. You will receive a final decision about two months later.

If you hear nothing

If you hear nothing from the agency within 28 days of it getting your letter, you can appeal to the Data Protection Commissioner in writing giving the following details:

- your full name and address
- the name and address of the credit reference agency
- details of the entry on your file which you want corrected
- why you want the entry corrected
- why you think you will suffer if it is not corrected
- the date you sent your note of correction to the agency.

The Data Protection Commissioner will look into your case and may ask the agency for its side of the story to help make a decision. If the Commissioner thinks you are right, the agency can be ordered to accept your note of correction. Whatever the decision, you will find out what it is after about two months.

Chapter 16

What to do about debt

Getting into debt is easy, getting out of debt is a struggle. If you find that you are having difficulty making ends meet, the one thing you should *not* do is ignore the problem. Doing nothing in the hope that your debts will disappear could result in you being taken to court, losing your home, having your gas, electricity and water cut off and – if you fail to pay your council tax (in England and Wales) – being sent to prison. These are the very real risks that you face if your debts get out of hand. However, unmanageable debts do not just happen overnight and letting yourself drift into debt without addressing the problem can have equally serious consequences.

This chapter tells you how to spot the warning signs of unmanageable debt and gives advice on how you can curb the problem. If your debts are more serious and you are having trouble coping, there is practical guidance on what to do about your mortgage, your essential bills and your other debts. You will also find details of who you can turn to for help and what to do if you are threatened with court action.

How to spot the warning signs

The best way to deal with a debt is to nip it in the bud before it gets out of hand. This means not being complacent about the warning signs which can suggest that you are heading for trouble. If you answer yes to some or all of the following questions, you should give serious thought to getting your finances sorted out.

- Are you always overdrawn?
- Do you repay only the minimum amount on your credit card each month?

- Does the amount you owe on your credit card go up every month?
- Do you put off paying bills until the final reminder arrives?
- Have you ever missed a repayment on your mortgage or other loan?
- Can you afford to buy things only by borrowing?

If you have answered yes to any of the questions above, before you drift any further into debt, you should take steps to become financially solvent. You can do this by:

- cutting back spending on inessentials by drawing up a budget which will also tell you how much you have available to pay off your debts (see Chapter 18)
- working out a monthly budget for all of your essential bills (see Chapter 11)
- checking that your overdraft is authorised and that you are not paying over the odds for it (see Chapter 2)
- transferring all your credit-card debts to a lower-charging card (see Chapter 3)
- diverting any savings you may have towards paying off your debts (see Chapter 4)
- finding a cheaper way to borrow for your other loans – but be wary of transferring loans which carry a penalty for early repayment (see Chapters 13 and 14)
- ensuring that you keep up repayments on your mortgage and other existing loans
- paying off the most expensive of the debts which you can clear first.

Warning

Personal crisis leads to financial crisis: divorce, redundancy or a serious accident can turn manageable borrowing into unmanageable debt. The more control you have over your finances, the less susceptible you will be to dramatic changes in your personal life.

It makes sense to act while your record of paying debts is still relatively good. If you get a record as a bad payer, your ability to get credit will suffer and you may not be able to switch to cheaper forms of borrowing. It is not wise to consolidate your debts if the only lender willing to give you a loan charges you more – which is very likely to be the case if you have serious debt problems.

Dealing with serious debt problems

Once you have decided to confront the problem, the first thing you should do is to contact your creditors – the organisations that you owe money to (which includes gas, electricity, water and telephone companies). The earlier you write to your creditors explaining that you are in financial difficulty, the more sympathetic and helpful they are likely to be. If you have already started to receive reminders and/or final demands, do not ignore them but get in contact as soon as possible to explain your situation. Your creditors may add the costs they incur in chasing you to the amount of the loan, so you will exacerbate the problem if you do nothing. You are also more likely to face court action (see pages 292–294).

You then need to take stock of your financial position so that you can work out how you are going to repay your debts. You should also seriously consider enlisting the help of a debt adviser, which you can do by contacting the Citizens' Advice Bureau,* a Money Advice Centre,* the Consumer Credit Counselling Service* or the National Debtline.* Getting outside help not only shows your creditors that you are serious about solving your problem, but you will also get advice about any state benefits and tax allowances to which you may be entitled, together with advice on drawing up a plan to help deal with your debt. Even if you do not get outside help you should follow the same procedure that a debt adviser would use. This is recognised by most creditors, and involves:

- sorting your debts into priority and non-priority debts
- working out how much you can afford to repay each month
- preparing a financial statement
- negotiating repayment plans with your creditors.

Getting your priorities right

Your priority debts are those which carry particularly serious consequences if they are not dealt with, such as court action or losing your home and other essential services. Priority debts include:

- mortgage or rent arrears
- council tax
- gas
- electricity
- water
- court fines
- maintenance payments
- income tax
- National Insurance.

Working out how much you can repay

Before you can start to tackle your debts, you need to work out how much you can afford to repay each month. List all sources of income and draw up a detailed breakdown of all your monthly spending. You can do this by filling in the personal budget calculator in Chapter 18. To find out how much money is left over for paying your debts, subtract your monthly spending from your monthly income. If you are left with a minus figure you need to find ways of either increasing your income or cutting back on your spending. Note that a debt adviser can take a dispassionate view of what is essential and what is not.

Preparing a financial statement

Drawing up a financial statement not only helps you to plan but it will also show your creditors what your financial position is and how much money is available for repaying your debts. If your creditors can see that you do not have money available to repay them in full, they may realise that it is not worth taking you to court to recover the money. A financial statement can also help to persuade creditors to freeze interest and to accept token payments while you concentrate on repaying your priority debts.

The financial statement below is in two parts: the first lists your income and outgoings and shows how much you have available for repaying your debts each month; the second shows your total debts and the amount you can repay each month.

Example of a financial statement

Name

Address

Income	Monthly amount
After-tax salary	
State benefits	
Other income	
Total income	
Outgoings	
Rent/mortgage	
Second mortgage	
Council tax	
Life insurance	
Water	
Gas	
Electricity	
Other fuel	
House insurance	
Housekeeping	
TV rental/licence	
Travelling expenses	
School meals/meals at work	
Clothing	
Prescriptions	
Childminding	
Other	
Total outgoings	

Money available for paying debts (total income less total outgoings)	£	
Priority debts	**Total amount owed**	**Monthly offer of repayment**
Mortgage/rent arrears		
Second mortgage arrears		
Council tax arrears		
Water rates arrears		
Money owed for gas		
Money owed for electricity		
Court fines outstanding		
Maintenance arrears		
Other		
Total monthly repayment of priority debts	£	
Monthly amount available for other creditors Money available for repaying debts less total monthly repayment of priority debts	£	
	Total amount owed	**Monthly offer of repayment**
Credit card		
Catalogues		
Bank loans		
Other loans		
Hire purchase		
Total	£	£

Negotiating with your creditors

Once you have drawn up a financial statement you will be in a position to negotiate a realistic repayment plan with your creditors, concentrating on your priority debts first.

Mortgage

If you have mortgage arrears you risk losing your home, so it is vital that you contact your lender to talk about how you can resolve the problem. If you miss instalments and ignore reminders and attempts to reach alternative arrangements for dealing with your mortgage arrears, your lender will repossess your home.

Mortgage lenders which subscribe to the Banking and/or Mortgage Code are committed to dealing with financial difficulties and mortgage arrears 'sympathetically and positively'. You need to show your lender your financial statement so that it can help you to draw up a realistic plan to clear the arrears (note that if you ask for a statement showing how the arrears have built up, you may be charged for this). If you ask them to, lenders will liaise directly with the debt counselling service from which you are getting help (if appropriate). Most lenders would rather avoid repossessing your home and may be willing to let you:

- **make interest-only payments**, which is only possible if you have a repayment mortgage (see Chapter 10) and you have started to pay off some of the loan as well as paying interest
- **suspend your payments**, which means that you may be allowed a short period when you pay less than you owe or are let off making payments altogether. This can give you useful breathing space but the catch is that the payments you do not make are added to your loan, so when you start paying in full again your repayments will have gone up. Your lender may also levy a 'suspension charge' for agreeing to reduced payments
- **extend the length of your loan**, which reduces your monthly payments but pushes up the cost of the loan overall. This may not be possible if it would mean that the mortgage would not be paid off before your retirement
- **add the arrears to the outstanding mortgage loan**, which spreads the overdue debt over the remainder of the mortgage term. However, this will be an option only if the value of your home is much higher than your mortgage and you can afford the increased monthly payments.

It is vital that the repayment plan you agree with your lender is realistic. If you break the agreement, you may face a 'broken arrears arrangement charge'. If you continue to break the agreement, you risk having your home repossessed and, on top of the repossession costs, may face the following charges:

- **final reminder charge** for the letter sent before legal action
- **referral charge** when the mortgage arrears are referred for legal action
- **seven-day letter charge** for the letter sent seven days before a court order to repossess the property is enforced
- **pre-eviction visit charge** for a visit undertaken to establish the occupancy of the property.

Warning

Never admit that a lender is entitled to the property. A court may believe that you are consenting to your eviction, which could lead to problems if you need the local authority to find you a home. You should also never hand back your keys to the lender because your name will automatically go on to a mortgage blacklist.

Essential bills

If you cannot pay your gas, electricity or water bills, the companies involved should try to come to an agreement on clearing the debt and will disconnect you only if this fails. Depending on the extent of your other debts, you may be allowed to pay off your outstanding bill in instalments before the next bill is due. However, if there is not enough money for you to do this ask if there is a monthly budget scheme which would enable you to spread what you owe over a period of time (depending on the size of the arrears). For gas and electricity, you could have prepayment meters installed. The meter is set to charge enough to clear what is outstanding as well as the normal cost of use and standing charges.

Other creditors

Once you have come to an arrangement with your priority creditors, you need to negotiate with your other creditors to agree how you will clear the debts you have with them (if you have money available for doing this after you have dealt with your priority debts). This means offering to make a reduced monthly repayment. To calculate how much you should offer each creditor:

- divide the amount you owe each creditor by the total amount of all your debts (including priority debts)
- multiply the result by the monthly amount available for other creditors (see the example of a financial statement on pages 288–289).

This is how a court would work out your repayments, so most creditors will accept your offer, especially if it is backed up by a detailed financial statement. Note that if there is no money available after meeting your priority debts, your offer will be zero. Once you have calculated how much you can afford to offer, write to each creditor enclosing a copy of your financial statement. Your letter should:

- explain why you cannot afford to make full repayment
- ask the creditor to accept a reduced repayment or, if your offer is zero and you cannot afford any repayment, to accept no payments
- make a request to have the interest on the debt frozen so that your debt does not increase
- explain that other creditors have accepted your offers (if this is true) – this can be a useful point in your favour
- explain that you will contact the creditor again when your circumstances improve and you are able to increase your repayments.

If your offer is rejected, try again and do not give up.

Warning

Do not make an offer to make a payment that you will not be able to keep up. Most lenders would rather have a small regular payment than a promise of payment which does not materialise.

Court action

If you do not succeed in renegotiating your repayments, fail to keep to your new repayment plan or do not act in time, your creditor may take court action; the court costs will add further to your debt.

However, this does not necessarily mean that you will have to go to court because most of the court procedure happens by post. At this point, if you have not already done so, you should seek advice from a debt counselling service – see page 286. You will be given advice on how to fill in all the forms and if you eventually have to go to court, help presenting your case.

The summons

If you receive a 'default summons', do not ignore it. If you have not already done so, get outside help. The summons will give details of how much the creditor says you owe. If you disagree with the amount, fill in the enclosed 'Defence and Counterclaim' form and send this back to the court as soon as possible.

If the amount of the debt is correct, fill in the reply form, following the instructions that come with it. If you have prepared a financial statement, this should be relatively straightforward because the form asks for the same sort of information. The completed form should be returned to the creditor – *not* the court – within 21 days of the postmark on the summons.

The court order

Once you have replied to the summons you will receive a written order from the court telling you how much you have to repay each month. If you do not agree with what the court proposes, you have 14 days (from receiving the court order) in which to ask for a hearing. The court will then send you a hearing date upon which you must attend. Take your financial statement with you, together with details of all your debts and proof of your earnings. The court will decide whether the amount of money owed has been correctly calculated, how it should be paid, and whether the creditor has the right to take possession of any security such as your home.

If you cannot pay the monthly amount ordered by the court, the creditor can take further action against you, such as getting a repossession order and sending the bailiffs in. If you cannot afford the repayments, you can ask for them to be reduced by filling in form N245, which is available from the court.

Administration orders

If your total debts are less than £5,000, you may be able to apply for an administration order, which is a way of bringing all your debts together. Instead of repaying each individual creditor, you make one monthly payment into the court which then shares it out among your creditors on your behalf. The advantage of doing this is that creditors cannot take any further action against you, but you should always seek advice before deciding on this course of action.

Your credit record

A court action not only adds to your debts through court costs – which is why it is so important to act to avoid it – but it will also affect your ability to get credit in the future. If the court orders you to pay, details will be recorded on the Register of County Court Judgements and passed to credit reference agencies. However, if you pay your debt in full within one month of the order you can have the entry removed, although there is a small fee for doing this.

Part 5

Practicalities

Chapter 17

How to check your tax

It is estimated that about six million people are paying too much tax, so finding out whether you are one of them should save you money. Checking that you are paying the right amount of tax means understanding the basic differences between what you and the tax rules regard as income, working out how much tax you do – and do not – have to pay on each part of it, and knowing which of your personal circumstances can help to reduce your tax bill. If you get a self-assessment tax return every year, you already have the opportunity to check that you are not paying too much tax. But if you do not, you have to rely on your employer, pension provider and/or your tax office so you need to check they have got it right.

This chapter deals with income tax and explains how to work out which kind of taxpayer you are; takes you through the calculations you need to do to work out your income tax bill; and tells you how to check that you are paying the right amount. To find out how tax affects you as a couple see Chapter 22, and if you have children, see

---

Tax facts

Income tax is an annual tax, so what you have to pay tax on and the amount you have to pay varies from year to year – depending on changes announced in the Budget. Your annual tax bill is generally based on the income you receive in a tax year – which runs from 6 April in one year to 5 April in the next – and is calculated according to the rules and rates that apply to that tax year. This chapter looks at the rules for the 1999–2000 tax year, which started on 6 April 1999 and ends on 5 April 2000.

Chapter 23. The special tax rules for people aged 65 and over are dealt with in Chapter 25.

Which sort of taxpayer are you?

Knowing which sort of taxpayer you are is essential when you are looking at the best way to save, how much your pension contributions are going to cost you, whether you should switch from having a company car, and whether it is worth rearranging your finances in a way that will save you tax. The calculator on see pages 308–309 will help you to do the sums, but before you can fill it in, you need to know how much of your money:

- can be ignored before you even start to work out your income tax bill (see below)
- counts for income tax purposes (see pages 299–301)
- will fall into your personal tax-free band of income (see page 301)
- falls into each of the three bands, which are taxed at 10, 23 and 40 per cent (see pages 301–302)
- is tax-free savings (see page 302)
- is taxable savings (see pages 302–303).

How much tax you pay will also be affected by the tax deductions you will be able to take off your tax bill (see page 305). In addition, you can save money by making sure that you are getting all the tax subsidies in the form of tax relief that are available (see pages 307–308).

Money you can ignore

Not all the money you have coming in counts as income for the purposes of working out your income tax bill so you can ignore it when working out what type of taxpayer you are. There are two reasons for ignoring certain types of money: either it does not count as income; or it does count as income but it can be ignored because it is zero-rated – i.e. it is tax free. Money that does not count as income includes:

- personal presents and small gifts (under £250)
- money gifted to you under a covenant

- some maintenance payments you receive
- money you borrow
- money you make selling something that has increased in value (for example shares) – although you may have to pay capital gains tax (see page 303)
- large gifts of money and money you inherit – although you may have to pay inheritance tax
- betting winnings (unless you are in the betting business)
- lottery winnings
- Premium Bond prizes (see Chapter 20)
- grants for education or certain home improvements
- scholarships
- court awards (or out-of-court settlements) for compensation and damages
- money from an insurance claim (with the exception of income-protection insurance provided by your employer).

Money that does count as income but which is tax free so it does not need to be included in your tax calculations includes:

- part of the income from an annuity you have bought (for further details see Chapter 25)
- some social security benefits (check with your benefit office)
- up to a total of £30,000 of redundancy pay (see Chapter 6)
- strike and unemployment pay from a trade union
- some earnings from working abroad (ask your employer)
- the first £4,250 of rent you get if you let a room in your home – for example, you have a lodger to help pay the mortgage.

What counts for income tax purposes

Once you have ignored money that does not enter the income-tax equation, you are left with income that does count for tax purposes – but this does not mean that you will necessarily pay tax on all of it. The main sources of income that are subject to income tax are:

- **money paid to you by an employer**, which includes not just your basic earnings but also commission, overtime pay, bonuses, sick pay and so on. Your employer has to give you a P60 each year, and this tells you how much pay is liable to tax, how much you have paid in pension contributions (if applicable) and how much tax has been deducted at source through the PAYE (pay-as-you-earn) tax collection system (see pages 310–312). If you get pay in the form of tips, these are not included on your P60 and so you should keep your own records

- **perks from your job** such as a company car or private medical insurance, which – unless they are tax free – the tax system converts into money by giving them a 'taxable value'. Your employer has to give you a form P11D every year, and this lists the taxable values of all your perks, but you should always check that it is correct – ask your employer and/or tax office if you think it is wrong

- **freelance earnings**, whether you are full-time freelance or you do occasional freelance work alongside your main job. The whole of your freelance income may not be liable to tax because you can deduct expenses involved in carrying out the work – for example, telephone calls or travel expenses to meet clients. If you are full-time freelance, you will usually count as being a self-employed business and so will need to keep formal records of your freelance earnings and expenditure

- **earnings from self-employment**, which are not what you pay yourself but your taxable profits. These are worked out by adding up all your business income and deducting business expenditure and capital allowances. If you are self-employed, you will get a tax return to fill in; the guide that accompanies it explains what you can and cannot include. If you have not told your tax office that you are self-employed, you should do so, otherwise you may face tax penalties

- **pension income**, which includes state pensions, income you get from an employer's pension scheme and/or the income from an annuity you bought with the proceeds of a personal pension plan or AVC (additional voluntary contributions) scheme, whether free-standing or an employer's scheme

- **rent from letting property** not all of which is taxable because you can deduct expenses involved in letting the property, including interest you pay on a loan to buy the property you let. If you rent a room in your home and the rent you get is £4,250 or less,

all the rental income can be tax free under the rent-a-room scheme – ask your tax office for details
- **social security benefits**, although not all benefits are taxable – check with your benefit office.

Your personal tax-free band of income

Even after you have worked out how much of your income is liable to tax, you will still not have to pay tax on all of it because you have a personal tax-free band, which is made up of:

- your personal allowance of £4,335 in the 1999–2000 tax year
- the blind person's allowance of £1,380 if you are registered as blind with a local authority in England and Wales; or unable to perform any work for which eyesight is essential in Scotland and Northern Ireland (where there is no register)
- an extra age-related allowance if you (or your spouse, if applicable) reaches the age of 65 at any time during the tax year (for more details, see Chapter 25)
- pension payments you make to an employer's scheme or a personal pension. Note that employees who make personal pension payments should divide the amount of the payments by 0.77 to arrive at the figure to include in their personal tax-free band
- gifts to charity you make as an employee through the payroll giving scheme (to find out how other gifts to charity are dealt with, see pages 307–308)
- interest on loans to pay an inheritance tax bill or some business-related loans – ask your tax office for more details.

Tax bands

The amount of income on which you pay tax – i.e. your 'taxable income' – is the income liable to tax after subtracting your personal tax-free band. This is then sliced into tax bands, each one attracting a different rate of tax. This highest band that your income falls into determines the type of taxpayer you are. In the 1999–2000 tax year, you pay tax at:

- the lower rate of 10 per cent on the first £1,500 of your taxable income

- the basic rate of 23 per cent on the next slice of £26,500
- the higher rate of 40 per cent on any taxable income over £28,000.

Tax on savings

Once you know what type of taxpayer you are you can work out how much tax you have to pay on your income from savings and investments. However, as with your other income, you can ignore savings that are tax free. These include:

- income from savings and investments held in the tax-free wrapper of an ISA (individual savings account) – see Chapters 4, 20 and 21
- interest on a National Savings Ordinary account – see Chapter 4
- proceeds from fixed-interest and index-linked savings certificates – see Chapter 20
- proceeds from Save-As-You-Earn contracts (which are no longer available to buy)
- money from insurance-based savings plans – see Chapter 20
- money from investments in a PEP (personal equity plan) – now replaced by the ISA
- proceeds from a TESSA (tax-exempt special savings account) – now replaced by the ISA
- proceeds from children's bonus bonds – see Chapter 23.

All other income from savings and investments is taxable. If your non-savings income comes to more than £28,000, all your savings income is taxed at the higher rate of savings tax, which is 40 per cent. However, if your non-savings income plus your taxable income from savings:

- comes to less than £28,000, your savings income is taxed at the lower rate of savings tax, which is 20 per cent. With the exception of savings income from National Savings★ and British government stocks (see Chapter 21), the tax you have to pay has already been deducted from the income before you get it
- straddles the £28,000 limit when added to your other income, the part below the limit is taxed at 20 per cent and the part over the limit at 40 per cent.

The 'How much tax on savings?' calculator on page 304 will help you to work out the tax bill on your income from savings. When filling it in, remember to ignore all tax-free savings. You will also need to know the before-tax amount of your savings that are taxable. If you know only the after-tax amount of interest, divide it by 0.8. The before-tax amount of share dividends and distributions from unit trust and OEICs (see Chapter 21) will be shown on the voucher you receive telling you how much income you have been paid.

Warning

If you are a lower-rate taxpayer and you have taxable savings income, you will still have to pay savings tax at 20 per cent even though your other income may be taxed at 10 per cent, so you should consider switching to tax-free savings, see opposite.

The other tax on savings

As well as paying tax on the income you get from savings and investments, you may also have to pay capital gains tax when you sell investments like shares, unit trusts and OEICs (see Chapter 21) held outside the tax-free wrapper of an ISA (individual savings account). The capital gain is the difference between the price you paid and the price at which you sold, less any costs (such as share-dealing commission) involved in buying and selling. If your total gains in the 1999–2000 tax year come to more than £7,100, you have to pay tax; otherwise, your gains are tax free. The rate of tax you have to pay is decided by adding the gains to your other income and income from savings. As with tax on savings income, if the total is less than £28,000, the gain is taxed at 20 per cent; if it is more, the gain is taxed at 40 per cent. If the gain straddles the £28,000 limit, the part below the limit is taxed at 20 per cent and the part above the limit at 40 per cent. If you have gains of over £7,100, there are ways in which you can reduce them, depending on when you bought the investment – you can ask your tax office for details.

How much tax on savings?

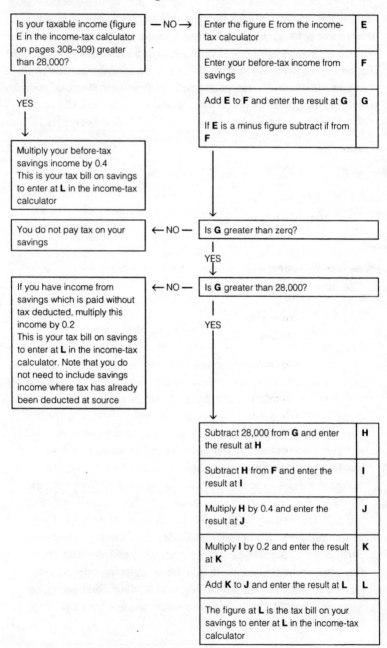

Tax deductions

The tax bands into which your income falls will determine both the amount of tax you pay on your main income and your income from savings. However, this may not be your final tax bill if you are able to knock off one of the following tax deductions in the form of personal allowances, which are fixed at the same rate for all types of taxpayer. In the 1999–2000 tax year, the value of the allowances given below is £197 (10 per cent of £1,970). You get the deduction provided that you tell your tax office that you want to claim the:

- **married couple's allowance** but note that if you share the allowance with your spouse or marry after 5 May, you get a lower deduction (see Chapter 22)
- **additional personal allowance** which you can claim if you are responsible for a child *and* are single, separated or married and your spouse is incapacitated (see Chapters 22 and 23)
- **widow's bereavement allowance** – note that a widow can claim this allowance for the tax year in which her husband dies and – unless she remarries – in the next tax year as well
- **maintenance deduction** because you are legally required to make maintenance payments to an ex-husband or ex-wife.

All the allowances listed above are due to be abolished from 6 April 2000. A new allowance for people who are responsible for children (the children's tax credit) – a proposed tax deduction of up to £416 – will replace the abolished allowances from 6 April 2001. Only couples who are entitled to age-related allowances on 5 April 2000 will continue to get a tax concession from marriage or for maintenance payments (see Chapter 25).

Tip

If you are entitled to an allowance, you can make sure you get it simply by phoning your tax office. If you have been entitled to an allowance for several years but you have not informed your tax office, you can ask for the deduction to be taken account of in your tax bills from the earlier years because it can be back-dated for up to six tax years.

Why income is not what it seems

Charlotte and Florence each made £20,000 in the 1999–2000 tax year but Florence pays less tax. This is why:	Charlotte	Florence
Income to ignore		
£200 a month from her lodger		£2,400
Premium Bond prize		£500
interest on savings in a cash mini-ISA		£100
What counts for income tax purposes		
earnings	£19,000	£17,000
taxable value of company car	£4,050	£0
freelance income	£850	£0
Income liable for tax	**£23,900**	**£17,000**
Personal tax-free band of income		
personal allowance	£4,335	£4,335
pension contributions of 4% of earnings	£0	£680
£10 a month payroll giving	£0	£120
Total tax-free band	**£4,335**	**£5,135**
Taxable income		
income liable for tax minus personal tax-free band	**£19,565**	**£11,865**
What sort of taxpayer?		
Both Charlotte and Florence are basic-rate taxpayers because their taxable income is less than £28,000.		
How much lower-rate tax?		
10% tax on the first £1,500	£150	£150
How much basic-rate tax?		
23% tax on taxable income minus the lower-rate band of £1,500	£4,154.95	£2,383.95
How much higher-rate tax?		
Charlotte and Florence do not pay higher-rate tax		
Tax bill on income		
lower-rate tax plus basic-rate tax	**£4,304.95**	**£2,533.95**
Tax on savings		
20% savings tax on £150 of building society interest	£30	
	£4,334.95	**£2,533.95**
Tax deductions		
half-share of married couple's allowance	£98.50	
Total tax bill	**£4,236.45**	**£2,533.95**

Tax subsidies

Tax subsidies do not have a direct effect on your tax bill, however they do help you to save money on certain payments. The tax subsidy is fixed at the same rate for all taxpayers and is given in the form of tax relief at source, which means that you make lower payments to whoever you are paying. Tax subsidies given at source include those on:

- payments into a personal pension plan or free-standing additional voluntary contribution (FSAVC) scheme made by employees (see Chapter 8); higher-rate taxpayers can claim extra relief
- interest on up to £30,000 of your mortgage, but this subsidy is being withdrawn from 6 April 2000 (see Chapter 10)
- study and examination fees for work-related vocational training – the person running a training course will know if the fees qualify for a tax subsidy. This subsidy will be replaced by the government's proposed 'individual learning accounts' from 6 April 2000.

Tax subsidies on donations to charity

Certain payments you make to charity also attract a tax subsidy and include donations through:

- **a covenant** which is capable of lasting longer than three years
- **the Gift Aid scheme**, where you make a single donation of at least £250 to the charity of your choice
- **the Millennium Gift Aid scheme**, where you make a donation of at least £100 (either as a lump sum or in instalments) before 31 December 2000 to a charity that works to support education and anti-poverty projects in the world's poorest countries; and also those working to relieve the Kosovo crisis.

In all these cases, if you are a basic-rate taxpayer, you do not get the subsidy – the charity receives it in the form of the tax you have paid on the income you used to make the donation. For example, if you make a donation of £100 out of taxed income, the before-tax amount would be just under £130 (i.e. £100 'grossed up' by dividing by 0.77) so the charity gets an extra £30 from the Inland Revenue.

> **Tip**
>
> Covenant payments to charity also affect how much age-related allowances you get if you (or your spouse) is over 65. For more details, see Chapter 25.

Note that if you do not pay tax or you pay it at the lower rate of 10 per cent, you should not make donations to charity by covenant because you may face a tax bill if you do.

However, if you are a higher-rate taxpayer, you get a subsidy of 17 per cent of the before-tax amount of the donation. The subsidy is given by subtracting 23 per cent of the before-tax amount of the donation from your tax bill. To calculate this, divide the amount you pay the charity by 0.77 then multiply the result by 0.23.

Income-tax calculator	
Step 1: Calculate your income for tax purposes	
Ignoring all the income that does not count (see page 301) and income from savings (see pages 302–304) add up all your income that *does* count for tax purposes (see pages 299–301)	A
If you are an employee, add up the taxable value of fringe benefits from your P11D (see page 300)	B
Add A to B and enter the result at C	C
Step 2: Calculate your personal tax-free band	
Add up your personal allowances and other payments you can include in your tax-free band (see page 301)	D
Step 3: Work out your taxable income	
To arrive at your taxable income, subtract D from C and enter the result at E	E
Step 4: What sort of taxpayer are you? The figure at E is your taxable income before savings. If E is zero or a minus figure, you are a non-taxpayer – go to Step 8 If E is above zero but less than £1,500, you are a lower-rate taxpayer If E is more than £1,500 but less than £26,500, you are a basic-rate taxpayer If E is more than £28,000, you are a higher-rate taxpayer.	

Step 5: How much lower-rate tax?	
If E is more than £1,500, enter £150 at F If E is less than £1,500, multiply E by 0.1 and enter the result at F then go to Step 8	F
Step 6: How much basic-rate tax?	
Subtract £1,500 from E and enter the result at G	G
If G is more than £26,500, enter £6,095 at H then go to Step 7 If G is less than £26,500, multiply G by 0.23 and enter the result at H then go to Step 8	H
Step 7: How much higher-rate tax?	
Subtract £26,500 from G and enter the result at I	I
Multiply I by 0.4 and enter the result at J	J
Step 8: Calculate your tax bill before deductions	
Add together any figures at F, H and J and enter the result at K If you are a non-taxpayer (see Step 4), enter zero	K
Step 9: Add tax on savings	
Enter the tax bill on your savings income from 'How much tax on savings' (see page 304)	L
Add L to K and enter the result at M	M
Step 10: Subtract your tax deductions	
Add up all the tax deductions you can make (see page 305) If you are a higher-rate taxpayer, include the subsidy for covenant or gift aid payments to charity (see page 307–308)	N
Subtract M from N and enter the result at O	O
The figure at O is your **total tax bill** If O is zero or a minus, you do not pay tax on any of your income.	

Have you paid the right amount of tax?

Once you know what your tax bill should be, you need to find out
if you have paid the right amount. If you are sent a tax return, by
filling it in you automatically get the chance to check that you are
paying the right amount of tax and to correct any under- or overpayments. However, if you do not receive a tax return (which is
likely if you are an employee or receive pension income and you do
not pay tax at the higher rate), you need to check that you are paying
the right amount of tax yourself.

To do this, you need to add up all the tax you have already paid during the tax year. Tax that has been deducted from your earnings (or pension) is shown on your P60 – a kind of annual payslip, which your employer (or pension provider) has to give you each year in May (the P60 you receive in May 2000 will show the tax you paid for the 1999–2000 tax year). Tax that has been deducted at source from savings income will be shown on annual interest certificates and vouchers, which the savings institution and/or investment company should send you.

Is your tax code wrong?

The system used to collect tax on a regular basis from earnings and pensions is called the PAYE (pay-as-you-earn) system. Your tax office gives your employer (or pension provider) a tax code, which is used to work out how much tax should be deducted every pay day.

Your tax code takes account of any tax allowances you are entitled to and also extra income you get, both in the form of the taxable values given to perks from your job and income from other sources (such as freelance income) that has not yet been taxed. If your code is wrong, you will not pay the right amount of tax. If you are sent a Coding Notice, you can check what is included in your code; if not, contact your tax office.

Too much tax

If the total amount of tax that you have already paid is about the same as the tax bill you have calculated, your tax code is right. If the tax bill you have calculated is lower than the tax you have paid, it is wrong. Since your tax code is only as good as the information given to your tax office, it may mean that your tax office does not know that:

- you are **entitled to a tax allowance** – you have married or had a baby, for example
- you have **stopped receiving a perk** – for example, you have given up your company car (see Chapter 14)
- you **no longer have untaxed income** – you have given up freelancing, for example, or you no longer have income from letting a property.

> **Tip**
>
> If your circumstances have changed in a way that affects your tax bill, let your tax office know so that the necessary adjustments to your tax code can be made. You can do this by phone, and your tax code can be changed straightaway. Any change will be back-dated to the month when the change occurred so you may get a rebate.

Too little tax

If the tax bill you have calculated is higher than the tax you have paid, the probable reason is that your tax office does not know that you have:

- **stopped being entitled to a tax allowance** – you have divorced, for example
- **started receiving untaxed income** from self-employment, for example
- **a new perk** – despite the fact that your employer is supposed to inform the Inland Revenue about perks provided for employees, you cannot be certain that it has done so (although it can be fined if it does not).

> **Warning**
>
> You must tell your tax office about changes in your circumstances that increase your tax bill. If you do not, and you pay less tax than you are required to, you face penalties and interest on the unpaid tax. You have until 5 October following the end of the tax year in which you received the extra income (5 October 2000 for new income in the 1999–2000 tax year) to tell your tax office but if you wait until then, you are more likely to have to pay the tax due in a lump sum rather than in instalments through your tax code.

How to contact your tax office

If you need to contact your tax office about an allowance to which you are now entitled or about income that should be taxed, you will find the correct address and a telephone number on any communication you have had from it. If you have not had dealings with your tax office in the past, ask your employer or pension provider. If you are self-employed, your tax office is usually the one nearest to your place of business. Wherever your tax office is, when you contact it, you will need to quote your tax reference or, failing that, your National Insurance number.

Chapter 18

How to budget

Drawing up a budget is about taking stock of your financial position and will help you to identify the changes you need to make to your financial arrangements. Budgeting is not just for people whose finances are out of control; it is also a useful exercise if you are solvent but you want to make good use of savings, put controls on your spending or you want to rearrange your spending to accommodate new plans or a change in your personal circumstances.

This chapter takes you through the budgeting process step by step, tells you how to analyse your financial position and gives practical advice on rearranging your finances to meet spending priorities. If you already have a clear idea of what you spend your money on and how you are going to cope with future spending plans but you would like to find a way of smoothing dips in your current account, you may find it useful to draw up a bill-paying budget (see Chapter 11).

Step 1: make a list

The essential first step in drawing up a budget is to make a list of everything you spend money on and also of what you need or would like to spend money on. Writing everything down helps to focus your mind and also prevents you from forgetting things. The more detailed the list, the more useful it will be, and it can be helpful to break it down into the different chunks, such as:

- household costs
- living expenses
- travel
- car

- personal spending
- leisure
- Christmas and birthdays
- savings
- children
- financial costs
- cash spending.

Tip

When dividing up your spending, make sure it reflects your spending patterns. You should count your weekly shop at the supermarket as one item, even though it includes things from a variety of different categories – for example food, household basics, such as light bulbs and cleaning materials, and personal spending, such as toiletries and magazines. If you try to separate these out, you will make the task a lot harder (as it will involve poring over a year's worth of supermarket receipts). Similarly, you will make life easier if you write down all the things you buy with cash under one heading of cash spending.

Step 2: establish your priorities

As well as breaking up your list into sections, you should divide your spending into two categories:

- **essential**, which covers the unavoidable and the necessary, such as your rent or mortgage, your bills, season ticket for getting to work, food, life insurance and so on
- **desirable**, which covers spending that is not *strictly* necessary (and at a push, you could do without) but which you regard as essential to your well being.

Step 3: collect data

You need to collect hard financial data before you can complete the next step. Depending on why you are drawing up a budget, this will be a combination of actual past spending and educated guesses at future spending.

If you can lay your hands on a year's worth of bank statements, fully completed cheque-book stubs, credit-, shop-card and other household bills, you already have a lot of the data you need to provide a detailed breakdown of your finances. If your records are less comprehensive, you may still be able to get a reasonable idea of where your money goes just from your bank statements and credit-card bills.

If you do not have any records or if you are drawing up a budget to see if you can afford something in particular – a house or a car, for example – you will have to estimate the figures.

Tip

You do not need to write down everything you pay for with cash if you know how much you withdraw each month (from your bank statement). If you want to know what you spend it on because you think you should cut back on cash spending, try using your credit or debit card instead for anything costing more than £10. Using a card will give you a ready-made record of where you spent your money. The alternative is to write down everything you spend in a little note book but this requires cast-iron discipline and may not be a very practical solution.

Step 4: enter the figures

Once you have collected all your data together, you can start to enter the figures against the items on your list. You will need two columns:

- **monthly** in which you should enter figures for items where you know the monthly cost such as your rent or monthly mortgage. If you want to set limits on your spending on certain items, enter the maximum you want to spend each month
- **yearly** for irregular spending on items such as clothes, holidays, and quarterly bills where you need to estimate how much you spend each year. You then divide the yearly figure by 12 and enter it under the monthly column (see example overleaf).

Once you have entered all the figures, add up those in each of the monthly columns for essential and desirable spending. This has the effect of smoothing your spending over the year to give you an average monthly spending figure for each of the categories. These can then be entered in the 'Personal budget calculator' below.

Tip

If you have a computer and spreadsheet software, you will save time if you enter your figures on a spreadsheet. This will also help if you need to adjust the figures or if you want to do 'what if?' calculations to see the effect of making changes to your budget.

Step 5: work out your average monthly income

Once you have worked out your average monthly spending, you need to work out your average monthly income. To do this:

- add up all sources of regular monthly income
- if you get weekly income (such as child benefit or state pension), multiply the weekly amount by 52 and divide by 12.
- add income you get in irregular amounts to lump sums you withdraw from savings and divide by 12.

The total of all these figures is your average monthly income, which you should enter in the 'Personal budget calculator' below.

Personal budget calculator	
Enter your average monthly income	A
Enter your average monthly spend on essentials	B
Subtract B from A and enter the result at C	C
The figure at C is what you have left after meeting essentials	
Enter your average monthly spend on desirables	D
Subtract D from C and enter the result at E	E
If **E** is zero or a plus figure, your desirable spending is covered. If **E** is a minus figure, your desirable spending is *not* covered	

Example of part of a budget breakdown

Household	Essential spending		Desirable spending	
	Yearly	Monthly	Yearly	Monthly
Mortgage		£250		
Council tax	£900	£75		
Water	£200	£17		
Electricity	£325	£27		
Gas	£240	£20		
Telephone	£300	£25		
Buildings insurance		£32		
Contents insurance		£23		
Boiler service	£60	£5		
Decorating			£600	£50
Gardening			£300	£25
Things for house			£240	£20
Supermarket		£200		
TV licence	£101	£9		
Sub-total		**£683**		**£95**
Personal				
Work clothes	£600	£50		
Other clothes			£600	£50
Going out				£200
CDs				£15
Books				£15
Gym		£33		
Holidays/savings				£100
Sub-total		**£83**		**£380**
Cash spending				
Video rental				£12
Newspapers				£15
Magazines				£10
Drinks				£60
Dry cleaning		£10		
Miscellaneous				£20
Sub-total		**£10**		**£117**

Analysing the results of your budget calculations

START HERE

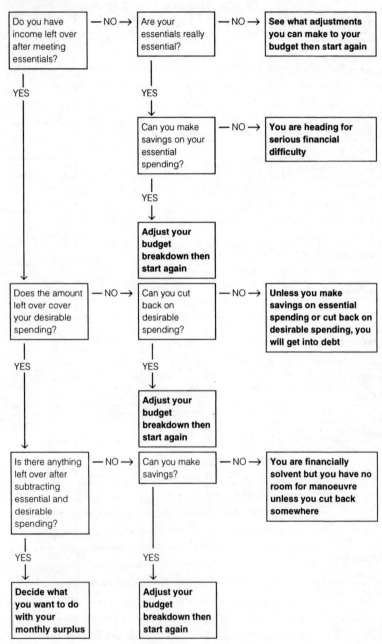

Chapter 19

Getting problems sorted out

It is not often that you will meet someone who has never had a problem with a financial institution – even if it is only a small gripe about a bank, building society, credit-card company, insurer, mortgage lender, tax office or pension provider. But whether the problem is large or small, there are always steps you can take to get the problem sorted out. And if the financial institution you are dealing with will not help, an independent referee often can.

This chapter looks at what you can do to make sure that your problem is dealt with as effectively as possible and explains, step by step, how to get an unresolved problem sorted out by taking your complaint further. If you think that you have been unfairly turned down for a loan or credit card, turn to Chapter 15; if you are worried about your own problems with your finances, see Chapter 16.

How to complain

If you have a problem with a financial institution, always try to get it sorted out at a local level first, either in person, by phone or by letter. Depending on the financial problem in question, your first port of call might be your bank branch, the person who sold you the insurance policy or investment, or you might make a telephone call to the customer enquiry line of a credit-card issuer or insurance company.

If this initial approach fails to get the problem sorted out, ask for details of any internal complaints procedure so that you know who to contact next. Following the internal complaints procedure is important if you need to take your complaint yet further (see pages

320–323). This is because most of the schemes available to help with unresolved problems make it a condition that you exhaust the formal complaints procedure before you are able to make use of their services.

You are likely to find that your complaint will be more successful if you act quickly and complain while the details are still fresh in your mind. It will also help if you:

- **complain in writing** with a clear explanation of what the problem is and what you want done about it
- **provide evidence** (credit-card receipts or photographs of damage for an insurance claim, for example) to back up your complaint
- **give a deadline** by when you expect a reply to your letter
- **chase letters with a phone call** if you do not get a reply by your stated deadline
- **keep records** of any communication to do with your complaint, including copies of all letters and, if you phone, a note of the name of the person you spoke to in addition to the time and date of your call
- **refer your complaint to a higher level** if you do not feel you are getting anywhere
- **do not make threats** that you do not mean to stick to
- **take the matter further** if you reach deadlock with the institution concerned (see below) – do not accept any offer that may be made if you plan to do this.

Taking the matter further

If you have reached deadlock and have exhausted the internal complaints procedure, you can take your problem to the ombudsman or arbitration scheme to which the institution belongs. Ombudsman schemes do not cost anything and they are there to help consumers by reaching an independent resolution of unresolved complaints.

As part of the streamlining of the regulation of the financial services industry, it has been proposed that all complaints and redress procedures should be brought under the authority of one single financial services ombudsman scheme, which is envisaged as a 'one-stop shop' for unresolved complaints. However, until that is set up (which may not be until late 1999 at the very earliest), who you should turn to for help depends on what your complaint is about and, to a certain extent, who sold the product/service to you.

Problems with investments

If your complaint is about an investment (which includes personal pensions and endowment policies sold with a mortgage – but not the mortgage itself) or about financial advice relating to an investment that is regulated by the Financial Services Act, the institution should tell you which ombudsman scheme it belongs to, otherwise contact the Financial Services Authority★ public enquiries helpline; until the Financial Services Ombudsman Scheme comes into being it will point you in the direction of:

- **the Personal Investment Authority (PIA) Ombudsman**,★ who deals with complaints about investment-type insurance, personal pensions and other long-term investments. Insurers which belong to this scheme can choose to join a voluntary part of it, so that the ombudsman can deal with complaints about other long-term insurance (ones that are not regulated by the Financial Services Act). The compulsory part currently has a limit on awards of £100,000 (plus up to £1,500 for distress and inconvenience). The voluntary part also has a limit of £100,000 but no restrictions on the awards for distress and inconvenience. You must make your complaint within six months of reaching deadlock with your insurer
- **the Investment Ombudsman**,★ who handles complaints about investments that are not covered by the PIA Ombudsman – these relate mostly to general financial advice and portfolio management. This ombudsman can make binding awards of up to £100,000 (plus up to £1,500 for distress and inconvenience). You must make your complaint within three years of reaching deadlock.

Problems with other financial products

If your complaint is about a financial product that is not covered by the Financial Services Act, your first point of contact should be one of the ombudsman schemes as shown in the following table and described below. These schemes not only deal with. unresolved complaints within their terms of reference but also act as clearing houses for complaints that are outside them. They will pass your complaint on to a scheme that will be able to help. These secondary sources of help are also set out in the table below.

Where to go for help

Problem	Who to approach first	Who you may be referred to
banking services current accounts credit cards	Banking Ombudsman Building Societies Ombudsman	
employer's pensions	Occupational Pensions Advisory Service	Pensions Ombudsman
insurance	Insurance Ombudsman's Bureau	Personal Insurance Arbitration Service PIA Ombudsman
loans	Banking Ombudsman Building Societies Ombudsman	Finance and Leasing Association Arbitration scheme Office of Fair Trading
mortgages	Banking Ombudsman Building Societies Ombudsman	The Mortgage Code Arbitration Scheme
personal pensions	PIA Ombudsman	
tax and national insurance	Inland Revenue Adjudicator	

- **the Banking Ombudsman***, who deals with complaints about all types of banking services except those about banks' general policies or lending decisions. The ombudsman can make awards of up to £100,000 that are binding on the bank. You must bring a complaint to the ombudsman within six years of identifying the problem and within six months of reaching deadlock with the bank concerned
- **the Building Society Ombudsman***, who covers most services offered by building societies. Like the banking scheme, it does not cover policy or lending decisions and it will not cover complaints about membership rights – such as your eligibility for a payout if the building society converts to a bank, for example. Awards can

be up to £100,000 but they are not binding – although it is extremely rare for societies to reject the ombudsman's decision. Complaints must be made within six months of your discovering the problem, excluding the time taken by your society to investigate your complaint

- **the Insurance Ombudsman's Bureau (IOB),** ★ to which most general insurers belong, deals with complaints about general insurance (such as car, house, travel and loan payment protection insurance). The Insurance Ombudsman's Bureau can make awards of up to £100,000 (£20,000 a year for awards relating to income-protection insurance), which are binding on the company. You must bring a complaint within six months of reaching deadlock.

If you are not happy with the decision of any of these schemes, you can take the matter to court.

Going to court

If the company at the centre of your financial complaint is not a member of an ombudsman or an arbitration scheme or if your complaint is outside their terms of reference, your other option is to pursue your complaint through the courts.

If your claim is for £5,000 or less (£1,000 in Northern Ireland; £750 in Scotland), you can use the small claims arbitration procedure. This is part of the county court (sheriff's court in Scotland), but the proceedings are informal and not heard in open court. You can represent yourself and you do not need to pay a lawyer. You can get details of court fees from your county court or sheriff's court.

To start a small claims action, you fill in a summons form – which is available from the court office together with an information booklet – giving details of:

- your name and address
- the other side's name and address
- a brief statement of your case.

You take or post your completed form to your local county or sheriff's court and pay the fee. The court then serves the summons and tells you what to do next. If you lose your case, the most you are likely to have to pay is the other side's expenses for attending the hearing (unless, for example, the court thinks that you caused unnecessary costs by making an unreasonable claim or by not attending the hearing).

If your claim is for more than £5,000, you cannot use the small claims procedure, and should take legal advice on whether you should pursue a court action, since this could be expensive if you lose. If this happens, you could have to pay your opponent's legal costs as well as your own so opt for this only as a last resort.

Chapter 20

How to build up savings

If you find that you have a surplus at the end of the month – whether it is every month or only every now and then – what you do with it will depend on how far you have got with your other financial plans. If you have not yet sorted out the basics by clearing expensive debts, building up an emergency fund, making other contingency plans and paying into a pension, go back to Chapter 1. If, on the other hand, you have taken care of all that, you can spend your surplus cash, pay more into your pension (see Chapter 8), use it to reduce your mortgage (see Chapter 10) or start to build up savings.

This chapter looks at suitable homes for small amounts of surplus cash and explains the decision-making process you need to go through to find the savings product which will suit you best both in terms of the amount of money you can save and your saving habits. Detailed descriptions of suitable vehicles for saving begin on page 329. Savings accounts which are suitable for an emergency fund are dealt with in Chapter 4. If you are more interested in the best ways of saving a lump sum and you have at least £1,000 to invest, go to Chapter 21. Savings for children are discussed in Chapter 23, and those particularly suited to older people are dealt with in Chapter 25.

How to build up savings

Saving involves setting aside money out of your regular income in order to build up a lump sum (or, in the case of paying off debts, to gradually reduce a lump sum to zero). If you have no particular plans for the lump sum that your savings will build up – and/or you plan to save as and when you can – you will increase the options open to you if you save in an ordinary savings account (see Chapter 4). Once you have at least £1,000 built up, you can think about investing it (see Chapter 21). This method of saving also has the advantage that investing a lump sum tends to be better value (as the charges involved tend to be lower) than saving small amounts on a regular basis.

However, regular saving is ideally suited to saving up for something specific, where you know how much money you require and when in the future you will need to it. Examples include saving up for:

- next year's summer holiday
- replacing your car in three years' time
- the deposit for a flat
- giving up work for a year to go travelling
- taking unpaid leave when your baby is born
- paying for your children's higher education.

If you have a clear idea of what you are saving for, you can then work out how much you should save each month to achieve the required lump sum at the appropriate time (the calculator below will help you). To do this you need to take account of the interest rate or rate of return you will get on your investment and the possible impact of inflation (currently around 2.5 per cent) on whatever you are saving for. If the amount of the lump sum you need in the future

How to convert a future lump sum into monthly savings	
Enter the interest rate or annual rate of return you expect to get on your savings after tax	A
If the cost of whatever you are saving for will rise in the future, enter your assumed inflation rate; enter zero if the cost will not rise	B
Subtract B from A' and enter the result at C	C
The figure at C is the rate of return you should assume	
Enter the current cost of whatever you are saving for	D
Enter the size of lump sum that savings of £10 a month (for the period until when you need the savings) gets you from the table on opposite page assuming the rate of return calculated at C	E
Divide D by E and enter the result at F	F
Multiply F by 10 and enter the result at G	G
The figure at G is the amount you need to save each month.	

The lump sum that savings of £10 a month gets you

Value of savings at the end of:	if the rate of return is:																				
	0%	0.5%	1%	1.5%	2%	2.5%	3%	3.5%	4%	4.5%	5%	5.5%	6%	6.5%	7%	7.5%	8%	8.5%	9%	9.5%	10%
Year 1	£120	£120	£121	£121	£121	£122	£122	£122	£123	£123	£123	£124	£124	£124	£125	£125	£125	£126	£126	£127	£127
Year 2	£240	£241	£243	£244	£245	£246	£248	£249	£250	£251	£253	£254	£255	£257	£258	£259	£261	£262	£263	£266	£266
Year 3	£360	£363	£366	£368	£371	£374	£377	£380	£383	£386	£389	£392	£395	£398	£401	£404	£407	£410	£413	£419	£419
Year 4	£480	£485	£490	£495	£500	£505	£510	£515	£521	£526	£531	£537	£542	£548	£553	£559	£565	£570	£576	£586	£588
Year 5	£600	£608	£615	£623	£631	£639	£648	£656	£664	£673	£681	£690	£699	£708	£717	£726	£735	£745	£754	£768	£774
Year 6	£720	£731	£742	£754	£765	£777	£789	£801	£813	£826	£839	£852	£865	£878	£892	£905	£919	£934	£948	£969	£978
Year 7	£840	£855	£870	£886	£902	£918	£935	£951	£969	£986	£1,004	£1,022	£1,041	£1,059	£1,079	£1,098	£1,118	£1,139	£1,159	£1,188	£1,202
Year 8	£960	£980	£1,000	£1,020	£1,041	£1,063	£1,085	£1,107	£1,130	£1,153	£1,177	£1,202	£1,227	£1,253	£1,279	£1,306	£1,333	£1,361	£1,390	£1,428	£1,449
Year 9	£1,080	£1,105	£1,130	£1,156	£1,183	£1,211	£1,239	£1,268	£1,298	£1,328	£1,360	£1,392	£1,425	£1,458	£1,493	£1,529	£1,565	£1,602	£1,641	£1,691	£1,721
Year 10	£1,200	£1,231	£1,262	£1,295	£1,328	£1,363	£1,398	£1,435	£1,472	£1,511	£1,551	£1,592	£1,634	£1,677	£1,722	£1,768	£1,816	£1,864	£1,915	£1,978	£2,019
Year 11	£1,320	£1,357	£1,396	£1,435	£1,476	£1,518	£1,562	£1,607	£1,654	£1,702	£1,752	£1,803	£1,856	£1,911	£1,967	£2,026	£2,086	£2,148	£2,213	£2,293	£2,348
Year 12	£1,440	£1,484	£1,530	£1,578	£1,627	£1,678	£1,731	£1,786	£1,843	£1,902	£1,963	£2,026	£2,091	£2,159	£2,230	£2,303	£2,378	£2,457	£2,538	£2,638	£2,709
Year 13	£1,560	£1,612	£1,666	£1,722	£1,781	£1,842	£1,905	£1,971	£2,039	£2,110	£2,184	£2,261	£2,341	£2,424	£2,511	£2,600	£2,694	£2,791	£2,892	£3,016	£3,107
Year 14	£1,680	£1,740	£1,803	£1,869	£1,938	£2,009	£2,084	£2,162	£2,243	£2,328	£2,417	£2,509	£2,605	£2,706	£2,811	£2,920	£3,035	£3,154	£3,279	£3,430	£3,545
Year 15	£1,800	£1,869	£1,942	£2,018	£2,098	£2,181	£2,268	£2,360	£2,456	£2,556	£2,661	£2,771	£2,886	£3,006	£3,132	£3,264	£3,403	£3,548	£3,700	£3,883	£4,026
Year 16	£1,920	£1,999	£2,082	£2,169	£2,261	£2,357	£2,458	£2,565	£2,676	£2,794	£2,917	£3,047	£3,183	£3,326	£3,476	£3,634	£3,801	£3,975	£4,159	£4,379	£4,555
Year 17	£2,040	£2,129	£2,224	£2,323	£2,428	£2,538	£2,654	£2,777	£2,906	£3,042	£3,186	£3,338	£3,498	£3,666	£3,844	£4,032	£4,230	£4,439	£4,659	£4,922	£5,137
Year 18	£2,160	£2,260	£2,367	£2,479	£2,597	£2,723	£2,856	£2,996	£3,145	£3,302	£3,469	£3,645	£3,831	£4,029	£4,238	£4,459	£4,694	£4,942	£5,205	£5,517	£5,778
Year 19	£2,280	£2,392	£2,511	£2,637	£2,771	£2,913	£3,063	£3,223	£3,393	£3,574	£3,765	£3,969	£4,185	£4,415	£4,659	£4,919	£5,194	£5,487	£5,799	£6,168	£6,482
Year 20	£2,400	£2,524	£2,657	£2,797	£2,947	£3,107	£3,277	£3,459	£3,652	£3,858	£4,077	£4,311	£4,560	£4,826	£5,110	£5,413	£5,735	£6,080	£6,447	£6,881	£7,257

will not rise – you are building up a lump sum to pay off the mortgage, for example – you do not need to worry about inflation.

If you have already decided how much you are going to save, you can use the table opposite to work out how big a lump sum your proposed monthly savings will get you. To do this:

- find the lump sum in the table which best matches the interest rate you expect to get and the number of years you plan to save for
- divide the monthly amount you propose to save by 10
- multiply the result by the lump-sum figure from the table.

Deciding how to save

Once you have worked out what you are going to do with your savings and how much you are going to save, you need to identify which savings product will provide the most suitable home for your savings. The route map overleaf gives an overview of the decision-making process and the questions you will need to answer. The importance of the questions is explained in more detail below.

Can you leave the money you save untouched?

If there is any chance that you will need to call on the money you are setting aside, you need quick access to your savings and should look at the savings accounts described in Chapter 4. You certainly should not commit yourself to saving a regular amount each month because you will not get the access to your cash that you need. However, if you are saving up for something specific, not being able to touch your savings could be useful.

Can you commit yourself to saving on a regular basis?

Aiming to save a fixed amount each month is good discipline, but any kind of regular-savings product will penalise you if you do not commit yourself for the length of time specified for the product. If you want the discipline but need flexibility, consider setting up a standing order (see Chapter 2) to an ordinary savings account (see Chapter 4) which you can cancel without penalty if you find that you cannot keep your savings going.

How should you build up your savings?

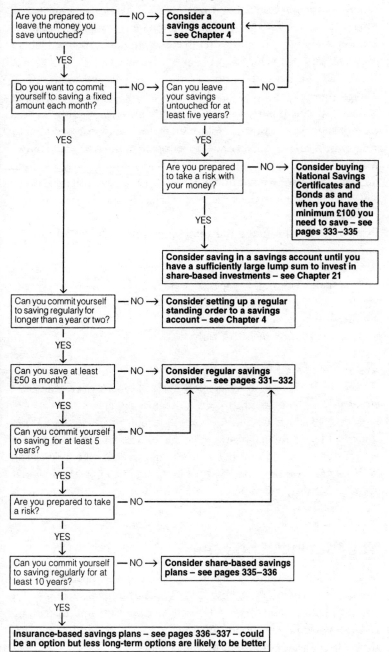

How long can you save for?

Regular-savings accounts (see pages 331–332) usually require you to commit to saving for two years, while insurance-based savings plans (see pages 336–337) require you to keep saving for at least ten. These plans are very bad value if you stop paying into them, and are best avoided if there is any possibility that you will not be able to keep your savings going. With share-based plans (see pages 335–336) no fixed period is specified, but you need to keep your savings going for five years or so to get a reasonable return on them. Committing yourself to long-term savings is not a good idea if you are unsure what the future will hold or if you know that you will face a drop in your monthly surplus – you plan to buy a home, for example, or you will need every penny you have got to meet the cost of bringing up children.

How long can you leave the lump sum you have saved tied up?

Some forms of saving such as Savings Certificates and Bonds offered by National Savings* (see pages 333–335) do not require a commitment to save a regular amount each month, but to get the best return you need to keep your savings tied up; you risk a lower return if you need to get your money back early.

Are you prepared to take a risk?

If you are not prepared to get less back than you have paid in – either because you failed to keep up regular savings or the value of your savings fluctuates – you should avoid the share-based and insurance-based savings plans which carry these risks. If you cannot commit to regular saving but you are prepared to take a risk with your money, consider building up a lump sum in an ordinary savings account and then investing the lump sum in share-based investments (see Chapter 21).

Your savings choices

Which savings product you choose will basically depend on the amount you have to save, how long you can tie up your money for and how much risk you are prepared to take. But note that if you can get a better return on your savings without restrictions, you should choose the better return.

If you do not want to take a risk with your money, the main choices open to you are:

- ordinary savings accounts (see Chapter 4)
- regular savings accounts (see below)
- Fixed-Interest Savings Certificates (see pages 332–333)
- Index-Linked Savings Certificates (see pages 333–334)
- Capital Bonds (see page 334)
- Premium Bonds (see page 335).

If you are prepared to take a risk with your savings but you do not have at least £1,000 which you could invest as a lump sum (see Chapter 21), your choices are:

- share-based savings plans (see pages 335–336)
- insurance-based savings plans (see pages 336–337).

Tax point

Most of the types of savings products described in this chapter are available within the tax-free wrapper of an individual savings account (ISA). This means that you do not have to pay tax on the money you make on your savings. However, because of this tax-free status, the amounts you can save are limited. In the 1999–2000 tax year, the overall limit is £7,000, which can either be used entirely for share-based savings or split between share-based savings, cash savings (up to a maximum of £3,000), and insurance-based savings (up to a maximum of £1,000). In the 2000–01 tax year, the limits will be lower: £5,000 overall and, within this overall limit, a maximum of £1,000 for cash and £1,000 for insurance-based savings (see table on page 347).

Regular savings accounts

Regular savings accounts from banks and building societies require you to save every or most months (in some cases for a fixed number of years). Your commitment to save regularly is typically rewarded with a higher rate of interest than you would get from an account without restrictions and bonus interest payments worked out as a percentage (typically 2 to 3 per cent) of your total savings. Do not opt for a regular savings account if you can get a better interest rate on an ordinary savings account (see Chapter 4).

- **How much can you save?** The minimum monthly amount you can save ranges from £10 to £100. If you want to change the amount you save, you may be able to do this only once a year although some accounts do not let you change it at all. Most accounts let you make additional payments on top of your regular monthly payment.
- **Do you have to leave the money untouched?** Yes, because you are allowed to withdraw your savings infrequently – once a year, say – or not at all.
- **Do you have to commit to regular saving?** Yes, although some accounts allow you to miss one month's payment each year.
- **How long do you have to save for?** Most accounts require you to save for at least a year or two, but it can be as long as five years.
- **Is there a risk?** If you do not keep to the terms and conditions of the account, you will have to pay a penalty. In most cases, this will mean losing the bonus interest or having interest docked from the amount you withdraw.

Tax point

Interest from a regular savings account is paid after deducting tax at 20 per cent. Higher-rate taxpayers have to pay further tax; non-taxpayers can reclaim the tax or can register to have the interest paid without tax deducted by completing form R85 (from the institution where the account is held or a tax office).

Fixed-Interest Savings Certificates

As the name suggests, Fixed–Interest Savings Certificates (which you buy at a post office or direct from National Savings) pay a fixed amount of interest which goes up each year that you hold the certificate. Certificates are available in 'issues', each of which has its own interest rate and maximum investment limit. The issue available in April 1999 was the 50th issue, which was paying 3.5 per cent for certificates held to maturity.

- **How much can you save?** The minimum you can save is £100; the maximum is £10,000.
- **Do you have to leave the money untouched?** Yes − if you want to get the full benefit of the guaranteed interest you need to leave the certificate untouched for five years.
- **Do you have to commit to regular saving?** No.
- **How long do you have to save for?** Once you have bought the certificate, you do not need to save any more unless you choose to.
- **Is there a risk?** If you cash in the certificate in the first year, you do not get any interest. After that, if you cash in before the five-year maturity, you get a reduced amount of interest.

Tax point

The interest you get on both Fixed-Interest Savings Certificates and Index-Linked Savings Certificates (see below) is tax free, so these forms of saving are particularly attractive for higher-rate taxpayers.

Index-Linked Savings Certificates

If you want a guarantee that the value of your savings will keep pace with prices inflation, you can buy Index-Linked Savings Certificates (at a post office or direct from National Savings). These certificates worked like Fixed-Interest Savings Certificates (see above) except that on top of a guaranteed fixed rate of 1.65 per cent (for the 15th issue available in April 1999), you get an extra percentage linked to inflation. This is called index-linking.

- **How much can you save?** The minimum you can save is £100; the maximum is £10,000.
- **Do you have to leave the money untouched?** Yes − if you want to get the full benefit of the guaranteed interest plus index-linking, you need to leave the certificate untouched for five years.

- **Do you have to commit to regular saving?** No.
- **How long do you have to save for?** Once you have bought the certificate, you do not need to save any more unless you choose to.
- **Is there a risk?** If you cash in the certificate in the first year, you do not get any interest. After that, if you cash in before the five-year maturity, you get a reduced amount of interest.

Capital Bonds

Buying a Capital Bond is another way of securing a guaranteed rate of interest on your savings. Interest is added to the value of your bond each year and the amount is fixed at the time you buy the bond (from a post office or direct from National Savings). The interest added increases each year giving an overall interest rate of 4.65 per cent (for Series P bonds available in April 1999).

- **How much can you save?** The minimum you can save is £100; the maximum is £250,000.
- **Do you have to leave the money untouched?** Yes – if you want to get the full benefit of the guaranteed interest, you need to leave the bond untouched for five years.
- **Do you have to commit to regular saving?** No.
- **How long do you have to save for?** Once you have bought the bond, you do not need to save any more unless you choose to.
- **Is there a risk?** If you cash in the bond in the first year, you do not get any interest. After that, if you cash in before the five-year maturity, you get a reduced amount of interest.

Tax point

Interest on Capital Bonds is taxable, although tax is not deducted from the interest, which is good for non-taxpayers. If you are a taxpayer, you have to pay tax on the interest each year even though the interest is not paid until the bond matures (or when you cash it in). You will receive a notice of interest credited to your bond each tax year which you need to keep as part of your tax records.

Premium Bonds

If you genuinely have no plans for your surplus cash and you want to take a modest gamble, you can buy Premium Bonds (available from a post office or direct from National Savings). Each £1 you save buys you a number which may win a prize after you have held the bond for at least a month. The prizes start at £50 and the most you can win is £1 million. The winning numbers are randomly selected by the Electronic Random Number Indicator Equipment (ERNIE) and announced on the first working day of each month.

- **How much can you save?** The minimum you can save is £100 (which buys 100 different numbers); the maximum holding is £20,000.
- **Do you have to leave the money untouched?** There is little point buying Premium Bonds if you cannot leave your money untouched.
- **Do you have to commit to regular saving?** No.
- **Is there a risk?** You might not win a prize but, unlike other forms of gambling, you are guaranteed to get your stake back, although the longer you leave it, the less it will be worth because its value will have been eroded by inflation.

Tax point

Premium Bond prizes are tax free.

Share-based savings plans

If you are prepared to take a risk with your money and you can tie your money up for at least five years, you could consider share-based savings plans, where the return you get is linked to the performance of the stock market. The money you save each month is invested in unit trusts, open-ended investment company shares (OEICs) or investment trusts (for more on how these work see Chapter 21). You can get free fact sheets on investment trusts from the Association of Investment Trust Companies.* For free leaflets on unit trusts and OEICs, contact the Association of Unit Trusts and Investment Funds.*

- **How much can you save?** Some companies accept as little as £20 a month, but £50 is more typical.
- **Do you have to leave the money untouched?** You need to be prepared to keep your money tied up for at least five years to allow the ups and downs of the stock market to even out. The charges on share-based savings plans also mean that you should try not to touch your savings.
- **Do you have to commit to regular saving?** Yes.
- **Is there a risk?** The main risk is that the value of your savings can fall as well as rise and if you need to get at your money in a hurry you take the risk that your savings will be worth less than you have paid in.

Tax point

The money you make on share-based savings is taxable. Tax is deducted from your savings so, unless you are a higher-rate taxpayer, no further tax is payable. Any money you make when you cash your savings in may be liable to capital gains tax (see Chapter 17). However, if you invest in share-based savings plans in an ISA the money you make is tax free.

Insurance-based savings plans

If you are prepared to save for at least ten years and you want to mix your savings with life insurance, you could consider an insurance-based savings plan – often called an 'endowment policy' – which you buy from an insurance company or friendly society. There are two sorts of plan: with-profits and unit-linked. Both are linked to investment on the stock market but a with-profits plan has an element of guarantee because when bonuses are added each year, they are guaranteed to be paid at the end of the plan. The value of unit-linked plans can fall and rise so they are as risky as share-based plans.

- **How much can you save?** You can save as little as £20 a month but because life insurance is part of the package, you will have to save more the older you are. If you buy from a friendly society the most you can save is £25 a month.

- **Do you have to leave the money untouched?** Yes, you certainly do because – especially in the first few years – you may get nothing back if you cash in (or 'surrender') early. Even in later years, the surrender value of your savings may be less than you paid in.
- **Do you have to commit to regular saving?** Yes, for at least ten years.
- **Is there a risk?** If you do not save the required monthly amount every month until the plan comes to an end, your savings may be non-existent at worse and worth less than what you have paid in at best. These types of savings plan are best avoided if you have even the slightest doubt about being able to keep up the savings commitment.

Tax point

The insurance company pays – on your behalf – income and capital gains tax on the money you make on your savings. So when you get the proceeds, you do not need to pay any further tax. If you save with a friendly society, the money you make on your savings is tax free. However, because of the charges involved, tax free does not necessarily mean it is good value.

Chapter 21

How to invest
a lump sum

If you have a lump sum which you genuinely have no other use for – which is likely to be the case if you have built it up by saving a monthly surplus – you can start to think about how to invest it. However, if your lump sum is an unexpected windfall, you should make sure that you sort out other areas of your finances first. This means paying off expensive overdrafts and credit-card debts, putting some cash aside in an emergency fund, boosting your pension and possibly buying insurance against loss of income. You should also think seriously about buying a home or paying off some of your mortgage (see Chapter 10). What is left over after dealing with the basics is what you have available to invest.

This chapter looks at the options open to you if you have a lump sum of at least £1,000 to invest, explains the factors which you should take into account when making your investment decisions and examines the benefits of tax-free investing through an ISA (individual savings account). Descriptions of the different investment

---

Tip

If you have a large lump sum to invest – you have a redundancy payment, for example, or you have inherited a large amount of money – and/or you want help in choosing particular investment products, you should consider getting independent financial advice. The Financial Services Authority* publishes a useful booklet entitled *FSA guide to financial advice*, which explains how to find an adviser, outlines what he or she should do and tells you what questions to ask when you are given advice.

vehicles start on page 348. If you do not have a lump sum of at least £1,000 or you want to save a monthly surplus, go back to Chapter 20 or to Chapter 4 for advice on building up an emergency fund. Investing for children is dealt with in Chapter 23 while investments for people over 60 are discussed in more detail in Chapter 25.

Deciding how to invest

The first step in whittling down your investment options is to decide what you want the lump sum to do for you. This means thinking about whether you want the lump sum to provide you with extra income (unlikely if you are still earning) or whether you simply want it to grow bigger – either to be available for future spending commitments or to provide an income in the future. Although many investments will suit both of these aims, some are particularly suited to providing an income, while others will be better for producing a larger lump sum at a future date. Once you have made this basic decision, you can use the most appropriate of the two route maps 'Going for growth' and 'Investing for income now' on pages 341–342 to identify the investment options open to you. The importance of the questions they ask is explained in more detail below.

Tip

If you have a lump sum which you want to invest for your retirement, the best way of doing this is by paying it into a pension. For more details, see Chapter 8.

How long can you leave the money untouched?

The longer you can leave your money untouched, the more choice you will have about how you invest it and the greater risk you can be prepared to take. Unless you can commit yourself to saving for at least five years without withdrawing any money, you will find that your options are limited to cash investments such as savings accounts and savings bonds (unless you are at least 65 – see Chapter 25). With some investments, you may have to leave your money untouched for at least five years to avoid paying a penalty for early withdrawal, so if you are not sure when you will need to get at your money you should avoid these sorts of investment.

Are you prepared to see the value of your lump sum rise and fall?

If you are not prepared to see the value of your lump sum rise and fall, you rule out all investments which provide capital growth – where the lump sum itself increases in value (as with shares) – rather than growing by having income added to it (as with a lump sum in a savings account). In general, you should avoid fluctuations in the value of your lump sum if you are not prepared to get back less than you have invested and/or you cannot leave your money untouched for at least five years.

However, if you do plan to leave your lump sum untouched for more than five years, ruling out the possibility of capital growth would leave you open to the risk of inflation eroding the value of your lump sum. This is a particularly important consideration if you want the lump sum to produce an income for a long period of time, because you need to ensure that the lump sum keeps increasing in value as well as paying an income. If you rule out capital growth because you cannot cope with fluctuations in the value of your lump sum, you also rule out investments which offer a degree of certainty if you hold them for a fixed period of time.

Do you want a degree of certainty?

With some investments, such as gilts (British government stocks), you have to be prepared to see the value of your lump sum rise and fall, but you can be certain of what you will get back after you have held the investment for a certain period of time. This sort of investment provides a half-way house between cash-based investment and the more risky share-based investments where there is no certainty about what you will get back. However, if you are prepared to do without the certainty of knowing what you will get back, share-based investments tend to produce a higher return. The longer you keep share-based investments (and the more flexible you are about when you need to get at your money), the lower the risk because the day-to-day fluctuations in the value of your lump sum will usually even out over a long period.

Going for growth

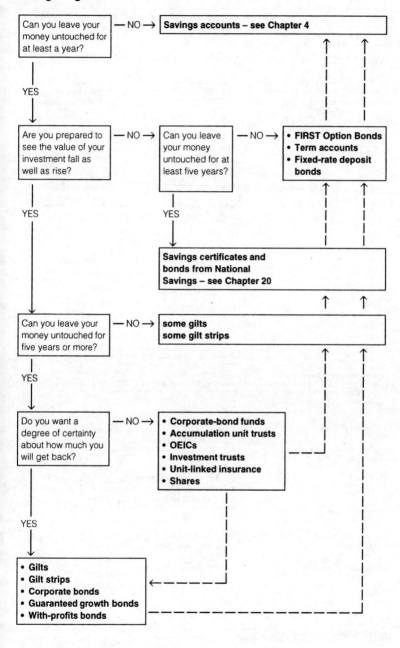

- - - - →   leads you to other investment options open to you

Investing for income now

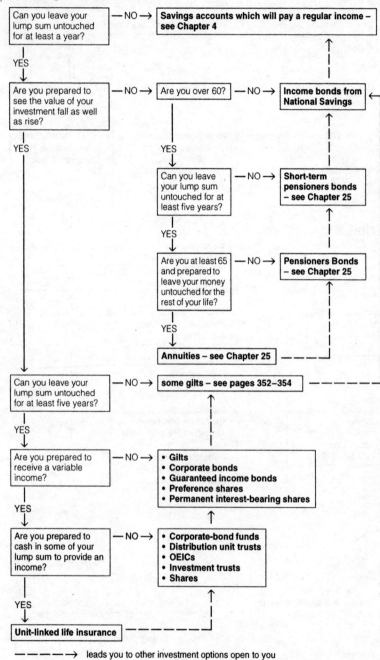

— — — — — → leads you to other investment options open to you

Choosing your investments

Knowing what you want your lump sum to do for you, how long you are prepared to keep your money untouched and how much risk you are prepared to take will help you to identify a shortlist of the investment options open to you. Which of the options will be most suitable for you depends on:

- how much you have to invest (see below)
- how you want your money to grow (see below)
- what type of return you want (see overleaf)
- the tax you will have to pay (see pages 344–345).

How much do you have to invest?

All the investments described in this chapter require a minimum investment of £1,000 but some investment options have a higher minimum than this. If you have a large amount of money to invest (i.e. several thousand pounds) you should consider sharing it between different types of investment as a way of balancing your risks.

With the exception of cash-based investments, you will also have to consider how the cost of making your investment will eat into the amount of money you have to invest. With direct investment in shares, corporate bonds and gilts, the cost of buying (and selling) is an up-front fee which is added to the amount you have available to invest. There are no further charges until you sell your investment. With pooled investments such as unit trusts and insurance-based investments, charges are taken off the amount you invest – both in the form of initial charges (and possibly commission to the person selling you the investment) and in the form of on-going charges for managing the investments. This can reduce the value of your investment, sometimes quite substantially.

How do you want your money to grow?

If you choose cash-based investments, your lump sum will grow only if you leave the interest it earns to be added to it – i.e. the interest is compounded. If you use a cash-based investment to pay you an income, your lump sum will not grow and will gradually fall in value

343

because of inflation. If you want your investment to increase in value and pay you an income, you will need to choose an investment which produces capital growth as well as income. If you do not particularly need income, consider investments where the income is reinvested and so adds to the value of your investment.

What type of return do you want?

The kind of return you choose will depend largely on how much certainty you want in what you get back from your investment. If the return is:

- **variable** you have to accept an element of unpredictability in what you get from your investment because the return is determined by general investment conditions
- **fixed** you get the certainty of knowing what you will get back, but you have to accept that you may not get as good a return as you would with an investment producing a variable return
- **index-linked** you have the guarantee that your investment will keep pace with inflation. You may not get the highest return (especially when inflation is lower than interest rates generally) but at least you will know that your money will not have lost any of its spending power.

How much tax will you have to pay?

The amount of tax you have to pay on the money you make from investments will affect the return you get, so the after-tax return is all-important. If you invest through an ISA (see pages 346–348), there will be no tax to pay on the money you make through your investments (until 2004, when ISA managers will no longer be able to reclaim the tax paid on dividends – but interest on cash will still be tax free). However, if you hold investments outside an ISA, the amount of tax you will have to pay – and the after-tax return – will depend on the type of investment you choose and which sort of taxpayer you are (if you do not know, see Chapter 17).

Unless an investment is tax free, the two taxes on the money you make on investments are:

- **income tax**, which everyone has to pay on income from shares, unit trusts, OEICs and investment trusts (non-taxpayers cannot reclaim this tax); higher-rate taxpayers have to pay extra tax (at a rate of 32.5 per cent of the before-tax amount of this sort of income) on top of the tax already deducted from the income before it is paid. With income from other investments, there is no tax to pay if you are a non-taxpayer and you can reclaim tax deducted at source; lower- and basic-rate taxpayers pay tax at 20 per cent and higher-rate taxpayers pay tax at 40 per cent. For more on working out the tax on investment income, see Chapter 17

- **capital gains tax**, which is a tax on the increase in the capital value of your investments, so only applies to investments which produce capital growth. However, unlike income tax, it is not an ongoing tax and so only really becomes an issue when you come to cash in your investments. Even then there may be no tax to pay if the gain (i.e. the proceeds from selling the investment, less the price you paid, less selling expenses) comes to less than £7,100 (in the 1999–2000 tax year). Some investments – for example, cash-based investments (including gilts) and stocks and shares held in an ISA (see pages 346–348) – do not attract capital gains tax at all. Note that there is no capital gains tax for *you* to pay on gains from insurance-based investments (because it has been paid by the insurance company on your behalf) but there may be income tax to pay.

Warning

You should not automatically assume that a tax-free return is better than a taxable return – particularly if you are a non-taxpayer for whom all income from savings is tax free (with the exception of dividend income outside an ISA). For example, if you are offered tax-free interest of 4 per cent, it would be worth having only if you could not find a similar investment offering before-tax interest of more than 5 per cent if you are a lower- or basic-rate taxpayer, or 6.67 per cent if you are a higher-rate taxpayer. To convert a tax-free return into a figure to compare with the before-tax return on a taxable investment, divide the tax-free return by 0.8 if you are a lower- or basic-rate taxpayer, or by 0.6 if you are a higher-rate taxpayer.

Investing in an ISA

An ISA is not an investment in itself; it is a way of sheltering cash, share- and insurance-based investments from tax. If you hold investments in the tax-free wrapper of an ISA, you do not have to pay tax on the money you make. However, because of this tax-free status, there are limits on the amount you can invest – see table opposite.

ISAs are run by 'ISA managers' – i.e. the financial institutions which offer them. Each tax year you can choose between having one maxi ISA or up to three mini ISAs – you cannot have both. If you opt for a maxi ISA, it means that you use one manager who must offer stocks and shares but does not have to offer the cash or insurance components. With a mini ISA, you choose a separate manager for each type of investment. So, for example, you could have a mini cash ISA with a bank or building society, a mini insurance ISA with an insurance company and a mini stocks and shares ISA with an investment house offering share-based investments.

CAT marks

CAT marks are the government's attempt to ensure that ISAs meet certain minimum standards. Therefore a CAT mark is not a guarantee that you are getting the best deal possible. CAT stands for: fair Charges, easy Access and decent Terms. In general, to meet CAT standards, an ISA cannot be bundled with other products or limited to existing customers, and the managers of CAT-marked ISAs cannot suddenly decide to withdraw them. The standards which apply to CAT-marked cash ISAs are described in Chapter 4. The standards which apply to share-based ISAs are that:

- the total charges for running the ISA must be no more than 1 per cent of the value of your investment each year
- you must be able to save as little as £50 a month or £500 in a lump sum
- the risks of investing in share-based investments must be made clear in any advertisement or marketing literature
- at least half the underlying investments of collective schemes (such as investment trusts, OEICs and unit trusts) must be invested in EU shares and bonds.

ISA limits for the 1999–2000 tax year

Maxi ISA limits if the ISA manager offers:	Stocks and shares	cash	Insurance
stocks and shares only	£7,000	n/a	n/a
stocks and shares plus cash	£4,000	£3,000 [1]	n/a
all three components	£3,000	£3,000 [1]	£1,000 [1]
Mini ISA limits:			
stocks and shares	£3,000	n/a	n/a
cash	n/a	£3,000	n/a
insurance	n/a	n/a	£1,000

ISA limits for the 2000–2001 tax year and beyond

Maxi ISA limits if the ISA manager offers:	Stocks and shares	cash	Insurance
stocks and shares only	£5,000	n/a	n/a
stocks and shares plus cash	£4,000	£1,000 [1]	n/a
all three components	£3,000	£1,000 [1]	£1,000 [1]
Mini ISA limits:			
stocks and shares	£3,000	n/a	n/a
cash	n/a	£1,000	n/a
insurance	n/a	n/a	£1,000

[1] In a maxi ISA, if you do not invest up to the limits for cash and insurance, you can put the whole of the excess into stocks and shares (up to the overall limit).

The standards applied to insurance-based CAT-marked ISAs are:

- the annual charge must be no more than 3 per cent of the value of the fund
- there must be no other charges apart from the annual charge
- you must be able to invest £25 a month or £250 as a lump sum
- the amount you get back if you cash in before three years must be directly linked to the value of the underlying fund
- if you cash in after three years, what you get back must be at least equal to what you have paid in.

What the CAT mark does not guarantee is how well your investment will perform. The Financial Services Authority★ publishes a helpful booklet on ISAs called *FSA guide to ISAs*, which explains the things you need to take into account when choosing an ISA as well as a list of questions to ask a financial adviser. For more details of the tax rules, ask your tax office (or the Inland Revenue★) for IR165: 'The new individual savings account (ISA): a guide for savers'.

Your investment options

Which investment – or combination of investments – you choose will ultimately depend on the degree of risk you are prepared to take, the length of time that you are prepared to leave your money untouched, and what you want the lump sum(s) to do for you – i.e. produce a bigger lump sum at a future date or pay you an income.

The next most important factor is the rate of return after taking tax into account. If you can get a better return without having to take a risk or tie up your money, you should take it – do not choose an investment just because it is tax free. At the time of writing, for example, National Savings products were paying relatively low rates of interest in comparison with taxable products such as term accounts and fixed-interest bonds from banks and building societies. However, rates change all the time so it is always worth comparing the returns you could expect to get from all the options open to you.

Tip

The descriptions that follow will give you a flavour of the main investment options open to you in terms of how they work, the amount of money you need to invest and the risks involved. If you want more in-depth information, as well as getting hold of the various leaflets and booklets mentioned, you may want to consult *Which? Way to Save and Invest* and the regular reports on investments published in *Which?* magazine★. The latter can point you in the direction of particular investment providers as well as giving up-to-date rates. The weekend personal finance pages of newspapers are also a good source of information.

Corporate bonds

Investing in corporate bonds is a way of lending money to a company for a fixed period of time for a fixed rate of interest (called the 'coupon'). At the end of the fixed period (at 'maturity') you get back a set amount of money (the bond's 'nominal value' when you bought it, or 'pounds nominal'). For example, if you have a £1,000 pounds nominal of 'Blue-chip Enterprises 8 per cent 2004' (the name of the bond) it will pay you £40 twice a year (i.e. 8 per cent of £1,000 divided by 2) until 2004 when the £1,000 is repaid. Corporate bonds are traded on the stock market, so if you want to get your money back before the maturity date, you have to sell the bond – the company will not repay the loan early.

- **How much do you need to invest?** At least £1,500 to £2,000 because of the dealing commission you will have to pay a stock broker, unless you invest in a new issue of bonds (these are advertised in the financial pages of the press) – in which case whatever minimum the company stipulates.
- **For how long do you have to leave the money untouched?** Until maturity – bonds are typically issued for ten years – or until you choose to sell the bond.
- **Does the value of the lump sum fluctuate?** Yes.
- **Will you get your lump sum back?** Yes – provided that the company does not go out of business before the bond matures. The risk of the company defaulting on its loan should be reasonably small if you buy bonds issued by large well-established companies (the measure for a company's standing is issued by agencies such as Standard and Poor's or Moody's, which give companies a rating: AAA – or triple A – is good, BBB less so). If you buy bonds issued by new companies or companies which have a low rating (sometimes referred to as 'junk' bonds), you take the risk that your bond will not be repaid and you will not get back what you paid in. If you do not want to risk not getting your money back, gilts (see pages 352–354) are probably a better option.
- **Is it designed to pay a regular income?** Yes – interest is usually paid twice a year. If you do not hold the bond to maturity and/or you bought it for less (or sell it for more) than its nominal value, there will also be some capital growth.

> **Tax point**
>
> The interest from corporate bonds and corporate-bond funds (see below) is paid after deducting tax at the lower savings rate of 20 per cent. Non-taxpayers can reclaim the tax (unlike the tax paid on income from share-based investments). Higher-rate tax-payers have extra tax to pay. In general, there is no capital gains tax to pay.

Corporate-bond funds

Investing in a corporate-bond fund is a way of investing in corporate bonds (see page 349) issued by a variety of companies. However, investing in bond funds does not offer the same certainty as buying a corporate bond yourself, where the income you get is fixed and you have the option to hold the bond to maturity. A bond fund will not mature at a fixed price and as the fund manager buys and sells bonds (and other types of company loans), the income you get will vary as will the value of your lump sum.

- **How much do you need to invest?** The minimum depends on the company which offers the fund, but £500 to £1,000 is typical. There may be a higher minimum investment if you want the fund to pay you an income.
- **For how long do you have to leave the money untouched?** You should aim to keep your money invested for at least five years. Early withdrawal can incur an exit charge.
- **Does the value of the lump sum fluctuate?** Yes – as does the income paid to you. Funds promising a high 'income yield' usually put your lump sum at greater risk than those promising a lower income yield.
- **Will you get your lump sum back?** This depends on how good the fund manager is and how much of your lump sum is used to pay charges. If the fund takes charges from your lump sum, it will gradually fall in value. If the fund takes charges from income, the income you get will be lower than if charges are taken from capital, but the value of your lump sum will not suffer as much. The figure to look at is the 'redemption yield' (some-

times called the 'total yield'), which includes any loss or increase in the value of your lump sum.

- **Is it designed to pay a regular income?** Most funds – particularly those promising a high income yield – aim to pay a regular income, but some funds reinvest the income so that your lump sum increases in value.

FIRST Option Bonds

FIRST (Fixed Interest Rate Savings Tax-paid) Option Bonds (which you buy from a post office or direct from National Savings*) pay a guaranteed amount of interest which is fixed for a year at a time. At the end of each year you can either cash in the bond or leave it for another year – the interest rate you get will be fixed for that year but will depend on the rates applying at the time. The guaranteed rate of interest for bonds in April 1999 was 4.65 per cent (3.72 per cent after tax at 20 per cent) for savings up to £20,000; 4.9 per cent (3.92 per cent after tax at 20 per cent) for savings over £20,000.

- **How much do you need to invest?** The minimum you can invest is £1,000; the maximum is £250,000.
- **For how long do you have to leave the money untouched?** For a year at a time.
- **Does the value of the lump sum fluctuate?** No.
- **Will you get your lump sum back?** Yes – but you will not get any interest if you cash in during the first year of holding the bond.
- **Is it designed to produce an income?** Not really – interest is added to your lump sum, although if you choose to keep your money invested for longer than one year you can withdraw interest by applying for a part-repayment equal to the interest earned.

Tax point

The interest paid on FIRST Option Bonds is paid with tax already deducted. Non-taxpayers can reclaim the tax while higher-rate taxpayers have to pay extra.

Fixed-rate deposit bonds

These are cash-based investments offered by banks and building societies which pay a fixed amount of interest for a fixed period of time. You have the certainty of knowing how much interest you will get, but if there is a general rise in interest rates you will not benefit because your money is locked into the fixed rate for the duration of the bond.

- **How much do you need to invest?** The minimum can be as low as £500, but is more typically £5,000 to £10,000.
- **For how long do you have to leave the money untouched?** Between one and five years, depending on the terms and conditions of the bond. Early withdrawals are heavily penalised.
- **Does the value of the lump sum fluctuate?** No.
- **Will you get your lump sum back?** Yes, and if the interest is added to it the lump sum will have grown. If the income is paid out, the lump sum will have lost some of its spending power.
- **Is it designed to pay a regular income?** Some bonds are; others are not.

Tax point

Interest is paid with tax at the lower savings rate of 20 per cent already deducted. Non-taxpayers can reclaim the tax; higher-rate taxpayers have to pay extra. Non-taxpayers can opt for interest to be paid without tax deducted by filling in form R85, available from the institution offering the account or your tax office.

Gilts

Investing in gilts (British government stocks) is a way of lending money to the government at a fixed rate of interest (the 'coupon') which is paid twice a year, usually for a fixed number of years. You make the loan by buying 'gilt-edged' stock (hence the name). Your loan is repaid (redeemed) for a set amount (the 'nominal value') at a set date in the future. For example, if you have a £1,000 nominal holding of 'Treasury 6.5 per cent 2003' it pays you £32.50 twice a year (i.e. 6.5 per cent of £1,000 divided by 2) until 2003 when the £1,000 is repaid. Gilts are divided into four types depending on how many years there are left to run:

- **shorts** have up to seven years left before redemption
- **mediums** have seven to fifteen years
- **longs** have over fifteen years
- **undated** have no fixed repayment date.

Gilts are traded on the stock market, so if you want to get your money back before the redemption date, you have to sell the gilt – the government does not repay the loan early. You can also buy gilts where both the income and the lump sum you get at maturity are linked to prices inflation (see 'Index-linked gilts' on pages 357–358).

If you want to look into gilts in more depth, the Debt Management Office (DMO)* produces an excellent booklet called *Investing in gilts: the private investor's guide to British government stock*, which is available by phoning the Bank of England free publications hotline.*

- **How much do you need to invest?** At least £1,000 if you buy new stock from the Debt Management Office when it is issued. For existing gilts there is no minimum, but there is a maximum of £25,000 a day if you buy by post from the Bank of England Brokerage Service,* which costs less but takes longer than buying through a stock broker.
- **For how long do you have to leave the money untouched?** This depends on when the gilt matures and on whether you decide to sell the gilt before maturity.
- **Does the value of the lump sum fluctuate?** Yes.
- **Will you get your lump sum back?** Yes, if you keep your investment to maturity.
- **Is it designed to produce an income?** Yes, and also capital growth if the amount you get back at redemption is more than what you paid for your gilt. High coupon gilts are better for producing income; low coupon gilts are better for achieving an increase in the value of your investment – i.e. a capital gain. (See also index-linked gilts.)

> **Tax point**
>
> The income you get from a gilt is taxable but the gain is tax free.
> You can have the income paid without tax deducted (this is
> automatic if you bought gilts after April 1998), which is useful if
> you are a non-taxpayer, or, if you do pay tax, you can ask for
> interest to be paid with the lower rate of savings tax deducted
> from your payment before you get it by applying to the Bank of
> England Registrar's Department.*

Gilt strips

Gilt strips give you a way of buying the promise of a definite
payment at a fixed date in the future. They are created by separating
a normal gilt (see pages 352–353) into single payments: one strip for
each single half-yearly interest payment and one strip for the final
payment at redemption. Each strip is traded separately on the stock
market. You make money by buying the future payment at a
discount. For example, if you buy the redemption payment strip of a
gilt maturing on 7 July 2004 which will make you a payment of
£10,000 on that date, you might buy it for £9,500. The increase in
the value of your investment is the difference between what you pay
now and what you will get in the future.

- **How much do you need to invest?** A minimum of £10,000.
  You have to buy through a stock broker; you cannot buy gilt
  strips by using the Bank of England Brokerage Service★ as you
  can when you buy normal gilts (see page 353).
- **For how long do you have to leave the money untouched?**
  Until the payment is due, unless you sell the strip before then.
- **Does the value of the lump sum fluctuate?** Yes.
- **Will you get your lump sum back?** Yes – if you hold the strip
  until the date when payment is due.
- **Is it designed to produce an income?** No – which is why
  strips are also referred to as 'non-interest-bearing bonds' or 'zero-
  coupon bonds'. However, if you bought a series of strips, each
  paying out on a different date, you can create the effect of
  receiving an income.

> **Tax point**
>
> The disadvantage of gilt strips compared with normal or index-linked gilts is that the gain you make is not tax free, and gains have to be calculated every year. However, the gain will be tax free if you invest through an ISA (see pages 346–348). There is no income tax to pay because gilt strips do not pay an income.

Guaranteed growth bonds

These are investments offered by life insurance companies which guarantee to return your lump sum plus a fixed amount of growth at the end of a fixed period.

- **How much do you need to invest?** It depends on the insurance company but could be anything from £1,000 to £10,000.
- **For how long do you have to leave the money untouched?** For a fixed period which can range from one year to ten years but is typically five years. Do not invest in one of these bonds if there is the remotest chance that you will want your lump sum back before the end of the fixed period.
- **Does the value of the lump sum fluctuate?** No.
- **Will you get your lump sum back?** Yes – plus the guaranteed growth – provided you keep the bond to the end of the fixed period. Otherwise there is no knowing what you will get back because it is up to the insurance company to decide the return if you cash in early.
- **Is it designed to pay a regular income?** No.

Guaranteed income bonds

These are investments offered by life insurance companies which guarantee to pay a fixed amount of income for a fixed period of time, and guarantee to pay back your lump sum at the end of the fixed period (unlike guaranteed high-income bonds – see overleaf).

- **How much do you need to invest?** At least £3,000.
- **For how long do you have to leave the money untouched?**

For a fixed period of anything between one and ten years, but most typically five years.

- **Does the value of the lump sum fluctuate?** No – but because the income is paid out to you, the value of your lump sum is gradually eroded by inflation.
- **Will you get your lump sum back?** Yes – provided you keep it invested for the whole of the fixed period. If you do not, it is up to the insurance company to decide what you get back, which could be a lot less than the amount you invested.
- **Is it designed to pay a regular income?** Yes – but you can probably find a better and less restrictive deal from a straightforward savings account.

Guaranteed high-income bonds

Not to be confused with a high-income fund, which is a type of unit trust (see pages 363–364), a guaranteed high-income bond is lump-sum (or 'single premium') investment-type life insurance offered by life insurance companies which guarantees to pay a high, fixed amount of income for a fixed period. However, unlike guaranteed income bonds the guarantee applies only to the income part – there is no guarantee that you will get the whole of your lump sum back at the end of the fixed period.

- **How much do you need to invest?** £5,000 to £10,000.
- **For how long do you have to leave the money untouched?** At least five years.
- **Does the value of the lump sum fluctuate?** Yes.
- **Will you get your lump sum back?** Not necessarily and certainly not if you pull out early.
- **Is it designed to pay a regular income?** Yes.

Tax point

The tax on guaranteed growth, income and high-income bonds is paid by the insurance company which offers them and you cannot get it back if you are a non-taxpayer. Higher-rate taxpayers have to pay extra tax.

Income bonds

As the name suggests, income bonds (which you can buy at a post office or direct from National Savings★) are bonds which pay you a regular monthly income in the form of variable interest on your lump-sum investment. Rates in April 1999 were 4.95 per cent on lump sums of up to £25,000 and 5.2 per cent on amounts over £25,000.

- **How much do you need to invest?** The minimum you can invest is £2,000 (after that you can invest in multiples of £1,000); the maximum is £250,000.
- **For how long do you have to leave the money untouched?** For as long as you want the income to be paid. If you want to cash in your bond you have to give at least three months' notice or pay a penalty of three months' interest. You can take part-repayments only in multiples of £1,000 and you must leave at least £2,000 invested – otherwise you have to take full repayment.
- **Does the value of the lump sum fluctuate?** No – but its value is gradually eroded by inflation.
- **Will you get your lump sum back?** Yes – unless you did not give the required notice, in which case penalty interest will be deducted from the lump-sum repayment.
- **How is income paid?** Monthly on the 5th (or nearest working day after) direct to the account you nominate when you buy the bond.

Tax point

Income from income bonds is taxable but tax is not deducted at source, which makes these bonds convenient for non-taxpayers.

Index-linked gilts

Index-linked gilts work like normal gilts (see pages 352–354) except that the interest payments are increased in line with prices inflation, as is the amount you get back if you hold the gilt until the redemption date. These can be useful if you want a safe home for your lump sum but do not want to see its spending power eroded.

- **How much do you need to invest?** At least £1,000 if you buy new stock from the Debt Management Office★ when it is issued. For existing gilts, there is no minimum but there is a maximum of £25,000 a day if you buy by post from the Bank of England Brokerage Service,★ which costs less but takes longer than buying through a stock broker.
- **For how long do you have to leave the money untouched?** This depends on when the gilt matures (which could be as long as 30 years) and on whether you decide to sell the gilt before maturity.
- **Does the value of the lump sum fluctuate?** Yes.
- **Will you get your lump sum back?** Yes, if you keep your investment to maturity – plus you get inflation-proofing.
- **Is it designed to produce an income?** Yes – and also capital growth if the amount you get back at redemption is more than what you paid for your gilt.

Tax point

The income you get from an index-linked gilt is taxable, but the gain is tax free. You can have the income paid with or without tax deducted from the payment before you get it.

Investment trusts

If you invest in an investment trust, you buy shares (see page 361) in an investment trust company whose business it is to invest in shares of other companies. This gives you a way of investing directly in the stock market while spreading your risk. You get income through dividends and capital growth if the value of your shares goes up. The value of the underlying investments that the company invests in can fluctuate, as can the share price of the investment trust itself, but the two will not necessarily fluctuate in line with each other. The main difference between an investment trust and a unit trust is that the investment trust can borrow money to invest (called 'gearing'). The effect of borrowing is to exaggerate ups and downs in the trust's share price. To find out more about investment trusts contact the Association of Investment Trust Companies (AITC)★ which produces free fact sheets and a directory of investment trust companies.

- **How much do you need to invest?** At least £1,500 to £2,000 because of the cost of buying shares through a stock broker. However, you can invest smaller amounts through a savings plan (see Chapter 20).
- **For how long do you have to leave the money untouched?** You should aim to invest for at least five years.
- **Does the value of the lump sum fluctuate?** Yes.
- **Will you get your lump sum back?** Only if you can sell your shares for more than you paid for them.
- **Is it designed to pay a regular income?** Income from your investment is paid in the form of dividends. Income trusts aim to pay a high income while growth trusts concentrate on capital growth.

Tax point

The dividend income you get from investment trusts, OEICs (see below), shares (see page 361) and unit trusts (pages 363–364) is paid to you after tax has been deducted, so unless you are a higher-rate taxpayer there is no further tax to pay. Any gains you make will be subject to capital gains tax. There is no income tax or capital gains tax to pay if you hold these investments in an ISA (see pages 346–348).

OEICs

OEICs (open-ended investment company shares) are a pooled investment similar to unit trusts (see pages 363–364), except that instead of quoting two prices – one for the buyer and one for the seller – only one price is quoted and charges are more transparent. The risks and rewards are the same as for any form of pooled investment. For free leaflets on unit trusts and OEICs, contact the Association of Unit Trusts and Investment Funds.★

Permanent interest-bearing shares

These are shares – PIBs for short – offered by building societies. They pay a fixed rate of interest for an unlimited period. Like any share (see opposite), they are bought and sold on the stock market and the value of your lump sum can rise and fall. The PIBs of ex-building societies are called PERPs (perpetual subordinated bonds) and work in the same way.

- **How much do you need to invest?** From £1,000 to £50,000, depending on the building society (or ex-building society) whose PIBs you want to buy.
- **For how long do you have to leave the money untouched?** At least five years, or as long as you want the fixed income to carry on being paid.
- **Does the value of the lump sum fluctuate?** Yes.
- **Will you get your lump sum back?** Only if you can sell the shares for more than you paid for them.
- **Is it designed to pay a regular income?** Yes.

Preference shares

Preference shares work like corporate bonds (see pages 349–350) in that they pay a fixed income and you get back your lump sum if you hold them to redemption. However, preference shares which do not have a redemption date carry the same risks as ordinary shares except that if the company goes out of business, preference shareholders get paid before ordinary shareholders but after holders of corporate bonds and debentures. This makes undated preference shares riskier than corporate bonds. Convertible preference shares give you the right to switch to ordinary shares in the company at a set price at or before a specified future date.

Shares

Buying ordinary shares – which are bought and sold on the stock market – gives you a way of investing in the fortunes of a particular company. The types of shares available range from those in old established companies through to shares in companies which have newly started up. There are two ways of making money from shares: through the income from dividends, which are usually paid twice a year – although some companies pay a quarterly dividend – or from the capital gain you hope to make when you finally sell the shares. It is important to remember that – apart from the dividend income – however much shares are worth on paper, they are worth nothing until you have actually sold them.

You can spread the risk of investing in shares by opting for a collective investment – such as OEICs (see pages 359–360), investment trusts (see pages 358–359) or unit trusts (see pages 363–364) – where you buy into a fund that invests in the shares of lots of different companies. Instead of having to judge when the time is right to buy and sell shares, the fund manager does it for you. For free leaflets on buying and selling shares, contact the London Stock Exchange.★

- **How much do you need to invest?** £1,500 to £2,000 because of dealing charges.
- **For how long do you have to leave the money untouched?** For at least five years, if you intend to smooth the effects of ups and downs in the stock market. However, there is nothing to stop you selling earlier if you can make money by doing so.
- **Does the value of the lump sum fluctuate?** Yes – which is why you have to be prepared to leave your money untouched.
- **Will you get your lump sum back?** Only if you can sell your shares for more than you paid for them and the company in which you hold shares does not go out of business. Ordinary shareholders are at the end of the queue of creditors when a business goes into liquidation.
- **Is it designed to pay a regular income?** You get a twice-yearly variable income in the form of dividends. However, if the company is going through a tough patch, you may not get a dividend at all.

Term accounts

These are cash-based investments which work like fixed-rate deposit bonds (see page 352) except that some pay a variable rate of interest and you may be able to have the income paid out to you rather than added to your lump sum. Like fixed-rate deposit bonds, unless you can leave your money untouched for the required term, you face stiff penalties for early withdrawal.

Unit-linked life insurance

Unit-linked life insurance works in the same way as other collective investments: OEICs (see pages 359–360), investment trusts (see pages 358–359) and unit trusts (see opposite). The difference is the money you invest buys units in various funds run by a life insurance company and you get some life insurance as well as an investment.

- **How much do you need to invest?** It depends on the insurance company – often £1,000 if you invest it as a lump sum. You can invest smaller amounts in a regular-savings plan – see Chapter 20.
- **For how long do you have to leave the money untouched?** At least five years.
- **Does the value of the lump sum fluctuate?** Yes.
- **Will you get your lump sum back?** You are unlikely to get it all back if you pull out early, and what you get back if you leave your investments for at least five years will depend on how well the fund performs.
- **Is it designed to pay a regular income?** No – but you can create the effect of an income by cashing in units.

Tax point

Capital gains tax (see page 345) is paid on your behalf by the fund, but if you are a higher-rate taxpayer you may have to pay tax when you cash the bond in. There is no tax to pay at the point when you cash units in to provide an 'income', provided you keep within certain limits – the insurance company will tell you what these are. There is no tax to pay if you invest unit-linked life insurance through an ISA (until 2004).

Unit trusts

Investing in a unit trust buys you units in a fund of investments run by fund managers. Buying units in the fund gives you a stake in a large number of shares and other investments. There is usually a choice of funds, each with a different profile, which is usually reflected in the name of the fund:

- **cash and gilt funds** invest in interest-bearing investments such as gilts (see pages 352–354) and bonds so are the least risky of unit-trust funds
- **tracker or index funds** aim to track the performance of a particular stock market – because these funds are not managed in the same way as other unit-trust funds, they tend to have lower charges
- **income and growth funds** are general funds which aim to produce a mixture of both income and growth
- **income funds** aim to produce income
- **growth funds** aim to increase the unit price and hence the value of your lump sum
- **specialist sector funds** look for capital growth by investing in the shares of companies in a particular industry
- **international funds** invest in stock markets overseas
- **specialist region funds** invest in a specific geographical region such as North America, Europe or the Far East.

The way you make money is by selling your units for more than you paid for them. The other way you make money is through distributions which are your share of the income from the fund's investments. For free leaflets on unit trusts and OEICs, contact the Association of Unit Trusts and Investment Funds.

- **How much do you need to invest?** This depends on the unit trust, but there is often a minimum of £500 to £1,000. You can invest smaller amounts in a regular-savings plan – see Chapter 20.
- **For how long do you have to leave the money untouched?** As with all share-based investments, at least five years to smooth the effects of ups and downs in the stock market.
- **Does the value of the lump sum fluctuate?** Yes.

- **Will you get your lump sum back?** Only if you sell your units for more than you paid for them.
- **Is it designed to pay a regular income?** Yes if you choose a 'distribution' unit trust which pays out the income; no if you choose an accumulation unit trust where the income from the fund is reinvested.

With-profits bonds

A with-profits bond is a form of unit-linked life insurance which offers a degree of certainty – although not a guarantee – about how much you will get back when you finally cash in your investment. The money you invest buys units in a life insurance company's with-profits fund. This differs from other unit-linked investment in that the price of each unit is not directly linked to the value of the investments held in the fund. Your lump sum grows by having bonuses added to it at regular intervals – either by increasing the value of the units or by adding bonus units. Once added, bonuses cannot be taken away apart from in very exceptional circumstances or if you cash in early. When you cash in, you may also get a final – or terminal – bonus, the size of which is unknown.

- **How much do you need to invest?** This depends on the insurance company, but a minimum of £3,000 to £5,000 is typical.
- **For how long do you have to leave the money untouched?** At least five years.
- **Does the value of the lump sum fluctuate?** Yes – but the fact that your lump sum grows by having bonuses added has the effect of smoothing the fluctuations.
- **Will you get your lump sum back?** If you cash in early, you are unlikely to get the whole of your lump sum back. So do not invest in one of these bonds if you cannot leave your money untouched for at least five years.
- **Is it designed to pay a regular income?** No – but you can create the effect of an income by cashing in units.

Part 6

Your personal circumstances

Chapter 22

Your finances as a couple

Sharing your life with someone does not necessarily mean sharing your finances, but if nothing else, taking time to talk about how you will organise your joint finances will spare you a few rows. According to a survey conducted early in 1998 for the relationship-counselling charity Relate,* money came top of the list of the reasons for arguments, with nearly half the people in the survey saying that it was their most common cause. The problem is that, with the exception of day-to-day finances, working out a joint financial strategy invariably means focusing on the less-than-romantic subjects of illness, death and splitting up. But if you choose to do nothing, the consequences if disaster does strike can be serious – and this is a particularly important consideration for couples who are not married.

This chapter examines the factors that affect your finances as a couple, explains how you can deal with your day-to-day finances and what you can do to ensure that your partner is protected from losing out financially if things go wrong. If you are planning on getting married, you will find information on how marriage will change your financial position together, with advice on the steps you can take to reduce your tax bill once you have tied the knot. The financial consequences of becoming a parent are dealt with in Chapter 23.

Day-to-day finances

If you have decided to set up home together, it makes sense to come to some sort of arrangement for sharing the household bills and other joint spending and it is worthwhile deciding:

- what you both agree is joint spending
- what you are each going to contribute to joint spending
- what you both agree is personal (and private) spending
- who is going to pay for what
- how you are going to share bills
- how you are going to share your assets – your home or shares, for example
- who will be in charge of the finances
- how you will agree spending priorities
- how you will make financial plans for the future – whether it is saving for a holiday or for when you have children.

Warning

According to Relate, lack of openness in financial arrangements can be a major source of friction and can even point to an underlying lack of trust in other areas of your relationship.

Sharing your finances

There is no reason why you should share your finances with your partner at all (except that it demonstrates a certain lack of trust if you don't) but if you choose to pool your resources to pay for what you have decided is joint spending, you may find it useful to open a joint bank account (for advice on setting up a bill-paying account, see Chapter 11). You can either run this alongside your own personal current accounts if you want to keep your personal spending separate and private, or you can arrange for both your salaries (if applicable) to be paid into a joint account and close your sole accounts. If you want to share everything with your partner but you do not want to close your sole account – because it is convenient for work, for example – an alternative is to make both your sole accounts joint ones.

You will have to open the joint account together, but whether you both have to sign cheques is up to you. Once the account is open, you will each get your own cheque book, cheque guarantee card (provided the bank is happy to provide this straightaway), payment and cash card. You will also become joint owners of the money in the account and jointly responsible for any debts (called 'joint and several liability'). This means that your current account provider can recover money to pay off debts from either account-holder regardless of who actually spent the money. For more on opening and running a current account – see Chapter 2.

Warning

If you have a very different attitude towards money from your partner – one of you is a saver while the other is a spendthrift, for example – you may find it less stressful to keep your financial arrangements separate.

Savings and investments

In addition to a joint account for bills, it could be worthwhile opening a savings account into which you both pay so that you can build up a fund for spending on large items such as furniture or home improvements. Whether you set it up as a joint account depends on the type of taxpayers you and your partner are. If one of you pays tax at a higher rate than the other, consider opening the account in the name of the lower-earning partner.

Planning for the unexpected

Even if you choose to keep your day-to-day finances completely separate from one another, you may still become financially inter-dependant – especially if you buy a home together. To ensure that your partner would not suffer if your income was no longer available you need to consider:

- **making a will** if you want your partner to get what you own – this is particularly important for couples who are not married because unless you make a will, your partner will get nothing
- **putting your home in joint names** if your partner has moved in with you and is contributing to the costs of running the home. There are two ways in which you can share ownership of a property: you can either own an equal half share of the property as 'tenants in common' or you can both own the whole property

jointly (owning the property jointly has the advantage that the whole property passes to your partner on your death and is not subject to inheritance tax)

- **taking out life insurance** if you do not already have enough as a perk from your job (in which case you should let your employer know that you want your partner to receive the proceeds). To work out exactly how much life insurance you need, see Chapter 7
- **taking out income-protection insurance** if you are worried about not having enough income as a result of long-term illness (see Chapter 5)
- **building up your own savings** so that you have a pot of money to fall back on if you do split up.

Tip

If you are worried that you would not be able to cope without your partner's income if he or she died, you do not need to wait for your partner to take out life insurance because you can buy a 'life of another policy' on his or her life, which belongs to you and will pay out if he or she dies (see Chapter 7).

Money and marriage

Marriage is unlikely to make much of a difference to your day-to-day finances but it does mean that from the moment you sign your marriage certificate, you will be allowed to pay slightly less tax, your pension entitlement will go up and you will be automatically entitled to at least some – if not all – of your spouse's wealth.

Before April 1990 a husband became responsible for his wife's tax affairs, and a wife's income from savings and investments was regarded as belonging to her husband and he had to pay the tax on it. These days, however, husband and wife are treated as individuals, each responsible for their own tax affairs, which means that you will still get your own slice of tax-free income (your personal allowance), pay your own tax bill and, if applicable, have to fill in your own tax return. Apart from having to tell your tax office if you change your name, in practical terms you will see very little difference in your dealings with the Inland Revenue. In financial terms, however, marriage will mean that:

- the amount of tax one (or both) of you pays will decrease because you will be able to claim a reduction in your tax bill in the form of the married couple's allowance
- you may be able to make extra tax savings on your mortgage payments
- any gifts you make to each other will be free of tax.

The married couple's allowance

Unless one of you will be 65 on 5 April 2000, the 1999–2000 tax year is the last year in which you will be able to claim the married couple's allowance (although if you were eligible to claim it in any of the last six tax years and have not done so, you can backdate your claim – contact your tax office). Despite its name, this married couple's allowance is automatically given to the husband unless you tell your tax office otherwise (see 'How to claim', overleaf).

How much married couple's allowance?

If the date of your marriage is between:	you will get an allowance of:	which represents a tax-saving of:
6 April and 5 May	£1,970	£197
6 May and 5 June	£1,806	£180.60
6 June and 5 July	£1,642	£164.20
6 July and 5 August	£1,478	£147.80
6 August and 5 September	£1,314	£131.40
6 September and 5 October	£1,150	£115.00
6 October and 5 November	£985	£98.50
6 November and 5 December	£821	£82.10
6 December and 5 January	£657	£65.70
6 January and 5 February	£493	£49.30
6 February and 5 March	£329	£32.90
6 March and 5 April	£165	£16.50

The figures are for the 1999–2000 tax year. Note that if you or your spouse is 65 or more at the start of the tax year in which you marry, you may be entitled to a higher married couple's allowance – see Chapter 25.

How much tax you save in the year you marry depends on the date of your wedding: the earlier in the tax year you marry, the more tax you save (see table on page 371). In the 1999–2000 tax year, the basic married couple's allowance for a full tax year is £1,970, which represents a maximum tax saving of £197 (to make the allowance worth the same to all taxpayers, the most you can deduct from your overall tax bill is 10 per cent of the allowance).

How to claim

If you want to get the benefit of the married couple's allowance, you have to let your tax office know that you are married, which you can do by phone or by letter. If you are an employee and so pay tax under the PAYE (pay-as-you-earn) system, your tax office will change the code that tells your employer how much tax to deduct from your pay, so you should see the effect of claiming the married couple's allowance quite quickly. If you are self-employed, the married couple's allowance will be taken into account when your tax bill for the year is calculated, provided that you fill in the relevant boxes in the allowances section of your tax return.

Although the allowance is automatically given to the husband, you can choose either to split it equally between you to make things fair (note that a wife can claim her half without her husband's consent) or to transfer the whole allowance to the wife. Electing for the wife to receive the whole allowance is a good idea if the wife is an employee and the husband is self-employed because you get the tax saving more quickly. There is no advantage if you are both self-employed or if the wife does not pay tax. If you want to change the way you share the allowance, you have until the end of the tax year in which you marry to notify your tax office.

Tip

Do not put off contacting your tax office because you do not like writing letters: claiming the married couple's allowance, changing the way it is shared between you or simply informing the tax office of the change in your marital status can all be done by phone. If you do not know the number, ask your employer or check any communications from your tax office.

When not to claim the married couple's allowance

If you had a child (or children) living with you before your marriage and you support that child (or children) financially, you can claim the additional personal allowance, which is worth the same as the full married couple's allowance (also due to be abolished in the 2000–2001 tax year). If you are a man, you will be better off continuing to claim the additional personal allowance if the wedding takes place on or after 6 May (when the married couple's allowance starts to decrease). If you are a woman, you can continue to claim the additional personal allowance for the rest of the tax year in which you married and you can also have half the married couple's allowance transferred to you.

Tip

If you have a child (or children) and you had not realised that you could have been claiming the additional personal allowance before your marriage, talk to your tax office. You can backdate claims for allowances for up to six tax years.

Transferring surplus allowances

If one of you does not have enough income to make full use of the tax savings that the married couple's allowance brings, you can transfer the unused part of the allowance to your spouse at any time during the tax year. It is also possible to transfer all – or any unused part – of the blind person's allowance (provided you qualify for it). If you get a tax return, you can transfer your allowances by completing the relevant boxes in the allowances section. If you do not get a tax return, contact your tax office so that it can make the necessary adjustments.

Extra tax savings on your mortgage

If you are planning to borrow to buy a home together, you will automatically save money on your mortgage payments because in the 1999–2000 tax year, the Inland Revenue will pay 10 per cent of the interest payments on the first £30,000 of the amount you borrow.

However, tax relief on mortgage interest will be abolished in the 2000–2001 tax year.

If you plan to sell your home either to buy a different joint home or because you are moving into your partner's home, you will carry on getting tax relief on your old home after the wedding until 5 April 2000 (when tax relief will be abolished) or until it is sold (whichever comes first). This is on top of the tax relief you will jointly get on the new home. If you are both selling up, you will each get tax relief on your old homes (until 5 April 2000) as well as tax relief on the mortgage for your new home.

Tax-free gifts

It may seem an odd concept that gifts attract tax at all, but they do – in the form of inheritance tax for the recipient and capital gains tax for the person making certain sorts of gift (in general, items that can rise and fall in value such as antiques, property and shares). The tax rules for gifts exist largely to deter people from giving away their wealth before they die as a way of avoiding inheritance tax, so it is unlikely that you will have to tell your tax office about all your wedding presents – although it may be interested if they are very valuable. As soon as you are married, you do not need to worry about tax on anything you give to your spouse because gifts between husband and wife – whatever the gift is and whatever it is worth – are exempt from both inheritance tax and capital gains tax; this can work to your advantage. The tax rules are also quite generous when it comes to wedding presents:

- before the wedding, the bride and groom can give each other gifts worth up to £2,500
- each parent of the bride or groom can give one or other of them a gift up to the value of £5,000
- a grandparent (or great-grandparent) can give up to £2,500
- anyone else can give £1,000.

Note that if a gift exceeds the limits given above and the person making the gift dies within seven years of making it, you may have to pay inheritance tax – but only if the donor's estate is worth more than a certain amount (£231,000 for deaths occurring in the

1999–2000 tax year). If the gifts fall within the limits given above, you will not have to pay inheritance tax.

Tip

Strictly speaking, to qualify for their tax-free status, wedding gifts have to be made 'in consideration of the marriage' and 'conditionally on the marriage taking place', so encourage generous relatives to write you a letter making the reason for their gift clear.

Marriage and your pension

If you belong to an employer's pension scheme, you are very likely to find that – without your having to increase your pension contributions – your spouse will automatically become entitled to receive a widow's or widower's pension and possibly a lump sum when you die. In its current form, the state pension scheme pays either a pension or an allowance and a small lump sum but only to widows (provided the husband has made sufficient National Insurance contributions throughout his working life). However, widowers will become entitled to receive state payments sometime in 2001 if government proposals go ahead.

If you have a personal pension, where your contributions build up a fund, this should be paid as a lump sum to your spouse in the event of your death before retirement. You can also arrange for your spouse to receive a pension if you die after retirement – for more details see Chapter 25.

Whichever sort of pension you have, make sure that the provider knows that you have married. You should tell the Contributions Agency★ (part of the Inland Revenue in charge of National Insurance contributions) that you are now married as a matter of course.

Marriage and inheritance

As soon as you marry, your spouse automatically becomes entitled to at least some of your possessions irrespective of any will you may have made as a single person. How much depends on where in the

UK you live. This is because your marriage automatically declares any will you may have made as a single person null and void (in legal parlance, your marriage 'revokes' the earlier will). If you want to be confident that your spouse will get all your worldly goods, you will have to make another will in his or her favour.

Making a new will is less urgent if your married home is your main asset and it is already in your joint names since half of it (if you are 'tenants in common') or the whole of it (if you are 'joint tenants') will automatically pass to your spouse when you die – and your spouse's share will not count as part of your estate.

Tip

If you want to avoid the problem of being without a will from your wedding day until you get around to making a new one, ask your legal adviser to draw up a specially-worded will which will not be automatically revoked by your marriage. This should say that the will is made in contemplation of marriage to a named person and it should also specifically state that the person whose will it is (the testator) intends that the will shall not be revoked by his or her marriage to the named person.

Who to tell that you have married

Marriage does not automatically mean that you have to change your name but you may find it convenient to do so even if you keep your maiden name for work purposes (but make sure that your employer knows your married name if this is what will appear on your bank account and/or passport – particularly if your job involves a lot of foreign travel). Whatever you decide to do about your surname, you will need to tell the following organisations that you are now married:

- your employer
- the Inland Revenue and Contributions Agency
- the Benefits Agency, which is part of the Department of Social Security (DSS)
- the passport office

- the DVLA (the Driver and Vehicle Licensing Agency) – to change your driving licence and vehicle registration documents
- bank
- building society
- credit-card companies
- insurer(s)
- pension providers (if you have a personal pension or contribute to an FSAVC (free-standing additional voluntary contribution) scheme
- your legal adviser
- your financial adviser.

If you do decide to change your name, you may be asked to produce your marriage certificate and/or provide examples of your new signature. Expect the changeover to take a few weeks.

Chapter 23

Financial planning for parents

Choosing to have children is likely to be one of the most expensive financial decisions you will ever make: estimates of how much it costs to bring up a child range from £50,000 to well over £200,000 if school fees enter the equation. Even if you would not consider private schooling, you are likely to have to pay at least a further £20,000 if you would like your child to go to university. How you cope with these costs will depend to a large extent on what plans you put in place to deal with the inevitable drop in your disposable income, how much help you can expect from the state and whether you decide to carry on working after your baby is born.

This chapter looks at the steps you can take to minimise the financial shock of having children, how you can best prepare for the cost of bringing them up and explains what changes you may need to make to your financial arrangements to cope with the extra responsibility of having dependants. You will also find advice on planning for the cost of education – whether it is to pay for your children's school fees or their living expenses at university – together with guidance on investing money on your children's behalf. If your children are already contemplating further education, you will find information on the help available for students in Chapter 24.

Plannning ahead

If you know that you want children at some point in the future but do not yet have firm plans about when, you are in the enviable position of being able to plan ahead. This means that you can:

- find out about maternity benefits (see below)
- assess the change in your income (see pages 381–384)
- start saving (see pages 384–385).

Maternity benefits

Knowing what maternity benefits you can expect to receive, which means both the amount of time you can take off (your maternity rights) and what you will be paid during that time (your maternity pay), is an important first step in your family planning. What you are entitled to depends on how long you have worked for an employer and on what your employer offers in addition to the minimum laid down by law (check your staff handbook or talk to your human resources department). Although it may sound callous, it makes sense to wait to have a baby until you have worked for your employer long enough to qualify for maternity benefits that are better than the legal minimum (see below).

Maternity rights

All women are entitled to return to the same job with the same terms and conditions after a minimum of 14 weeks' maternity leave no matter how long they have been with their employer. However, if you have worked for the same employer for at least two years and eleven weeks before the expected date of birth, you are entitled to return to work after 40 weeks' extended maternity leave. The exception to this is if you work for an employer who has fewer than five employees. In this case you lose your right to return to your old job after extended maternity leave (but not after the legal minimum of 14 weeks).

Note that if government proposals go through, the minimum maternity leave will be 18 weeks for all women, and extended maternity leave of 40 weeks will be available to women who have worked for an employer for one year and eleven weeks. Fathers will be entitled to three months' unpaid paternity leave. Adoptive parents will become entitled to three months' unpaid parental leave – although some employers may grant adoptive parents the same rights to paid leave as natural parents.

> **Warning**
>
> You have a legal right to keep your perks and other employment benefits only for the first 14 weeks of maternity leave. If you are able to take extended maternity leave, whether you keep your perks beyond the 14-week period is entirely in the hands of your employer.

Maternity pay

How much you are paid while on maternity leave depends on what your employer offers. The minimum you will receive by law depends on how much you earn and on how long you have worked for an employer. You will get:

- **statutory maternity pay** if you earn at least £66 a week (in the 1999–2000 tax year) and you have worked for the same employer for at least 41 weeks before the baby is due. For the first six weeks of maternity leave, you receive 90 per cent of your normal weekly earnings. After that you get a basic £59.55 a week (in the 1999–2000 tax year) for the rest of your maternity leave or the next 12 weeks if you are on extended maternity leave
- **maternity allowance** if you do not qualify for statutory maternity pay but you earn at least £66 a week and you have been earning for at least 26 weeks in the 66 weeks leading up to the date the baby is due. You get £59.55 a week if you were working in the 41st week before the baby is due or the lower rate of £51.70 if you were not. Self-employed women will get maternity allowance if they earn at least £30 a week.

Both statutory maternity pay and maternity allowance are paid for a maximum of 18 weeks from the start of maternity leave (which cannot start earlier than 11 weeks before the baby is due). So if you are entitled to take extended maternity leave, you will have to find some way of supplementing your income after maternity pay stops – unless your employer offers a maternity package that is more generous than the legal minimum.

If you do not qualify for either statutory maternity pay or maternity allowance, you may be eligible to claim incapacity benefit (which is paid for only eight weeks) if you have paid sufficient National Insurance contributions. If you have not, you may be able to claim other benefits – check with your benefit office.

Tax point

Statutory maternity pay – which is paid to you by your employer – is taxable. Maternity allowance, which is paid by the Benefits Agency,* is not taxable, but incapacity benefit (which you may get if you cannot claim the maternity allowance) is taxable.

How your income will change

Knowing what maternity benefits you would be entitled to will tell you how much of a drop in income you can expect while you are on maternity leave. How your income will be affected once maternity leave comes to an end depends to a large extent on the:

- extra income you can expect to receive
- extra expenses you will incur.

Extra income

As soon as your baby is born, you will see a modest increase in income because the state will pay you child benefit (see the table below). This is a flat-rate benefit (paid every four weeks in cash at a post office or direct to a bank account) for children under the age of 16 or under 19 if still in full-time education. From April 2000, child benefit is due to increase to £15 a week for the first child and £10 a week for subsequent children.

Rates of child benefit in the 1999–2000 tax year

	weekly	four-weekly	yearly
Rates for couples			
Eldest child	£14.40	£57.60	£748.80
Subsequent children	£9.60	£38.40	£499.20
Rates for lone parents			
Eldest child	£17.10	£68.40	£889.20
Subsequent children	£9.60	£38.40	£499.20

In addition to child benefit, you may be entitled to a reduction in your tax bill. In the 1999–2000 tax year, you will see a reduction of £197 in your yearly tax bill (about £16 a month) only if you are unmarried and you tell your tax office that you have had a baby – and so are given the additional personal allowance. Married couples get the same reduction in the form of the married couple's allowance irrespective of whether they have children. However, neither the married couple's allowance nor the additional personal allowance will be available in the 2000–2001 tax year. From the 2001–2002 tax year, these allowances will be replaced by the children's tax credit, which will mean a reduction of £416 a year (about £35 a month) for lower- and basic-rate taxpayers who have children under the age of 16. Higher-rate taxpayers will have the children's tax credit reduced by £1 for every £15 above the level at which they start to pay higher-rate tax. For more details on working out the rate of tax you pay, see Chapter 17.

Extra expenses

How much it will cost to bring up your child will depend entirely on your personal preferences: for example, if you choose to indulge in the latest designer baby-wear you will obviously spend more than someone who is happy to make do with cast-off baby kit and hand-me-down clothes. However, as a rough guide, if you buy everything new, you can expect to spend upwards of £1,000 on the basic equipment – such as a pram, pushchair, car seat, bath, changing mat, feeding accessories, baby-proofing your home and so on – and then at least £100 a month for the consumables such as food, nappies and clothes.

If you plan to go back to work after the baby has been born – unless you have a relative or friend who is prepared to look after your child for free – one of the biggest costs you will face is that of childcare. Expect this to cost at least £100 a week – although if you employ a full-time nanny, you could pay from £350 a week (which does not include the tax and National Insurance, which you will be responsible for collecting on behalf of the Inland Revenue).

Extra income for lower-paid families

Until October 1999, families with low earnings can claim family credit which is a social security benefit paid through the Benefits Agency. From October 1999, family benefit will be replaced by the working families tax credit and administered by the Inland Revenue. You will be able to choose whether the tax credit is paid to you or your partner (whether you are married or not). The effect of the new tax credit will be to increase the amount of money you can earn before you start to pay tax. You will be eligible if all the following apply:

- you are a single parent or couple (married or not)
- you have one or more children living with you
- you and/or your partner work at least 16 hours a week
- you and/or your partner are resident and work in the UK.

The working families tax credit, which is expected to apply from October 1999, will be made up as follows:

- a basic tax credit of £51.30 for each family
- a 30-hour tax credit of £11.05 paid where one earner works at least 30 hours a week
- a tax credit of £19.85 for each child under 11
- a tax credit of £20.90 for each child over 11 (paid from the September following the child's 11th birthday)
- a tax credit of £25.95 for children aged 16 to 19 (paid from the September following the child's 16th birthday until the day before his or her 19th birthday)
- a childcare tax credit of up to 70 per cent of eligible childcare costs – such as a childminder registered with the local authority, and after-school clubs – up to a maximum of £100 for one child and £150 a week for two or more children.

The total amount of tax credits actually paid will depend on a family's earnings and other income after tax and National Insurance. If this net income is above £90 a week, the maximum tax credit is reduced.

> **Tip**
>
> You may find it helpful to work out a pre-child and post-child budget (see Chapter 18 for how to budget) to see how your finances overall will be affected by parenthood and where you will need to make adjustments to the amount you spend on other things.

Start saving

Once you have estimated the costs and the likely effect on your income, you can work out how much you will need to save – although as a rough guide, you should aim to save about six months' worth of after-tax income to tide you over in the first year of having a child. Prospective fathers who hope to take advantage of the government's proposed right to unpaid paternity leave should also consider saving enough money to be able to do this. As well as putting money aside to cover the costs of having a child, you also need to consider whether you need to make additional savings to meet the costs of:

- **moving home** if you will need a bigger home once you have a child
- **replacing perks** such as a company car and private medical insurance if you decide not to go back to work (or if these would be withdrawn after 14 weeks of maternity leave)
- **boosting your pension** particularly if your earnings will fall after having children either because you go back to work part-time or because you will give up paid employment altogether
- **your child's education** if you want to have money put aside to help your child through university or if you want your children to be educated privately (for more details on planning for the costs of education, see pages 387–389).

> **Tip**
>
> If you are part of a two-income household and you are not sure that you would want to return to work after your child has arrived – or you want to see if giving up work would be a viable option – consider trying to live on the income of the person who would carry on working and saving the other income.

What to do when the baby is due

If you have not already done so, find out about the maternity benefits on offer from your employer (if applicable) and start saving. All pregnant employees are entitled to paid time off to attend antenatal care but you will be able to take advantage of your right to maternity benefits only if you follow certain procedures. At least 21 days before you want to start your maternity leave you must give your employer written notification of:

- the fact that you are pregnant as well as confirmation of the expected week of childbirth; around the 26th week of pregnancy, your doctor or mid-wife should issue you with your maternity certificate (form MAT B1), which gives this information
- the date on which you intend to go on maternity leave – which can be as late as the week in which your baby is due or as early (but no earlier than) 11 weeks before the baby is expected to be born
- the date on which you will start to receive statutory maternity pay – if you are eligible. If you are not, you should claim maternity allowance 14 weeks before the baby is due
- the fact that you intend to return to work after extended maternity leave (if you are eligible for it) – this does not mean that you cannot change your mind later.

If you are eligible for extended maternity leave, you must give written notice of your intention to return to work 21 days before you do so. If you are entitled to only the 14-week statutory minimum maternity leave, you have to inform your employer of your intention to return only if you plan to return early.

Warning

If you do not follow the procedures for notifying your employer, you may lose your right to return after maternity leave (whether extended or not) and your right to statutory maternity pay. You also risk losing your rights if you work beyond the week in which your baby is due.

Updating your finances

As well as making sure that you get the maternity benefits to which you are entitled, as soon as you know that you are pregnant, you should review your life insurance needs. Although death may not be at the forefront of your mind when planning for this happy event, you should make some sort of financial provision for your children in case one or both of you dies. It may be an unpleasant thought but arranging life insurance before the birth means that money will be available for looking after your child if you die in childbirth. Full details of how to calculate the amount of life insurance you need are given in Chapter 7.

You should also make sure that your will is up-to-date or make one if you have not already done so. This is particularly important if you are not married or if you have children from an earlier relationship or you are divorced and you have not updated your will since the divorce.

You should also consider appointing legal guardians for your children, otherwise you will have no say in who looks after them if you (and your partner) die.

When your child is born

You should claim your child benefit as soon as possible after the birth of your child – or the time when the child comes to live with you if you are adopting. Natural mothers should receive a claim pack automatically but if you do not, you can get one from your social security office.

> **Tip**
>
> It is very important that the person who will be caring for the child at home – even if only temporarily – is the person who claims child benefit. This is because you will automatically get 'Home responsibilities protection', which is a scheme that protects your entitlement to the basic state retirement pension even though you are not paying National Insurance. You can get more information by asking the Department Of Social Security for leaflet CF411 'How to protect your state Retirement Pension if you are looking after someone at home'; the leaflet is also available from local social security offices.

Planning for the cost of education

Making plans to pay for education in the future is no different from any other kind of saving for future spending. Provided you know the cost of what you want to buy and how long it is until you will need to spend the money and you can estimate how much your money will earn, you can work out how much you need to save each month (see the calculator 'How to convert a lump sum into monthly savings' in Chapter 20), or if you have a lump sum, how you should invest it (see the route maps in Chapter 21).

Planning for the cost of university

Although primary and secondary education are free in the state sector, higher education is not. So unless you want your son or daughter to start life after university with a large debt you should consider putting money aside now to help with their living expenses in the future.

At current prices, it is estimated that a student needs in the region of £20,000 to live on during a standard three-year course – but if your child wants to do a longer course, for example languages, medicine, dentistry or architecture, it will cost more.

> **Tip**
>
> If you manage to save all your child benefit from the time your child is born to the time when he or she will be 18 – and off to college – you will amass a lump sum of over £25,000, assuming that you achieve a rate of return on your savings of 5 per cent and that child benefit increases by 2.5 per cent each year.

Planning for school fees

If you want your child to have a private education, the sooner you start putting money aside to pay for it the better. Even if you plan only to pay for a secondary education in the private sector, at today's prices, you can expect to pay a minimum of £3,500 a year for a day school rising to over £15,000 a year for the most expensive boarding schools. Those figures are just the fees and do not include the cost of kitting out your child with uniform and sports' equipment or paying for other extras such as school trips. When planning for school fees, you also need to take into account the fact that fees generally rise at a higher rate than prices inflation; in recent years, fees have risen by about 5 to 6 per cent per year.

Paying fees

If you have time to plan ahead, it is worth doing so even if you do not manage to save the full amount of the fees. Although you can use specially designed school-fee plans, there is no particular reason to do so. They are simply a way of investing money in order to make a set of payments some time in the future. They may take the hassle out of planning for school fees – and introduce an element of discipline to your savings – but there is no reason why you cannot come up with a do-it-yourself plan using other investments, which can be more tax efficient, especially if you invest through an ISA (individual savings account).

Another reason for avoiding special school-fee plans is that because they are usually based on insurance-based savings plans (see Chapter 20), they require a commitment to save a fixed amount of money for a fixed amount of time, so they lack the flexibility of other savings plans. You should definitely avoid these plans if you cannot save on a regular basis or if there is a chance that you will have to stop or reduce your savings – for example, your income falls when another child arrives.

If you have a lump sum that you can set aside for school fees, instead of investing it (see Chapter 21), you may also be able to prepay the fees if you have a particular school in mind. The bursar of the school will be able to tell you if the school runs what is often called a 'composition fee scheme'. The advantage is that you may be able to buy fees at today's prices; the disadvantage is that if your child does not pass the entrance exam, you may find that you get back less than you paid unless you can use the money to pay the fees for another child.

If you do not have enough time to plan ahead, you will either need to borrow to pay the fees (see Chapter 13 for how you can cut the cost of borrowing) or you will have to pay the fees out of your income. However, careful budgeting and a thorough review of your existing savings could mean that this is less daunting than you first thought.

Cutting the cost

Many schools offer scholarships to academically, musically or artistically gifted children, subject to entrance exam results. Information on scholarships and grants – and on the cost of fees – is available from the Independent Schools Information Service (ISIS).★

Some employers' professional associations offer help with fees for the children of their employees or members (especially if staff are posted overseas), as do trade unions. But such financial help may be viewed as a taxable perk so check with your tax office (although tax on the benefit will still cost you less than paying the fees yourself). Parents working in the Diplomatic Service or serving in HM Forces may be eligible for help with fees while serving overseas.

Investing for your children

You may also want to consider saving money to create a nest-egg for your child to spend when he or she is older – or you may be in the happy position of having to make decisions about how to invest gifts of money from generous relatives and friends until your child is old enough to take an interest in his or her own financial affairs. While your child is still a baby, the main thing you need to concentrate on is tax.

Once your child is old enough to take an interest, you will also need to consider how much control you want to exercise over what he or she does with the money.

Tax on your children's savings

From the moment your child is born, he or she is a potential taxpayer and as a result has his or her own tax-free slice of income in the form of the personal allowance of £4,335 in the 1999–2000 tax year as well as an ability to make tax-free capital gains of £7,100. What counts as the income that can be included in your child's own tax-free slice depends on who gives him or her the money.

Any gifts of money from other people count as the child's income so any interest earned on the money is tax free until your child's money earns more than £4,335 (which is only likely to happen once he or she has accumulated a lump sum of about £100,000). From a practical point of view, this means that however you decide to invest money given to your child by other people – provided you invest in the child's name – it is likely to be tax free even if the investment is normally taxable. The exception to this is income from share-based investments where tax has already been paid by the time the child gets the income and it cannot be reclaimed.

Tip

If you decide to put your child's money into an interest-paying savings account, make sure that the account is in the child's name and that you have the interest paid without tax being deducted by completing form R85, which the bank or building society should be able to give you; alternatively ask your tax office. If relatives and friends give large sums of money, ask them to send a letter making it clear that the money is a gift to the child.

If you give money to your child or invest your own money in your child's name, any income it produces counts as yours for income tax purposes. However, there will be no tax for you to pay on it unless the income your child receives is greater than £100 per year (£200 if both parents give money). However, you are likely to go over the £100 limit only if you give your child more than £2,000 to £3,000.

If you do want to save substantial amounts of money in your child's name, you should choose tax-free investments or investments that produce capital gains – such as gilts or share-based investments. Note that you cannot open an ISA (individual savings account) in a child's name.

Tax-free children's savings

As well as tax-free savings which are open to everyone (see Chapters 20 and 21), there are two ways of making tax-free savings that are aimed specifically at children:

- **baby bonds**, which are insurance-based savings plans offered by friendly societies (see Chapter 20). You can invest up to £25 a month (or £270 a year) either in a with-profits fund or a unit-linked fund. However, the charges on these plans tend to be high and can wipe out the tax-free benefits. You could be better off investing in a share-based savings plan such as a unit trust, OEIC or investment trust
- **Children's Bonus Bonds** from National Savings,* which anyone over 16 can buy for any child under 16. The minimum investment is £25; the maximum is £1,000 in each issue. The bonds earn a set amount of interest which is fixed for five years at a time; at each five-year anniversary a bonus is added and a new guaranteed rate of interest (and bonus) is set for the next five-year period. The bond stops earning interest when the child reaches 21.

Control over your child's savings

If you invest in your child's name – unless you go to the expense of setting up a trust fund for your child (or children), which is generally not worth doing unless you have a spare £10,000 or so – you have to accept that at some point they will be able to do as they please with the money, so if you do not want them to touch the money before they are:

- **18 years old** choose gilts shares and other share-based investments
- **16 years old** choose Children's Bonus Bonds and Premium Bonds.

If you are uncomfortable about giving up control, do not invest in the child's name (or do not tell him or her that he or she has investments). However, you should give up control if you want to teach your child how to handle money – in which case most savings accounts from banks, building societies and National Savings are ideal because they allow children to operate an account themselves as soon as they are able to reproduce their signature satisfactorily (generally at age 7).

Tip

If you are keen to teach your children about money, it is important that you let them make their own decisions about which account they open. If they display a healthy disregard for loyalty to a particular financial institution and open several accounts with the minimum amount necessary to get the free gifts often available to young savers, so be it. If the counter staff are unfriendly and uncooperative at their chosen institution, they will soon learn to take their business to somewhere that offers the kind of service they feel comfortable with.

Chapter 24

Student money

Going on to higher education is not simply a question of finding a course you like and obtaining the right grades. Since the introduction of student loans and, more recently, the demise of the student grant at the end of the 1998–99 academic year, it has become a serious financial decision. Students starting a course – or going into their second year – in September 1999 will either have to rely on their parents (or spouse) for financial support or they will have to borrow or work to obtain the money to pay for college.

This chapter looks at the costs involved with being a student, the main sources of funding available for meeting those costs and explains how the new system of student loans works. There is information on how to choose a current account as well as advice on running your finances. If you are a parent and want to plan ahead for the cost of higher education, see Chapter 23. Note that the rules described in this chapter are the new rules that apply from the 1999–2000 academic year.

What being a student costs

The two main costs you face as a student are tuition fees and living costs. How much you – or your parents (or spouse) – will have to pay towards these depends on whether you are eligible for financial support from the state and how much help you are entitled to.

Tuition fees

Since the start of the 1998 academic year, most full-time students have had to contribute something towards the cost of their tuition.

The maximum fee for the 1999–2000 academic year is £1,025. For certain designated courses at privately funded institutions the fee is £960.

You may be able to pay a lower contribution of £510 towards your tuition if:

- you are on the placement year of a sandwich course where the placement lasts one year, or 12 months spread over two or more academic years
- you are on a part-time initial teacher-training course (which is not a post-graduate course)
- you spend a year at a college abroad as part of your UK course.

Note that if you are a student whose out-of-term home is in Scotland and you also study in Scotland, you will not be asked to pay the tuition fees for your final year if your course is a year longer than a comparable course in England and Wales.

Living costs

As well as having to meet the cost of tuition fees you will need money to live on – and the main help with meeting living costs that is now available from the state is in the form of student loans. However, some non-repayable funding is available for trainee teachers and health professionals, see page 400. According to the National Union of Students (NUS)* – unless you live at home or can live rent free – by far the largest part of your budget (more than half in most cases) will be the cost of accommodation. The table opposite shows the costs of the most expensive accommodation and other basic essentials if you choose to live in college accommodation but cook for yourself (note that halls outside London are usually less expensive than those inside London). If you choose to live in private rented accommodation, the costs can be far higher – not least because you may have to pay rent during the holidays.

Financial support for students

The financial help from the state which is available to you depends on a number of factors, including your personal circumstances, your

Student living costs

	outside London	inside London
Rent	£2,660	£2,432
Food/household costs	£1,011	£1,203
Laundry	£97	£97
Insurance	£55	£92
Clothing	£174	£201
Travel	£309	£661
Books/equipment	£443	£443
Leisure	£578	£721
Total	**£5,327**	**£5,850**

Based on an academic year of 38 weeks (including Christmas and Easter holidays) for the most expensive self-catered halls.

Source: National Union of Students

Tip

If you want to find out more about the cost of student living at the universities you are thinking of applying to, get hold of a copy of the *PUSH Guide to Which University 2000** (published in June). The guide covers facts and figures on student numbers, drop-out rates, the average cost of accommodation (both university-provided and rent in the private sector), travel and entertainment as well as average student debt. A summary of the statistical information in the guide is available from the National Union of Students.*

---

choice of course and a means test of your income and that of your parents or spouse. The main sources of state help are:

- help with tuition fees (see page 397)
- student loans (see page 398)
- extra grants (see page 400).

Who you contact to find out whether you are eligible for help (and to get more information on the help available) depends on where you currently live even if you will be studying in a different part of the UK. If you live in

- England and Wales you should apply to your local education authority (LEA), which should send you a booklet called *Financial Support for Students 1999/2000* (which is also available direct from the Department for Education and Employment)★
- Northern Ireland you should contact the Department of Education for Northern Ireland,★ which publishes its own booklet called *Financial Support for Students in Higher Education in 1999/2000*
- Scotland you should apply to the Student Awards Agency for Scotland,★ which should send you a booklet called *Student Support in Scotland*.

The body that is relevant to your home town is responsible for assessing your eligibility for state help, determining how much help you will be entitled to and telling you how to claim your financial support. In general, you will be eligible for state help if:

- you are resident in the UK (and have been for three years before starting your course)
- you are under 50 (or aged 50 to 54 provided you are intending to return to work after your course)
- you have not received support for a course of higher education in the past (although there are exceptions).

In addition, you must have a place at an approved institution on a full-time (part-time if it is initial teacher training) course in the UK that leads to one of the following qualifications:

- a first degree such as a BA, BSc or BEd
- a Diploma of Higher Education (DipEd)
- a Higher National Diploma (HND)
- a Higher National Certificate (HNC)
- a Postgraduate Certificate of Education (PGCE)
- qualified teacher status (QTS)
- an NVQ at level 4 where this is awarded with a first degree, DipHE or HND.

You will also be eligible to apply for help for the foundation year of a course leading to one of the above qualifications (provided you sign up for the full degree or diploma from the outset) and also if you take a course that prepares you for an exam that is of a higher standard than GCE level, Scottish Higher, National Certificate or National Diploma.

Tip

You can apply for financial support as soon as you have received a conditional offer of a place. The earlier you apply, the greater the chance of your money being made available on the first day of term.

Help with tuition fees

Help with tuition fees is means tested (see pages 401–405), but if your parents (or spouse) are not asked to contribute at all, your tuition fees will be paid in full. You will have to meet only part of the cost of the fees if you or your parents (or spouse) are asked to contribute an amount that is less than the fees you have to pay. For example, if your parents are asked to contribute £720, that is the most you will have to pay towards your fees. The remaining £305 (i.e. £1,025 minus £720) will be paid for you by whichever body you applied to for financial support. You will not have to pay tuition fees if:

- you started your course before the 1998–99 academic year
- you started a degree course in 1998–99 immediately after completing an HND or DipHE in the 1997–98 academic year. Note that you lose this benefit if you take a year off
- you had an offer of a place by 1 August 1997 and the grades to enable you to take it up but you chose to take a gap year
- you could not start a course in 1997–98 because your grades were not good enough but you were able to start in 1998–99 having had your grades raised as the result of an appeal
- you are a student on a post-graduate full-time or part-time course which leads to QTS such as a PGCE
- you are studying to become a teacher under the Secondary Shortage Subject Scheme (in England) and the Priority Subject Recruitment Initiative (in Wales)

- you are eligible for an NHS or Department of Health bursary (see page 400)
- you spend an entire year on ERASMUS exchange.

Student loans

The main source of financial help with living costs is student loans. For most students starting a course – or going into their second year – in the 1999–2000 academic year, the amount they can borrow will depend on a means test of their income and that of their parents (or spouse). The body that assesses your eligibility for help with tuition fees (see page 396) will also assess how much you are entitled to borrow and will ask you to say how much of it you want. You can apply as soon as you have a conditional offer of a place. The loan will be paid in three separate instalments (one for each term) by the Student Loans Company.

All students who are eligible for help can borrow about 75 per cent of the maximum amount of loan available (see table below); the remaining amount will be means tested (see pages 401–405).

Student loans in the 1999–2000 academic year

	Non-means-tested part of loan	Means-tested part [2]	Maximum loan available
Full-year loans			
London [1]	£3,360	£1,120	£4,480
Elsewhere	£2,725	£910	£3,635
You live at home	£2,155	£720	£2,875
Final-year loans			
London [1]	£2,910	£975	£3,885
Elsewhere	£2,360	£790	£3,150
You live at home	£1,880	£630	£2,510

[1] London is defined as the area covered by the City of London and the Metropolitan Police District

[2] An extra means-tested amount may be available if your course is longer than the normal academic year

If the amount your parents (or spouse) are asked to contribute is equal to the means-tested part of the loan, you can borrow only up to the figure given for the non-means-tested part. How much you can borrow also depends on where you study and whether or not you live at home. Loans are lower in the final year of study because they do not cover the summer holidays.

A higher rate of loan may be available if you study abroad for a continuous period of eight weeks or more. An extra weekly amount (means tested) may also be available if your course is longer than the standard 38 weeks (including Christmas and Easter Holidays). Check with the body that assesses your eligibility.

Tip

Although a student loan is not an interest-free loan, it is a low-interest loan because the amount you owe is increased each year only in line with inflation. Even if you do not plan to use the money, it is worth taking the maximum loan you are allowed and putting it in a savings account that pays interest at a higher rate than inflation (currently about 2.5 per cent). For more on choosing a suitable savings account, see Chapter 4.

Repaying the loan

You do not have to start repaying your loan until the April after you have finished your course, and then only if your salary is more than £10,000. The most you will have to repay each year will be 9 per cent of your income above £10,000. So if you are earning £13,000, your monthly repayments will be 9 per cent of £3,000 divided by 12. Payments will be collected by the Inland Revenue either direct from your salary if you become an employee or by being added to your tax bill if you become self-employed. If your income never rises above £10,000 throughout your working life, you will not have to repay any part of the loan. If you are still repaying the loan when you reach 65, the loan will be cancelled as it will be if you become permanently disabled or die.

The way in which you repay a loan if you started a course before the 1998–99 academic year (or if you took a gap year during

1997–98) is slightly different. You have to start repaying the loan only when your earnings reach 85 per cent of National Average Earnings, and the repayments are usually calculated as 60 instalments of the amount you owe – although the amount outstanding is recalculated each year to take account of inflation.

Extra grants

As well as student loans, some students may also be entitled to grants (which do not have to be paid back). Extra grants may be available if:

- you are disabled and you incur extra costs or expenses as a result of your disability in attending your course
- you have dependants – for example, children, or an adult relative or spouse who depends on you financially
- you are a lone parent
- you have to travel abroad as part of your course
- you were in care immediately before you started your course or you were in care at the time you finished compulsory schooling at age 16
- you are training to be a health professional
- you are training to be a teacher.

With the exception of grants for disabled students, all the grants mentioned above are means-tested. For more details of grants available for disabled students, ask for the booklet *Bridging the Gap* from the DfEE.★

For more details of other grants and bursaries, contact the body responsible for assessing your entitlement to financial support, or the college where you are planning to study if you are training to be a health professional or teacher.

Help from your college

If you are eligible to take out a student loan, you may be able to get extra support once you have started at college if you find yourself in financial difficulties. Your student support or student services office should be able to tell you if you can apply for:

- **a hardship loan** up to a maximum of £250. However, you will get this only if you have already received the first instalment of your main student loan and you can satisfy your college that you are in financial difficulty
- **Access Funds**, which are aimed both at students who may be put off going into higher education because of the costs involved and at students who have serious financial difficulties. You must normally be eligible for a student loan and have applied for a hardship loan as well to qualify for this.

The means test

When the body responsible for assessing you has told you that you and your chosen course are eligible for financial support, it will also send you a financial form to fill in. This will ask for details of your income, that of your parents (whether natural or adoptive) or that of your spouse (if applicable). Your parents' income will not be taken account of in this means test if you are permanently estranged from them, they cannot be traced, you are in care or if you are an independent student. You are considered to be an independent student if:

- you are 25 or over before the start of the academic year for which you are applying
- you have been married for at least two years before the start of the academic year for which you are applying
- you have supported yourself (or were unemployed and receiving benefit or on a government training scheme) for at least three years before the start of your course.

When income is assessed not all of it is taken into account because of what are called 'disregards'. These are deducted from your full income, and the amount left after this has been done is called the 'residual' income, which is the figure that determines how much help you are entitled to. Note that the means test does not take the income of a step-parent or guardian into account (unless they have adopted you). If your parents no longer live together, it will be up to your assessment body to decide which of your parent's income will be taken into account.

Your income

Your assessment body will ask you to give details of what you estimate your income will be for the academic year. However, in the assessment of your income, the following items will be disregarded:

- the first £1,000 of money from a scholarship
- the first £1,000 of payments you get from an employer
- any income from casual or part-time work you do while you are at college or during the holidays
- any NHS bursary
- the first £1,855 of income you get from a trust
- any teacher-training incentive payment from the government
- the first £3,105 of any pension (excluding a disability pension)
- most social security benefits
- money from student loans
- payments from an Access Fund
- hardship loans
- payments under the SOCRATES (ERASMUS) programme
- the first £820 of income from other sources (£1,780 if you are single and have dependants).

Any support you are entitled to will be reduced by £1 for every £1 your income goes over the amounts given above.

Tax point

If you work while you are at college and/or during the holidays, you can make sure that no tax is deducted from your earnings if you and your employer complete form P38(S). However, your taxable income for the whole year must not exceed the personal allowance of £4,335 in the 1999–2000 tax year. You can also arrange to have any interest on savings paid without tax being deducted by filling in form R85, which is available from your tax office.

Your parents' or spouse's income

Although you are asked to give an estimate of your income for the coming academic year, your parents (or spouse) will be asked to give details of before-tax income from the past financial year. However, if their income is likely to be lower in the coming year, they can ask to have their income assessed on the estimated lower figure provided the drop in income is permanent and unexpected (so voluntary redundancy or early retirement do not count). To arrive at the residual income figure, the following items will be subtracted from the before-tax figure:

- pension contributions and other payments that qualify for tax relief such as interest until 6 April 2000 (see Chapter 17)
- the first £1,720 if they pay for domestic help
- £2,195 if they support a dependant adult (other than you or their spouse)
- £890 if one of your parents holds a statutory award.

What are you entitled to?

The residual income figure – arrived at after taking into account disregards – will determine how much your parents (or spouse) will have to contribute to your tuition fees and living expenses and how big a student loan you will be able to take out.

What your parents will have to contribute

If your parents' residual income is less than £17,370, they will not have to contribute anything and your tuition fee will be met in full by your assessment body. However, if their residual income is greater than £17,370, they will be expected to contribute a minimum of £45 plus £1 for every:

- £13 of residual income between £17,371 and £22,199
- £9.20 of residual income between £22,200 and £32,634
- £7.50 of residual income over £32,634.

The maximum contribution is £6,280, which means that you will be expected to pay your tuition fees in full, you will not be able to borrow the means-tested part of the student loan (see page 398) and it is unlikely that you will be able to claim any of the extra means-tested grants (see pages 398–399). How much of the maximum contribution is actually paid by your parents rather than you is up to you to negotiate. The parental contribution will also be reduced by £75 for each of your brothers and sisters (if applicable) who is still living at home and financially dependant. If you have a sibling who is also a student, the assessment body will work out a total parental contribution and then share it between you.

What your spouse will have to contribute

Although his or her residual income calculation is worked out in the same way as for your parents, the amount your spouse will have to contribute is different. If he or she has residual income of £14,700 or less, no contribution will be necessary and your tuition fee will be met in full by your assessment body. However, if your spouse's residual income is more than £14,700 he or she will be expected to contribute a minimum of £45 plus £1 for every:

- £9.80 of residual income between £14,701 and £22,199
- £7.05 of residual income between £22,200 and £32,634
- £5.60 of residual income over £32,634.

The most your spouse can be asked to contribute is the same as the maximum parental contribution except that instead of getting a reduction for brothers and sisters, you get a £75 reduction for each dependent child you and your spouse have.

What the contribution pays for

Any contribution your parents (or spouse) are asked to make always gets set against your tuition fees first. Anything left over will reduce the amount of loan you can apply for and/or any extra grants for which you may be eligible. For example, if your parents are asked to contribute £900, all of this will go towards your fees, and your assessment body will pay what is left of your fee. You will be able to borrow the maximum loan applicable to your circumstances. However, if the parental contribution is more than your tuition fees – £2,000 for example – the first £1,025 will be used to pay your fee and the remaining £975 will reduce the amount of student loan you can take out.

Tip

If your financial circumstances – or those of your parents (or spouse) – change during the year, always let your assessing body know. It may reassess your entitlement to financial help.

Choosing a bank account

If you do not already have a bank account, you will need to open one – but even if you do already have one, it makes sense to open a student account because of the free overdrafts that banks offer to students. Ignore the gimmicky free gifts and concentrate on:

- **the size of the overdraft** The bigger the free overdraft limit the better, even if you do not intend to use it
- **what it costs for a bigger overdraft** Some banks start to charge extra if you arrange a larger overdraft than their standard limit, and all banks will charge a lot extra if you go over an agreed limit without asking first
- **running costs** There are usually no charges but it is worth checking
- **the terms after you graduate** Some banks extend the free overdraft facility for up to a year or two after graduation, which is when you are most likely to need it
- **the availability of cash machines** near to where you plan to study.

For more on choosing and running a current account, see Chapter 2.

Managing your money

Managing on the money made available to students is no mean feat. Even if you are eligible for help with tuition fees and you can take out the maximum student loan, according to NUS figures you are likely to find yourself with a shortfall at the end of each term unless you can top up what you receive with earnings or money you have saved before going to college.

If you already have some experience of managing your money, you will have worked out for yourself that if you spend all your money in the first week, you will be in financial difficulty for the rest of term and you probably have a fair idea of how you are going to budget. However, if you find the prospect of having to make a large lump sum last for the next three months or so (including holidays) slightly daunting, you may find it useful to go through the following exercise:

- work out the minimum you will need to survive on each week in the holidays
- multiply that figure by the number of weeks in the holidays
- subtract the result from your termly income
- subtract essential term-time spending – such as rent – from what is left of your termly income
- divide what is left over by the number of weeks you will be at college.

What is left is your weekly budget for books, food, travel home, clothes and going out. If the weekly figure does not look enough, try adjusting your estimate for what you will need to live on in the holidays. Once you know what your weekly budget is, try to stick to it and keep track by keeping an accurate running balance of your current account spending (see Chapter 2 for more details). It is also a good idea to set aside money for holidays and essentials in a savings account where it can earn interest and where you may be less tempted to spend it. For more information on financial survival as a student, contact the NUS* or consult the *PUSH Guide to Which University 2000*.

Chapter 25

Your finances in later life

Whether you are relishing the prospect of retirement or dreading it, one thing is certain: your income will fall. The amount by which it will decrease will depend on how much attention you have paid to your pension planning throughout your working life, what you have in the way of other savings and investments and how old you will be when you retire. If you still have a few years to go until then, it would certainly be worth drawing up a detailed plan of your potential retirement situation so that you can take steps to improve it.

The main way to plan for retirement is by paying into a pension, which is dealt with in detail in Chapter 8 –– where you will find advice on how to work out how much you should be paying into your pension to achieve the retirement income you want. This chapter looks at your retirement income as a whole, shows you how to work out your post-retirement tax bill and explains how to rearrange your finances to make the most of age-related tax allowances. If you are very near to retirement, you can follow the advice on making the right choices when you take your pension, and on ensuring that you get the best deal if you have to buy an annuity (which you will do if you have a personal pension or have been making additional voluntary contributions alongside your employer's main scheme). If it is too late to boost your pension, there is advice on other ways of increasing your retirement income, with a particular look at investments aimed at the over 60s.

Preparing for retirement

Ideally, as soon as you start paying into a pension (see Chapter 8) you should review your potential pension income and expected retirement spending every year but the nearer you are to retirement, the more accurate you can be about estimating your post-retirement expenditure. You may find it helpful to draw up a detailed budget (see Chapter 18), which takes into account likely reductions in spending, such as no longer having to pay the mortgage or buy work clothes – and likely increases – such as paying for more holidays or insurance that you will no longer get through your job. Before you can compare your likely income with your likely expenditure you need to know how much income you will have after taking tax into account. If you plan to retire before you reach 65, you can use the calculator in Chapter 17 to work out your after-tax retirement income. However, if you will not retire until you are 65, you need to work out whether you will get the higher age-related allowances for people over 65, which increase the amount of income you can have before you start to pay tax.

Tip

If it is still several years until you retire, not only can you take steps to improve your retirement income by paying more into your pension (see Chapter 8) but you may also benefit from aiming to make mortgage overpayments (see Chapter 10). This will be particularly worthwhile if you have an interest-only mortgage (such as an endowment mortgage) because the lower the amount of your outstanding mortgage loan, the more of the investment designed to pay it off you will be able to keep as savings. Paying off other loans (see Chapter 13) before retirement will also help to reduce post-retirement spending needs. If you have a company car, it could be worthwhile switching to a car of your own before you retire (see Chapter 14) both for the tax savings and to dull the financial shock of buying a car by doing so while your income is higher than it will be in retirement. If you will need to replace free life insurance from your job (see Chapter 7), buying it before you retire could also save you money, especially if you are worried about your health deteriorating as you get older.

Age-related allowances

If you turn 65 at any time during the tax year, you may qualify for a higher personal allowance, which applies for the whole of the tax year. The allowance can be even higher if you turn 75 during the tax year. The maximum amounts of the higher personal allowances for the 1999–2000 tax year are:

- £5,720 for those aged at least 65
- £5,980 for those aged at least 75.

Whether you qualify for the full amount of the age-related personal allowance or a reduced amount depends on what the tax rules call your 'total income'. This is calculated by adding up the before-tax amounts of income from all sources – including pensions, part-time earnings and income from savings and investments – then subtracting certain tax-allowable deductions, such as payments you make to charity.

If your total income comes to more than £16,800 (in the 1999–2000 tax year), the amount of age allowance you get is reduced by £1 for every £2 your total income is over the £16,800 limit until it reaches the amount of the basic personal allowance of £4,335 (in the 1999–2000 tax year) to which everyone is entitled. The calculator on page 412 will help you to work out how much allowance you may be able to claim. Once you know the size of your personal allowance after retirement, you can use the calculator in Chapter 17 to work out your retirement income after tax.

Extra deductions for married couples

In addition to possibly getting a higher personal allowance, which increases the amount of income you can have before you start to pay tax, married couples may also be able to reduce their tax bill by claiming the higher married couple's allowance, which (in the 1999–2000 tax year) is given as a fixed deduction of 10 per cent of up to:

- £5,125 if either spouse is aged 65 (a maximum deduction of £512.50)

- £5,195 if either spouse is aged 75 (a maximum deduction of £519.50).

Although a husband and wife each get a personal allowance based on their own age and their own total income, the higher married couple's allowance (which is always given to the husband) is available if either partner reaches the relevant age. The amount of the allowance is calculated on the husband's total income. When a married man starts to lose the extra allowance (which happens if his total income comes to more than £16,800), it is his personal allowance that is reduced first. When it has been reduced to the level of the basic personal allowance, he may then start to lose the extra married couple's allowance. However, the married couple's allowance will not be reduced below the level of the basic married couple's allowance of £1,970 in the 1999–2000 tax year. The calculator on page 412 will help you to work out exactly how big a deduction you will be able to make from your post-retirement tax bill.

Note that from the start of the 2000–2001 tax year, the higher married couple's allowance will be available only to couples where one partner was aged 65 on 5 April 2000. This deadline also applies to people paying legally enforceable maintenance payments to an ex-spouse.

Working out your age-related allowances

The calculator on page 412 will help you to work out your total income for the 1999–2000 tax year and then the amount of age-related allowance you should be getting. Before you can fill in the calculator you need to know the total figures for:

- your before-tax income
- payments you make that qualify for tax relief.

Your before-tax income

As well as income from pensions and earnings from a job, your total before-tax income should include the before-tax amount of any bank or building society interest (if you know only the after-tax amount, divide this by 0.8). You should also include share dividends, distributions from unit trusts and open-ended investment companies (add the tax credit – shown on the voucher you get – to the income to arrive at the before-tax amount). If you have made a gain by cashing in a life insurance policy which you bought with a lump sum, add the gain to your total. Finally, add on any other income such as rent on a property and taxable maintenance payments you receive. Do not include tax-free income (see Chapter 17).

Payments you make that qualify for tax relief

Some payments you make benefit from tax relief and can be used to reduce the amount of your total income. To arrive at the figure to enter in the calculator overleaf, add up all your:

- payments to charity made under a deed of covenant and donations under the Gift Aid scheme or Millennium Gift Aid (divide the total of payments of this kind by 0.77 to get the figure to enter in the calculator)
- charitable donations made under the payroll giving scheme (the figure you need is the amount deducted from your pay)
- interest payments on a loan to pay an inheritance tax bill
- contributions you make to an employer's pension scheme (including extra payments to an AVC or FSAVC scheme) or personal pension. Note that if you are an employee paying into a personal pension you will need to divide the amount you pay the pension provider by 0.77 to arrive at the amount before tax relief
- maintenance payments that qualify for full tax relief (broadly payments made under a legally binding agreement that was in place before 15 March 1988)
- payments made for your own training (divide the amount you pay by 0.77).

Tip

If your tax office tells you that you cannot deduct covenant payments to charity (or those made under either of the gift aid schemes) when calculating your total income, the tax office is wrong.

How to calculate your age-related allowances

What is your total income?

Enter your total before-tax income	A
Enter the total of all payments you make which qualify for tax relief	B
Subtract B from A and enter the result at C	C

The figure at C is your 'total income'
If C is less than £16,801, you will get the maximum amount of the age-related personal allowances for your age (see below)
If C is greater than £16,800, you will need to work out the reduced amount of the allowance.

How much personal allowance?

Enter £16,800 at D	D
Subtract D from C and enter the result at E	E
Divide E by 2 and enter the result at F	F
If you will be 65 in the 1999–2000 tax year enter £5,720 If you will be 75 in the 1999–2000 tax year enter £5,980	G
Subtract F from G and enter the result at H	H

If H is £4,335 or more, this is your reduced amount of personal allowance and (if applicable) you will get the full deduction for the married couple's allowance
If H is less than £4,335, your personal allowance is £4,335 and if you are a married man you will need to work out the reduced amount of married couple's allowance

How much married couple's allowance?

Enter £4,335 at I	I
Subtract H from I and enter the result at J	J
If you (or your wife) will be 65 in the 1999–2000 tax year enter £5,125 If you (or your wife) will be 75 in the 1999–2000 tax year enter £5,195	K
Subtract J from K and enter the result at L	L
Multiply L by 0.1 and enter the result at M	M

If the figure at M is £197 or more, this is the amount you will be able to deduct from your tax bill. If M is less than £197, the amount you can deduct from your tax bill is £197.

Making the most of age-related allowances

If you have worked through the calculator above and it looks as though your total income will exceed £16,800, and so you will get a reduced amount of the higher allowance (or none at all), it will be worthwhile looking at ways of reducing your total income, which you can do by:

- switching from savings and investments that produce a taxable income to tax-free investments – such as those held in an ISA and some National Savings products (see Chapters 20 and 21)
- arranging to make any donations to charity through a covenant or by way of the Gift Aid or Millennium Gift Aid schemes (the charity you give to will be able to supply the necessary forms)
- rearranging your joint investments if you are a couple and your partner's total income is well below the total income limit but yours is above it
- choosing to buy an annuity, where part of the income is tax free (see pages 415–417 for more details)

Taking your pension

The decisions you make when you come to take your pension will affect your income – and that of your dependants – for the rest of your life. One of the main decisions you have to make is whether or not you swap part of your pension for a tax-free lump sum. Whether you should do this depends to a large extent on whether your pension is linked to your salary at retirement or whether your pension will be provided by an annuity, which you will have to buy with the fund you have built up.

Taking cash from a final-salary scheme

Unless your scheme is set up to provide you with a lump sum at retirement automatically (such as those in the public sector) you will usually be able to swap part of your pension for cash (called 'commuting' your pension) but you will get a smaller pension by doing this. Although the idea of a tax-free lump sum may sound attractive, you should be wary of taking the cash if:

- the smaller pension will not cover your estimated post-retirement spending

413

- the increases in the pension you are paid are likely to be generous – the income you can buy from investing the cash is unlikely to match such a benefit
- you expect to live to a ripe old age (taking the cash may be a better option if you do not expect to live for a long time after retirement.)

However, if the smaller pension you will get by taking the cash will be enough to live on and you want the flexibility of being able to choose how you invest (or spend) the lump sum, taking the cash may be worthwhile.

Tip

To be absolutely certain that you are making the right choice regarding the option of a tax-free lump sum, compare the after-tax income you could get by using the lump sum to buy an annuity with the after-tax income you would give up by taking the lump sum. If the income you would give up is greater than the income an annuity would pay you, taking the cash will leave you worse off.

Taking cash from your pension fund

If you belong to an employer's pension scheme that is not linked to your salary or you have a personal pension, the tax-free lump sum you can have comes from the fund you have built up. The rest of the fund eventually has to be used to buy an annuity (referred to as a 'compulsory purchase' annuity), which is the investment that will provide your pension income (but you can decide to delay the purchase of an annuity in some circumstances – see page 417). In this case, taking the cash can make sense (but see the 'Warning' opposite) even if you use the cash to buy another annuity to top up your pension income. The reason for this is that all the income you get from a compulsory purchase annuity is taxable while part of the income you get from an annuity you choose to buy (called a 'purchased life' annuity) is tax free.

Warning

If you took out a personal pension (or retirement annuity contract, as they were called before July 1988) before 1994, do not make a decision about your retirement income without first scouring the small print (or asking an annuity specialist to do it for you). Many pensions sold until 1993 carry an annuity rate guarantee. This is a promise by the pension provider to pay a definite amount of income if annuity rates fall below a certain level. Since annuity rates *have* fallen dramatically, the guaranteed rate is well worth having because you will get a higher income to live on in retirement. Ask your pension provider to tell you if your plan carries a guarantee and consider *not* taking cash from your pension unless you do not need to maximise your pension income.

Choosing an annuity

Once you have bought an annuity to provide your pension there is no turning back: the income from it is fixed at the outset and you do not get the lump sum back. The income you get from the annuity depends on:

- **your age** The older you are when you buy the annuity, the higher the income
- **your gender** The income paid to women is lower than that paid to men of the same age because women live longer
- **your state of health** Smokers, very overweight people and those who have health problems that are likely to lower their life expectancy get higher rates than people in good health
- **the type of annuity** you choose to buy.

Which type of annuity?

The type of annuity you choose depends on how you want the income to be paid and on whether you need to provide a pension for your partner after your death. The more income you want in the future, the lower the starting pension will be:

- **level annuities** pay a fixed amount of income that never changes so these are not a good idea if you want your income to keep pace with inflation
- **escalating annuities** pay an income that increases each year either by a fixed percentage (which you decide at the outset) or in line with inflation (so these are sometimes referred to as 'index-linked' annuities). The income you get in the first few years will be lower than that paid by a level annuity but the value of your income will keep pace with inflation
- **joint life annuities** pay you income while you live and then carry on paying out that income – or a proportion of it, typically a half or two thirds – to your surviving partner until his or her death
- **impaired life annuities** pay out a higher income to people who have a shorter life expectancy than normal, such as smokers or people with a serious illness
- **Investment-linked annuities** are linked either to an investment fund so the income paid is not guaranteed and fluctuates according to how well (or how badly) the investment fund performs. With-profits annuities tend to be less risky than unit-linked annuities.

Getting the most from your annuity

Once you have decided on the type of annuity you want, you need to find the one that will pay the biggest income for the lump sum you have available. The difference between the best annuity and the worst can be as much as 25 per cent of your retirement income – in money terms that is the difference between being paid a pension of £8,000 and £10,000. To make sure that you get the best income possible, it would be worth your while approaching a specialist adviser such as the Annuity Bureau★ and Annuity Direct,★ both of which keep up-to-date databases on the whole market.

Warning

Do not take the annuity offered by your employer's scheme or from the company with whom you built up a personal pension until you have checked the rates available from other annuity providers: you may be able to do much better.

Delaying the purchase

You do not have to buy an annuity on the day that you retire – you can put off doing so until you are 75. If you have a fund of at least £250,000 and your pension provider offers an 'annuity deferral' or 'income drawdown' option, you can leave your fund invested but withdraw an income from it within limits set by the Inland Revenue (broadly the income you take cannot be more than what you would have got if you had bought an annuity). You are still allowed to take some of your fund at retirement as a tax-free cash lump sum but you must decide to do this when you start drawing the income – you cannot change your mind later. The risks you take if you choose the income draw-down option are that annuity rates will fall still further and that the fund you leave invested will fall in value.

Boosting your income in retirement

If you have a lump sum but do not like the idea of parting with it entirely by buying an annuity, there are other ways in which the lump sum can be used to produce extra income. Investments that are particularly suited to producing income are dealt with in Chapter 21, where you will find guidance on choosing a lump-sum investment in terms of the length of time you can tie the money up and the amount of risk you are prepared to take. An option that is available only to people of 60 and over is discussed in more detail below.

Pensioners Bonds

Pensioners Bonds (available from a post office or direct from National Savings*) provide a guaranteed regular income that is fixed for five years at a time (although there are plans to introduce sometime in 1999 a similar bond that will tie up your money for a shorter period). Provided you are at least 60, you can invest from £500 up to a maximum of £50,000 (£100,000 if you and your partner have a joint holding). Although the monthly interest is taxable, it is paid without tax deducted from it at source. The rate being paid by five-year Pensioner Bonds in April 1999 was 4.65 per cent (3.72 per cent after tax at the lower rate of 20 per cent). The advantage that these bonds have over Income Bonds from National Savings, which are not restricted to the over-60s, is that the minimum investment is lower and they pay a fixed rate of interest so you can be certain of the income you will get each month. However, the interest rate is slightly lower. You can cash in Pensioners Bonds before the five years are up but you will lose interest if you do.

Raising money from your home

If you do not have a lump sum that can be used to provide an income but you own your own home, there are several ways in which your home can be used to provide extra income. You can:

- **sell your home** and move to a smaller one; this would indirectly boost your income because it is likely to be cheaper to run a smaller home
- take out a **home income plan** where you borrow against the value of your home. The loan buys an annuity which provides the income that is paid to you after the tax and the interest on the loan have been deducted. These plans are suitable only if you are in your 70s and they are less attractive since the March 1999 Budget, in which tax relief on the interest payments was withdrawn
- take out an **interest–only mortgage** where you raise a lump sum by taking out a mortgage on your home. The lump sum can be invested to provide an income (the investment does not have to be an annuity). The loan is paid after your death by selling the home; during your lifetime you pay only the interest
- investigate a **home reversion** scheme where you sell part of your house but retain the right to live there for the rest of your life. These schemes are worth considering (when they are available) because they provide a higher income than other options, and because you are not borrowing you do not have to pay interest.

Tip

If you want more help and advice about planning your life in retirement both Age Concern* and Help the Aged* produce free fact sheets and leaflets about all aspects of retirement planning. You may also find it helpful to consult *The Which? Guide to an Active Retirement* published by Which? Books.*

Addresses

Age Concern England
Astral House, 1268 London Road,
London SW16 4ER
Tel: 0181-765 7200
Fax: 0181-765 7211
Email: e.infodep@ace.org.uk
Web site: www.ace.org.uk

Age Concern Northern Ireland
3 Lower Crescent, Belfast BT7 1NR
Tel: (01232) 245729
Fax: (01232) 235497
Email: ageconcern.ni@bt.internet.com
Web site: www.btinternet.com/
~ageconcern.ni

Age Concern Scotland
113 Rose Street, Edinburgh
EH2 3DT
Tel: 0131-2203345
Fax: 0131-220 2779
Email: acs@ccis.org.uk

Age Concern Wales
4th floor, 1 Cathedral Road,
Cardiff CF1 9SD
Tel: (01222) 371566
Fax: (01222) 399562
Email: accymru@ace.org.uk
Web site: www.accymru.org.uk

Annuity Bureau
Enterprise House, 59–65 Upper
Ground, London SE1 9PQ
Tel: 0171-620 4090
Fax: 0171-261 1888
Email: enquiry@annuity-bureau.co.uk
Web site: www.annuity-bureau.co.uk
*Independent financial adviser specialising
in annuities*

Annuity Direct
32 Scrutton Street, London
EC2A 4RQ
Tel: 0171-684 5000
Fax: 0171-684 5001
*Independent financial adviser specialising
in annuities*

Association of British Credit Unions
Co-Operative Union, Hanover Street,
Manchester, Lancashire M60 0AS
Tel: 0161-832 3694
Fax: 0161-832 3706
Email: info@abcul.org

Association of British Insurers (ABI)
51 Gresham Street, London
EC2V 7HQ
Tel: 0171-600 3333
Fax: 0171-696 8996
Email: info@abi.org.uk
Web site: www.abi.org.uk
Written enquiries preferred

Association of Investment Trust Companies
Third floor, Durrant House, 8–13
Chiswell Street, London EC1Y 4YY
Tel: 0171-282 5555
Factsheet orderline: 0171-431 5222
Fax: 0171-282 5556
Email: info@aitc.co.uk
Web site: www.iii.co.uk/aitc

Association of Residential Letting Agents (ARLA)
Maple House, 53–55 Woodside
Road, Amersham, Buckinghamshire
HP6 6AA
Tel: (01494) 431680
Fax: (01494) 431530
Email: info@arla.co.uk
Web site: www.arla.co.uk

Association of Unit Trusts and Investment Funds
65 Kingsway, London WC2B 6TD
Tel: 0171-831 0898
Factsheet orderline: 0181-207 1361
Fax: 0171-831 9975
Email: autif@investmentfunds.org.uk
Web site: www.investmentfunds.org.uk

Banking Ombudsman Scheme
The Office of the Banking
Ombudsman, 70 Grays Inn Road,
London WC1X 8NB
Tel: 0171-404 9944
Fax: 0171-405 5052
Enquiries: (0345) 660902
Email: bankingombudsman@obo.
org.uk
Web site: www.obo.org.uk

Bank of England Brokerage Service
Bank of England Registrars
PO Box 333, Gloucester,
Gloucestershire GL1 1ZY
Tel: (01452) 398333
Fax: (01452) 398027
Email: admin@registrarsdept.demon.
co.uk
Web site: www.bankofengland.co.uk

Bank of England Registrar's Department
See 'Bank of England Brokerage
Service'

Benefits Agency
Look in the phone book for your
local office

Building Societies Ombudsman Scheme
The Office of the Building Societies
Ombudsman, Millbank Tower,
Millbank, London SW1P 4XS
Tel: 0171-931 0044
Fax: 0171-931 8485
Complaints: 0171 233 9836
Email: blgsocombudsman@easynet.
co.uk

Citizens' Advice Bureau
Look in the phone book for your
local office

Consumer Credit Counselling Service
Tel: (0800) 138111

Contributions Agency
Inland Revenue
Look in phone book for local one

Council of Mortgage Lenders
3 Savile Row, London W1X 1AF
Tel: 0171-437 0075
Tel: 0171-440 2255 (for ordering
factsheets)
Fax: 0171-434 3791
Email: info@cml.org.uk
Web site: www.cml.org.uk

Data Protection Commissioner
Wycliffe House, Water Lane,
Wilmslow, Cheshire SK9 5AF
Tel: (01625) 545740 (switchboard)
Tel: (01625) 545745 (information
line)
Fax: (01625) 524510
Email: data@wycliffe.demon.co.uk
Web site: www.open.gov.uk

Debt Management Office
Cheapside House, 138 Cheapside,
London EC2V 6BB
Tel: 0171-862 6500
Fax: 0171-862 6509
Web site: www.dmo.gov.uk
For general enquiries on gilts

**Department for Education and
Employment**
Tel: (0800) 731 9133 (student support
information line)
Email: info@dfee.gov.uk
Web site: www.open.gov.uk/dfee

**Department of Education for Northern
Ireland**
Rathgael House, Balloo Road,
Bangor, County Down BT19 7PR
Tel: (01247) 279279
Fax: (01247) 279100
Web site: www.irlgov.ie/educ/

**Department of the Environment,
Transport and the Regions**
Eland House, Bressenden Place,
London SW1E 5DU
Tel: 0171-890 3000
Web site: www.detr.gov.uk

DSS Pensions
FREEPOST BS5555/1, Bristol
BS99 1BL
Pensions Info-Line: (0345) 31 32 33
(24 hours, calls charged at local rate)
Web site: www.dss.gov.uk

Energy Saving Trust
21 Dartmouth Street, London
SW1H 9BP
Tel: 0171-222 0101
Energy efficiency hotline: (0345) 277200
Web site: www.est.org.uk/saving/
index.htm

Equifax Europe
Dept 1E, PO Box 3001, Glasgow
G81 2DT
Tel: (0990) 783783
Email: enquiries@equifax.co.uk
Web site: www.infocheck.co.uk

Experian Ltd
Consumer Help Service, PO Box
8000, Nottingham NG1 5GX
Tel: 0115-976 8747
*One of the two main credit reference
agencies in the UK*

**Finance and Leasing Association
Arbitration Scheme**
Imperial House, 15–19 Kingsway,
London WC2 6UN
Tel: 0171-836 6511
Web site: www.fla.co.uk
Written or telephoned enquiries preferred

Financial Services Authority (FSA)
25 The North Colonnade, Canary
Wharf, London E14 5HS
Tel: 0171-676 1000
Leaflets line: (0800) 917 3311
(freephone)
Public enquiries helpline: (0845)
6061234 (calls charged at local rate)
Fax: 0171-676 1099
Email: enquiries@fsa.co.uk
Web site: www.fsa.gov.uk

Help the Aged
St James Walk, London EC1R 0BE
Home Owners' Income Plan: 0171-253
0253
Tax services: (0800) 0565535
Retirement property services: (0800)
592605
Insurance quotes: (0800) 413180
Care Fees Advisory Services: (0500)
767476
SeniorLine: (0808) 8006565 (general
advice)
Fax: 0171-250 4474
Email: hta@dial.pipex.com
Web site: www.helptheaged.org.uk

Housing Corporation
149 Tottenham Court Road, London
W1P 0BN
Tel: 0171-393 2000
Fax: 0171-393 2111
Email: webmaster@hcorp.demon.
co.uk
Web site: www.open.gov.uk

IFA Promotion
28 Greville Street, London
EC1N 8SU
Tel: 0171-831 4027
Consumer hotline: 0117-971 1177
Fax: 0171-831 4920
Email: contact@ifap.org.uk
Web site: www.ifap.org.uk

**Incorporated Society of Valuers and
Auctioneers (ISVA)**
3 Cadogan Gate, London SW1X 0AP
Tel: 0171-235 2282
Fax: 0171-235 4390
Email: hq@isva.co.uk
Web site: www.isva.co.uk

**Independent Review Body for the
Banking and Mortgage Codes**
Pinners Hall, 105–108 Old Broad
Street, London EC2N 1EX
Tel: 0171-216 8840
Fax: 0171-216 8811
Web site: www.bankfacts.org.uk

**Independent Schools Information
Service (ISIS)**
Grosvenor Gardens House, 35–37
Grosvenor Gardens, London
SW1W 0BS
Tel: 0171-798 1500
Fax: 0171-798 1501
Email: national@isis.org.uk
Web site: www.isis.org.uk

Inland Revenue Adjudicator
Adjudicator's Office, Haymarket
House, 28 Haymarket, London
SW1Y 4SP
Tel: 0171-930 2292
Fax: 0171-930 2298
Email: adjudicators@gtnet.gov.uk
Web site: www.open.gov.uk/adjoff/
aodemo1.htm

Insurance Ombudsman Bureau
City Gate One, 135 Park Street,
London SE1 9EA
Tel: (0845) 600 6666 (freephone)
Tel: 0171-902 8144
Fax: 0171-902 8197
Email: complaint@theiob.org.uk
        advice@theiob.org.uk
Web site: www.theiob.org.uk

Investment Ombudsman
6 Frederick's Place, London
EC2R 8BT
Tel: 0171-796 3065
Fax: 0171-726 0574

London Stock Exchange
Public information department,
London Stock Exchange, Old Broad
Street, London EC2N 1HP
Tel: 0171-797 1372
Web site: www.londonstockex.co.uk

Money Advice Centres
Look in the phone book for your
local centre

Money Management National Register
of Fee-based Advisers
C/o Matrix Data Ltd, FREEPOST 22
(SW1565), London W1E 7EZ
Tel: 0117-976 9444

Mortgage Code Arbitration Scheme
Chartered Institute of Arbitrators,
24 Angel Gate, City Road, London
EC1V 2RS
Tel: 0171-837 4483
Fax: 0171-837 4185
Written enquiries preferred

Mortgage Code Register of
Intermediaries
Festival Way, Festival Park, Etruria,
Stoke on Trent, Staffordshire
ST1 5TA
Tel: (01782) 216300
Fax: (01782) 216350

National Association of Estate Agents
(NAEA)
Arbon House, 21 Jury Street,
Warwick, Warwickshire CV34 4EH
Tel: (01926) 496800
Fax: (01926) 400953
Web site: www.naea.co.uk

National Association of Pension Funds
(NAPF)
12 Grosvenor Gardens, London
SW1W 0DH
Tel: 0171-730 0585
Web site: www.napf.co.uk

National Debtline
Birmingham Settlement, 318 Summer
Lane, Birmingham B19 3RL
Tel: (0645) 500511

National Savings
Sales Information Unit, National
Savings, FREEPOST BJ2092,
Blackpool FY3 9XR
Tel: (0645) 645000
Email: customerenquiries@national
savings.co.uk
Web site: www.nationalsavings.co.uk
Written or telephoned enquiries preferred

National Union of Students
461 Holloway Road, London N7 6LJ
Tel: 0171-272 8900
Fax: 0171-263 5718
Email: nusuk@nus.org.uk
Web site: www.nus.org.uk

Occupational Pensions Advisory
Service (OPAS)
11 Belgrave Road
London SW1V 1RB
Tel: 0171-233 8080
Fax: 0171-233 8016
Email: opas@iclweb.com
Web site: www.opas.org.uk
Written enquiries preferred

Office of Electricity Regulation (Offer)
Hagley House, Hagley Road,
Birmingham B16 8QG
Tel: 0121-456 2100
Fax: 0121-456 4664
Email: enquiries@offer.gov.uk
Web site: www.open.gov.uk/offer/

Office of Fair Trading (OFT)
Consumer Information Line
Field House, 15–25 Breams Buildings,
London EC4A 1PR
Tel: (0345) 224499
Tel: 0171-211 8000 (general
switchboard)
Fax: 0171-211 8800
Email: enquiries@oft.gov.uk
Web site: www.oft.gov.uk
*For guidance on where to get practical help
if problems arise when buying financial
products. For OFT products see
'Publications'*

Office of Gas Supply (Ofgas)
Ofgas Consumer Affairs
4th Floor
16 Palace Street, London SW1E 5JD
Tel: (0800) 887777 (freephone)
Fax: 0171 932 1666
Web site: www.ofgas.gov.uk

Pensions Ombudsman
11 Belgrave Road, London
SW1V 1RB
Tel: 0171-834 9144
Fax: 0171-821 0065
Email: pensions.ombudsman@iclweb.
com

Pensions Schemes Registry
PO Box 1NN, Newcastle upon
Tyne, Tyne and Wear NE99 1NN
Tel: 0191-225 6393/4
Fax: 0191-225 6390 (surnames A—
Je), 0191-225 6391 (surnames Jf to Z)
Web site: www.opra.co.uk

Personal Insurance Arbitration Service (PIAS)
Chartered Institute of Arbitrators,
24 Angel Gate, City Road, London
EC1V 2RS
Tel: 0171-837 4483
Fax: 0171-837 4185
Email: 71411.2735@compuserve.com
Web site: www.arbitrators.org

Personal Investment Authority (PIA) Ombudsman
See 'Financial Services Authority (FSA)'

Relate
Herbert Gray College, Little Church
Street, Rugby, Warwickshire
CV21 3AP
Tel: (01788) 573241
Fax: (01788) 535007
Web site: www.relate.org.uk

Retirement Pension Forecasting and Advice Service
Room TB001, Timeview Park,
Whitley Road, Newcastle upon Tyne
NE98 1BA
Tel: 0191-218 7585
Fax: 0191-218 7006
Web site: www.dss.gov.uk

Royal Institution of Chartered Surveyors (RICS)
12 Great George Street, Parliament
Square, London SW1P 3AD
Tel: 0171-222 7000
Fax: 0171-695 1505
Email: info@rics.org.uk
Web site: www.rics.org.uk

Self Assessment Orderline
PO Box 37, St Austell, Cornwall
PL25 5YN
Tel: (0645) 000404
Fax: (0645) 000604
Email: saorderline.ir@gtnet.gov.uk
Web site: www.open.gov.uk/inrev/sa

Shared Ownership Advice Line
Tel: 0171-963 0246

Student Awards Agency for Scotland
Gyleview House, 3 Redheughs Rigg,
South Gyle, Edinburgh EH12 9YT
Tel: 0131-476 8212
Fax: 0131-244 5887
Web site: www.student-support-saas.gov.uk

Welsh Office Education Department
FHE1 Division, Welsh Office
Education Department, Cathays Park,
Cardiff CF10 3NQ
Tel: (01222) 825831
Fax: (01222) 825823

Publications

Bank of England
Publications hotline: (0800) 818614

Department of the Environment,
Transport and the Regions
PO Box 236, Wetherby LS23 7NB
Tel: (0870) 1226236
Fax: (0870) 1226237
For free DETR literature

Money Management *magazine*
FT Finance, PO Box 387, Haywards
Heath, West Sussex RH16 3GS
Tel: (01444) 445520
Fax: (01444) 445599

Office of Fair Trading (OFT)
PO Box 366, Hayes UB3 1XB
Tel/fax: (0870) 6060321
Email: oft@echristian.co.uk
Web site: www.oft.gov.uk

**The PUSH Guide to Which
University 2000**
Web site: www.push.co.uk
*Available from Letts Educational, tel
0181-740 2266 or from bookshops*

Which? *and Which? Books*
PO Box 44, Hertford X, SG14 1LH
Tel: (0800) 252100
Fax: (0800) 533053
Web site: www.which.net

Index

The Which? Guide to Insurance

Insurance – the buying and selling of risk – is big business. Every year consumers spend billions of pounds on their policies. But how much of it do they really need and could they be paying less for any of it?

The Which? Guide to Insurance explains what to take into consideration before buying insurance so that you can avoid under- and over-insuring, and duplicating, and points out what to look for in the small print. It covers the range of policies from house contents and buildings to travel, health and car insurance. It also examines insurance, including life insurance, as an investment.

Using a no-nonsense, step-by-step approach, this guide shows you how to: work out how much insurance you need; buy the right insurance for your circumstances; cut the cost of your current insurance policies; make payments in the most cost-effective way; keep your insurance up to date; complain if your claim is unreasonably rejected.

Sound, money-saving tips on what to insure and how, plus tried and tested advice on how to take on an insurance company and win, with case histories to illustrate, make this book a great investment for anyone who needs insurance.

Paperback   216 x 135mm   320 pages   £10.99

Available from bookshops, and by post from
Which?, Dept TAZM, Castlemead,
Gascoyne Way, Hertford X, SG14 1LH

You can also order using your credit card
by phoning FREE on (0800) 252100
(quoting Dept TAZM)

The Which? Guide to Shares

In Britain, nearly one adult in every three has become a share-owner, having responded to privatisation issues and, more recently, windfall shares from building society conversions. If you already have one or two shareholdings, or you are considering shares for the first time, this book will show you how these fascinating and versatile investments can help you achieve your financial ambitions.

It covers the role of shares in financial planning; how to buy and sell shares in the high street, through a traditional broker, or over the Internet; the range of shares available; risk – and how to turn it to your advantage; how shares are taxed, and how, legitimately, to avoid tax; portfolios for every pocket; the perks that accompany some shares; mastering rights issues, takeover bids, and so on; and how to play the stock market without even buying any shares.

The Which? Guide to Shares is a detailed introduction to the intriguing, fun and potentially rewarding world of share ownership, complete with extensive glossary and a useful address section.

Paperback   216 x 135mm   256 pages   £9.99

Available from bookshops, and by post from
Which?, Dept TAZM, Castlemead,
Gascoyne Way, Hertford X, SG14 1LH

You can also order using your credit card
by phoning FREE on (0800) 252100
(quoting Dept TAZM)

Which? Way to Save Tax

With self-assessment in place and a new tax regime in operation, the taxpayer now, more than ever, needs guiding through the complexities of the British tax system. *Which? Way to Save Tax*, fully updated each year to reflect Budget changes, helps you to ensure that you are paying the right amount of tax.

Written for the non-specialist, this book helps you to understand and make the most of the new tax rules. It guides investors through the overhaul of capital gains tax – essential reading for the millions of new shareholders created by the conversion of building societies to banks – and explains the biggest shake-up in tax-free investment for over a decade. It offers reliable and independent advice on tax as it affects employment, families, homes, investments, inheritance, pensions and the self-assessment regime.

Which? Way to Save Tax contains the answers to common tax questions, and should also help you work out whether some of the estimated billions of pounds of overpaid tax belong to you.

Paperback   210 x 120mm   352 pages   £14.99